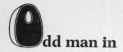Odd man in

ODD man in

ODD MAN in

ODD MAN IN

Societies of deviants in America
by Edward Sagarin
Chicago · Quadrangle Books

to Robert E. Bierstedt
and Donal E. J. MacNamara:
in each of you I have found
a friend, scholar, teacher,
and humanitarian

Acknowledgments

The debts a man owes are many, and he can only hope that, after he has discharged them, there will be some small residue which he can contemplate and say that it belongs to him.

This is the work of a man who was a college dropout. For a quarter of a century, from the time of my legal maturity until my mid-forties, I looked at the world of scholarship from the outside, peering in with wonderment and envy. At the prodding of my son, I returned to college at the age of forty-five. Today, many years of study and research later, to those who have opened up the world of learning for me I return a small payment toward a great debt.

My first debts are to my son, Fred, who showed me the road that I must follow, and to my wife, Gertrude, who encouraged me to travel it.

The professors who aided me in my research and writing are so numerous that I shall confine myself to mentioning those who helped me specifically with this work. Robert Bierstedt, formerly chairman of the Department of Sociology at New York University, discussed with me many aspects of my work as it proceeded. If

I could summarize my debt to Professor Bierstedt in one sentence, I would say that from him I learned a humanistic approach toward the nature of relationships that bind people together in a social order. Erwin O. Smigel led me to impose upon this humanism an empirical approach by which I would view the people in this study as members of voluntary associations, not merely as individuals involved in a deviant behavior pattern. It was from this intermingling of the organizational and socio-psychological frames of reference that this work emerged. For this, my debt to Professors Bierstedt and Smigel cannot be overstated.

At New York University, Professor H. Laurence Ross (later of the University of Denver) and Professor Joseph Bram offered many worthwhile suggestions. Several people, some of whom are mentioned in the text, discussed the manuscript with me, read parts of it, and supplied me with suggestions and information. I make the usual disclaimer on their behalf: they are in no way responsible for anything I have (mis)stated, but I do wish to thank them for their aid. They include Dr. Alvin B. Balaban, a psychiatrist, and Mrs. Balaban, both founders of Human Growth, Inc.; Dr. John Bauer, psychologist, Baruch College; Dr. Harry Benjamin, physician and sexologist.

Also Dr. Irving Bieber, psychoanalyst; Dr. Albert Ellis, the executive director of the Institute for Advanced Study in Rational Psychotherapy; Professor John Gagnon, sociologist at the State University of New York at Stony Brook, and formerly associated with the Institute for Sex Research, founded by the late Alfred Kinsey; Dr. Paul Gebhard, present head of the Institute for Sex Research; Dr. Jon Geis, director of fellowship training program of the Institute for Advanced Study in Rational Psycotherapy; Dr. Alfred A. Gross, executive secretary of the George W. Henry Foundation; and Dr. Henry Guze, psychotherapist.

Also Professor Donal E. J. MacNamara, criminologist at John Jay College of Criminal Justice; R. E. L. Masters, author of several works dealing with some of the phenomena discussed in this book; Dr. Wardell B. Pomeroy, psychotherapist and former director of the Institute for Sex Research; and Dr. Fredric Wertham, psychotherapist and former director of a clinic devoted to work in the area of homosexuality.

I have discussed all or parts of this book with so many people that I can hardly recall all the ideas I obtained from them. I would include, in addition to those already listed, Irving P. Gell-

11 Acknowledgments

man, John Mann, Richard Quinney, and Dennis Wrong, all of New York University; David W. McKinney, Jr., of Wellington College; Peter L. Berger of the New School for Social Research; and David L. Sills. Most important is a dear friend and colleague at Muhlenberg College, Roger Baldwin.

I received remarkable cooperation from many organizations, from their leaders, members, and ex-members, and from those presently or formerly active in similar groups. They completed questionnaires, and many of them spent hours talking with me; I was present at meetings, frequently closed meetings and executive committees; a few even read (I'm sure with dismay) material for this book as it came from the typewriter. It is in the nature of a study of this sort, and fundamental to an understanding of it, that all these people must remain anonymous. Whenever I quote from a document, even one that has been distributed publicly, the proper name which I use is almost invariably a pseudonym that I have supplied, when it is not a pseudonym supplied by the member of the organization. Those who use their actual names in most of these organizations (exceptions would be the Little People of America and the Self-Development Group) should not, I feel, be further jeopardized by the revelation of their names in these pages.

I have frequently mentioned writers in the text whose work has proved particularly illuminating to me. One cannot seriously write a book without betraying the influence of everything that he has read—even of many works that he may not yet have opened, perhaps not even heard of. Of the influences on my thinking that I'm aware of, those that seem most pertinent to the book include the work of Alfred Schutz, Erving Goffman, Edwin M. Lemert, David Truman, Robert K. Merton, Albert Ellis, and, going back a few years, Robert Michels and Karl Mannheim.

Several people read this manuscript in full and offered me many suggestions. I wish to thank Robert Boyers, editor of *Salmagundi;* Professors Charles Winick and Bernard Rosenberg of the City College of New York; and Fred and Pat Sagarin.

Some of the research for this book was made possible under a Summer Faculty Research Grant of the City University of New York. Two of the chapters should more properly be called collaborations; several others were written with the aid of information gathered for me by researchers. My collaborators are George L. Kirkham, who investigated COG and wrote the chapter on transvestites and transsexuals with me; and William C. Kuehn, who investigated the Self-Development Group and wrote the chapter on ex-convicts with me. W. Boyd Littrell, then at the University of Denver, made a study of Illegitimates Anonymous which serves as the basis for the brief discussion of that organization; Howard Ramer, then at the University of Connecticut, met with Robert Glazier and studied The Inn; and Marvin Schechter, then at City College, studied an Alateen group in New York.

These, then, are my debts. I hope my repayment has begun and that this book will contribute to an understanding of a set of complex and often tragic problems in modern life.

Contents

ODD MAN IN

1. Organizations of deviants in a nation of joiners

> *Congress shall make no law ... abridging ...*
> *the right of the people peaceably to assemble.*
> *—Article I, Amendments to the*
> *Constitution of the United States*

In recent years America has witnessed the growth of an important social movement. It embodies the idea of open, formal, and structured organizations (what sociologists call voluntary associations) among people whom society has characterized as deviant—people who are subject to scorn, discrimination, gossip, sometimes pity, and sometimes punishment, because they carry a stigma. That many of these people have been apparently successful in hiding their stigmatizing characteristic—concealment made possible by low visibility—makes the fact of these organizations all the more remarkable.

From the familiar Alcoholics Anonymous to Gamblers and Schizophrenics Anonymous; from TOPS and KOPS (Take—and Keep—Off Pounds Sensibly) to the Little People of America; from the highly publicized Mattachine Society to a motor-bike club that quite obviously resembles Mattachine in that its major area of interest is homosexuality; from the lesbian Daughters of Bilitis to an organization of transsexuals; and from self-help groups of former mental patients to a struggling Self-Development Group which utilizes convicts and ex-convicts as therapists and rehabilitation guides, this movement reveals sources that lie deep in the country's past and incorporates activities that reach into many unexpected sectors of American society.

Apart from these strictly deviant or stigmatized groups —but perhaps, by their very existence, encouraging their formation—there have always been numerous oddball and peculiar organizations in America; many are unpopular in one way or another, frequently because their goals and values are unshared, if not entirely scorned, by most Americans. Some groups are merely laughed at, some vigorously opposed, others completely ignored. Among these associations, one has been organized to discourage or prevent the name of Smith from being used in hypothetical instances. You don't have to be named Smith to be eligible to join; you simply have to recognize an injustice to people saying "Take John Smith, for instance," when they could use John Doe or Joe Blow for their example. Other people have become deeply distressed over the disappearance of the alphabet from telephone numbers. They have formed an organization, and gained a considerable number of adherents, to prevent, for instance, YU–7 from becoming 987, a change in which the Anti-Digit Dialing League sees many dangers to the American way of life.[1] The compilers of the Encyclopedia of Associations, which lists 12,910 national organizations, cite such unusual groups as the Simpler Spelling Association, whose members, interested in and inaugurating spelling reforms, include filologists, etimologists, and foneticions (but why not fonetishuns?); the Count Dracula Society, whose members are devoted to the study of horror literature; and Caterpillar Clubs consisting of airmen who have saved their lives by a parachute jump.[2]

People of macabre tastes, rare hobbies, and extraordinary achievements are as much a part of organizational life as are members of a local political club, the PTA, or a suburban women's society. Many organizations are secret, some by choice, others because they function in an atmosphere of semi-legality. Secret societies arose early in American history: denounced by those who saw in them a danger to the open democratic ideals of the new nation, they were nevertheless espoused by many of the nation's founders and leaders, and were often the subject of rumors and scandals, even investigations into disappearances and murders. But these societies survived; the secrecy of many like the Masons, Elks, and Odd Fellows centered mainly around some harmless oaths, jabberwocky, and hocus-pocus, plus the vow of aid to fellow members in distress.[3]

In contrast, the relatively recent associations of deviants are not characterized either by secrecy or ritual—although at times they contain an element of both—nor by their being groups of unusual people with tastes and predilections shared by few. Alcoholics, compulsive gamblers, schizophrenics and neurotics (or those characterizing themselves as such and assuming the label), former mental patients and ex-convicts, homosexuals and transvestites, together with those suffering from certain types of physical ailments—all the deviant groups—seem to have one distinguishing feature in common. What separates them from the unpopular, the oddball, the marginal, and the outsider, those who form organizations of snake cultists, fire buffs, fans of the Japanese game of Go, and collectors of cigar bands, is that, whereas both types of groups represent numerical minorities, and sometimes even unpopular ones, only members of the former are specifically looked upon as pariahs and subjected to social opprobrium, while members of the latter are viewed as more quaint than evil.

When one compares the societies of alcoholics or homosexuals with such socially condemned associations as the "lunatic fringe" of far left and far right or the Ku Klux Klan (to give a clearer example of unpopularity, let's say the Klan in a northern community where, ostensibly, it has little sympathy from nonmembers), the latter are seen as people who become outcasts and fall into disgrace (to the extent that they do) simply because they join an organization. The alcoholics and homosexuals, on the other hand, form organizations because they already are in trouble with society or themselves—at least they would be if their predilections and habits were known. Thus they seek association with others like themselves to assist in the handling of their problem.

This difference is crucial in many respects, but particularly from such viewpoints as self-image and self-righteousness, the voluntariness or involuntariness of one's status, and the nature of one's expectations from the group. Within the deviant organizations, the members are deviant and stigmatized before joining; the act of joining does not increase the social condemnation—although it may indeed make them more vulnerable to it. In extremely unpopular religious, political, racial, and social organizations, the members are deviant (to the extent that they are) because they are members of the group; in the anonymous organizations, they are members of the group because they are deviant. In slightly different terms, one can say that the alcoholic takes his stigma to AA and hopes to lose it there. Although he does not define his situation as stigmatizing, the racist, on the other hand, gets his stigma from the KKK and keeps it there.

21 Organizations of deviants in a nation of joiners

Essentially, the organizations of deviant and stigmatized people fall into two types, but not without overlapping. What most differentiates some groups from others may well be the goal of the organization in the eyes of the individual member. In forming, supporting, or joining a group the deviant always seeks to escape his stigma, but he does so by seeking either (1) to conform to the norms of society, or (2) to change those norms to include acceptance of his own behavior. In the first instance, he renounces his deviant behavior; in the second, he changes not himself but the rule-making order.

In taking the step of joining with others who are similarly labeled deviants, an individual may actually increase his stigma by enhancing his visibility as a member of a socially disapproved category; he thus calls public attention to his own deviant existence. This difficulty is countered in three ways: by protecting the individual through anonymity; by using the greater visibility as a mechanism to reduce social disapproval; and by concealing the nature of the organization behind a neutral name.

One can make several statements about groups in which individuals seek to reduce their deviant behavior and in this way escape from deviance. They gain wide approval from society-at-large—except, of course, from persons who are geographically and in other ways so close to the deviants that their congregation becomes threatening. These groups function very much on group therapy lines; they often turn to religious or pseudo-religious concepts for reinforcement; and, while scoffing at the hypocrisy of the middle class which rejects and opposes them, they nevertheless embrace many middle-class aims in order to return to a life of propriety. Finally, such groups paint deviants as worthwhile individuals, souls to be saved; but they view deviance itself as immoral, sinful, and self-defeating.

Frowning on members who stray, the deviance-reducing groups exert extreme pressure through inner group loyalty; they thus develop a pattern of overconformity in suppressing the controversial behavior itself. This last characteristic in fact results in a harsher condemnation of deviance than is found in the general population; the groups fear any enlightened, liberal, or permissive view, and they buttress this fear by moralistic stances, reinforced by religion. For those seeking to relinquish their deviance, any suggestion that the consequences of that deviance would be less severe if only social attitudes were changed becomes a threat to the organization and its program, and, to the members, a temptation to return to the abandoned pattern.

People attracted to groups fostering an escape from deviance are often in need of authority figures and ego-reinforcement. Compliant and submissive, they nevertheless have a strong component of aggression which they transfer from self- and society-direction to group-direction during the therapeutic process. As penitents, they both comply and gripe, willingly accept and let off steam.

The second type of deviant group, consisting of those who are seeking to modify the definition of their condition as deviant, shares some of the foregoing attributes, but not all. Even when it does share them, it is for entirely different reasons and hence with different consequences. Seeking to change the public attitude toward their particular deviance, such groups may turn to religion —not, however, for moral support, but for a respectable front and useful ally. They advocate a reinforcement of the ego, not through group therapy but through mutual reinforcement of deviant values and deviant ways of structuring reality. They scoff at middle-class norms but do not entirely reject them: acceptance by society is easier to achieve if members are moralistic, law-abiding, and conforming in most respects.

Groups seeking to change social attitudes thumb their noses at society in order to foster pride in the deviant; at the same time they become obsequious before society in order the better to elicit acceptance. While such organizations are likely to attract rebels and nonconformists, they nevertheless use respectable front men as façades and window dressing. They vacillate between the ultra-conformity of those anticipating social acceptance and the rebellion and rejection of those reacting against the society that has thrown them out.

Because of the enhanced stigmatization that ensues when one joins an organization of this type, the groups are likely to attract neurotics and personality misfits who require social disapproval and ridicule, as well as rebels who relish a battle with the world of respectability. The unceasing aggressive nature of the struggle against society and the small degree of resultant success leads to considerable membership turnover in such groups, as well as to fission, bitter internecine battles for leadership, and general skullduggery.

Thus the two types of organizations hold irreconcilable attitudes toward the deviance with which each is involved. The first type condemns sternly, both moralistically and scientifically, pointing to the road of eternal damnation that awaits anyone who slips backward; the second type likewise invokes science, philosophy, and ideology, but conversely for the eternal condemnation of those who condemn them. This latter type seeks to convince the world without, as well as the members within, that their particular deviance (a word to be shunned) is normal, natural, moral, and socially useful. All who deem otherwise are deluded and ignorant hypocrites, if not repressed deviants themselves. On the other hand, the former type

views its members almost as saints because they are re-
nouncing deviance; their devils are both the lost souls
who have not seen the light and their opponents in the
world of respectability. In the end, both types of organizations present distorted images of themselves. They fall
victim to the temptation, almost inherent in the nature
of such organizations, to project a self-image that both
glorifies and "prettifies."

In organizations of alcoholics, gamblers, ex-convicts,
and homosexuals, there is a convergence of three concepts: stigma, deviance, and voluntary association or
formal organization. Although stigma and deviance are
highly related, until recently little attention was given to
the former. Stigma, Erving Goffman points out in a book
of that title,[4] is a Greek word, originally referring to
bodily signs designed to expose something unusual and
bad about the moral status of the signifier:

> The signs were cut or burnt into the body and
> advertised that the bearer was a slave, a criminal,
> or a traitor—a blemished person, ritually polluted,
> to be avoided, especially in public places. . . . Today
> the term is . . . applied more to the disgrace itself
> than to the bodily evidence of it.[5]

Pointing out that the category to which a person belongs
and the attributes that he possesses could be called his
actual social identity, Goffman refers to the stigmatized
person as one having "spoiled identity," a characteristic
that reduces the individual, in the minds of others, "from
a whole and usual person to a tainted, discounted one."
In short, the term stigma is used "to refer to an attribute
that is deeply discrediting. . . . [It] is a special kind of relationship between attribute and stereotype."[6] Stigma is
a defect, physical, mental, characterological, and behav-

ioral; and it remains a defect both so long as it is seen as a defect by others, and so long as they deeply discredit the individual for having it. Usually a stigmatized person either internalizes the view of the discrediting society or expends great energy in seeking to fight it.

Deviance, likewise, is discrediting behavior; or, perhaps, to draw a fine distinction, it is socially condemned behavior. One might speak of the fascist or communist in a democratically oriented society as being deviant, but hardly as stigmatized. A conscientious objector living in the fervor of a jingoistic climate could be viewed as deviant, but he would probably not be said to carry a stigma: his anti-war activity would be considered too self-righteous and too voluntary to involve "spoiled identity." On the other hand, being a Negro, an outcast, or a member of some other racial or ethnic collectivity that is condemned can be stigmatizing, but not really deviant. What, then, is deviance?

On the broadest level, deviance is a category of behavior or status that is socially defined in a negative manner. For Marshall Clinard, social disapproval is one criterion for defining behavior as deviant. "Only those situations in which behavior is in a disapproved direction, and of sufficient degree to exceed the tolerance limit of the community, constitute deviant behavior."[7] Along somewhat similar lines, Albert Cohen offers a definition most useful as a point of departure, namely that any behavior is deviant "which violates . . . expectations which are shared and recognized as legitimate within a social system."[8]

A deviant group, then, is a collectivity of persons who share some trait, characteristic, or behavior pattern in common—in fine, any attribute that is defined negatively and that is of enough significance to themselves and to others to differentiate them from all those persons not sharing the attribute. Such a negative definition, however, is one of disapproval, as with intoxication, rather than one of disadvantage, as with blindness.[9] When the attitude is also a deeply discrediting one, we are then dealing with the meeting point of deviance and stigma. And, once these deviant and stigmatized people organize to assist each other with their problems, deviant societies are born.

That deviant societies should have originated in America may be due to many factors, not the least of which is the country's tradition of associations. For over a century, both foreign- and American-born observers have taken note of what has come to be described as the "proliferation of associations" in "a nation of joiners." The first and classic example of such a commentary was made by Alexis de Tocqueville who, in an oft-quoted passage, wrote: "Americans of all ages, all conditions, and all dispositions constantly form associations." These groups, he noted, were "religious, moral, serious, futile, general or restricted, enormous or diminutive."[10] De Tocqueville also emphasized the extreme importance of this phenomenon: "Nothing, in my opinion, is more deserving of our attention than the intellectual and moral associations of America."[11] Voluntary association in America has continued to attract the attention of travelers, historians, social philosophers, and sociologists. Close to the present day, Herbert Maccoby has provided a good general description and definition of these associations:

> The distinguishing characteristics of the voluntary association are that it be private, nonprofit, voluntary in that entrance rests on mutual consent while exit is at the will of either party, and formal in that there are offices to be filled in accordance with stipulated rules. These traits serve to differentiate the voluntary association from public and

governmental bodies; profit-making corporations and partnerships; family, clan, church, nation and other groups into which the individual is born; informal friendship groups, cliques, or gangs.[12]

Voluntary associations seem to have existed before the American Revolution; they even played a role in making the Revolution possible and in founding the Republic. Their existence was later protected by the doctrine of freedom of assembly expressed in the First Amendment to the Constitution. Nor is the organizational effort of people supporting an unpopular cause, or crusading for social change, a recent phenomenon. The 1820's and early 1830's saw the formation of several militant and noisy voluntary associations dedicated to different types of social reform. Abolitionists, temperance advocates, sabbatarians, and early feminists each took to the streets in demonstrations using tactics which gave many observers the impression of movements in which literally hundreds of thousands of people, and not a mere handful, were involved.[13]

But whence this abundance of associations? Many forces have led to the proliferation noted by visitors and native observers. They might be summarized under the headings of industrialization, geographic and social mobility, urbanization, immigration, pluralism, pragmatism, and religious and political (later labor) traditions.

America, with its cultural heterogeneity, brought together large numbers of immigrants whose ethnic origins differentiated them from the rest of the society. For these people, associations provided some of the features denied them by the society into which they were not yet assimilated; at the same time they served as transitional bridges to the new culture. The faceless anonymity of the city first provided a need for people to search out others of like interest; then—particularly in a nation where freedom of association had been specifically granted to the populace—that same anonymity provided the atmosphere in which the associations could flourish. The lack of rigid class distinctions in America gave rise to social mobility which, in turn, encouraged the formation of organizations that granted status to the joiner. The decline of both the large and the agricultural family saw an increasing number of functions once performed within the home brought elsewhere; organizational life was one of the methods for filling the gap left by the changing nature of the family. In addition, there was a well-established activist, pragmatist tradition in this country: people had not only to cherish their beliefs but to translate them into action. Josiah Royce once stated: "It is useless to call my feelings loyal unless my muscles somehow express this loyalty."[14]

If, then, there is so strong a tradition of association in the United States, if groups of all types have flourished for so long, one is tempted to ask not why organizations of deviants appeared at all, but why they did not appear much earlier in the history of America. There were, in fact, a few prototypes of current groups in the nineteenth century, the most famous of which was probably the Washingtonians, a sort of Alcoholics Anonymous that came on the scene some hundred years before the present group.

But why not more early groups? Since people with spoiled identities have always needed help, and since, in many instances, they could not receive it from others, why did they not get together sooner? The answer can probably be found, above all, in the strength of the individual's sense of stigma or discreditation, one so strong that he was forced to accept society's judgment and internalize the negative view of himself. Furthermore, there was a *modus vivendi* between society and many deviants, a sort of tacit contract, which would have been upset had the deviants come into the open. By increasing visibility, organizations would have adversely affected the small degree of tolerance by which, while always vulnerable, the deviant was nevertheless often protected.

Several factors seem to have converged in the second quarter of the twentieth century in America to encourage the formation of deviant societies. Certainly urbanism, combined with geographic mobility, allowed the deviant to meet with others of like nature under conditions of anonymity and protection. The so-called secret society had long been a part of the American tradition, but the term itself was somewhat of a misnomer: usually neither the organization nor its membership was hidden from public knowledge, only some rituals, oaths, and a few somewhat trivial activities. Urbanism, however, made possible secrecy of a new type: a man could organize and join an association, go to its meetings, and then return to the quiet surroundings of his home and neighbors with few people knowing about his membership. Thus the anonymous society—as opposed to the secret one—was born. Now, when the stigmatizing problem is not too visible (as is frequently the case with alcoholism), one can be protected from the sanctions of society, from scorn, gossip, and employment discrimination, while at the same time he gains the advantage of joining hands with others.

The 1920's also saw the emergence of two important and, to deviants, relevant social forces in America: Prohibition and psychoanalysis. The Eighteenth Amendment made America more alcohol-conscious than ever, more aware of the millions of men and perhaps not inconsiderable number of women who could not control their drinking and thus could not function either in their families or on their jobs. With this vast number of alcoholics abandoned to their drinking by repeal—all efforts to aid them by cutting off their source of liquor had been conceded to be a complete failure—the time was ripe for constructive social action.

The period between the First and Second World Wars also saw America become increasingly aware of the psychological ramifications of behavioral problems. At least the upper and middle strata of society were becoming sympathetic to those afflicted with emotional difficulties and disorders, particularly when the afflicted made an effort to handle and control them. The twenties and thirties were the heyday of Freud: people spoke of going to their analyst as they would of going to their endocrinologist or internist. Later, the respectability of psychoanalysis even served to diminish the shame and stigma of mental retardation and sexual deviance.

Now, it is one of the curious ironies of deviant organizations that the formation of AA and other groups—all essentially hostile to psychotherapy of every type but their own distinctive brand—was actually aided by the popularity of psychotherapy at this particular stage of American history. What Freud and his followers—novelists and educators, journalists and scenarists—did for the deviant was to popularize two distinct concepts about behavioral disorders and peculiarities: first, that they are within the area of human control, and second, that they should be looked upon with the same blameless compassion and sympathy that is extended to most victims of physical disorders.

With the repeal of Prohibition, America was again confronted with the problem of its problem drinkers; with the advent of psychoanalysis, all mental and social aberrations could be discussed, and, it was hoped, handled. It was in this social climate that two seemingly hopeless alcoholics, a medical man known as Dr. Bob and a layman known as Bill or W. W., met and formed a small fellowship for mutual self-help. Organizing and proselytizing, these two men who had "seen the truth" were able to form a few small groups of true believers and followers. And thus AA might have remained—small and obscure, reveling in its little successes—had a writer for the *Saturday Evening Post* not discovered it and catapulted Alcoholics Anonymous into national fame.[15] Almost three decades have passed since that one popular article made AA a household word in America. Today the organization claims 300,000 members (who are not accurately "members" of what cannot accurately be described as an organization), and boasts branches in many nations and on all continents.

Once AA succeeded, its technique was open to emulation; once Kinsey came on the scene, even sexual deviance became a matter of open discussion. Influenced by these developments, deviants began to doubt if their situation was really as hopeless as it had appeared; everyone was organizing, demonstrating, picketing, fighting for his rights—so why not they? The 1960's became the decade of activism: civil rights, civil disobedience, youth and student movements. Beards grew, hippies turned on and dropped out: an air of restlessness prevailed in America. In fact, this decade epitomizes the social climate that has produced in this country a truly remarkable proliferation of organizations of deviant and stigmatized people.

2. Alcoholics:
from the twenty-first amendment
to the twelfth step

> *They reel to and fro, and stagger like a*
> *drunken man; and are at their wit's end.*
> *So when they cry unto the Lord in their*
> *trouble: he delivereth them out*
> *of their distress.   —Psalms, 107:27–28*

Of all the self-help movements among deviants, Alcoholics Anonymous has been by far the best publicized and the most influential; most observers agree that it has also had the greatest degree of success. These attainments are reflected not only in the considerable prestige the organization enjoys in America, but in its emulators, who are numerous and readily recognized. Its predecessors, however, are less well known. Although the organization itself usually begins its history with the meeting of two alcoholics in Ohio in the 1930's, that meeting would not have led so easily to AA's formation had there not already existed in America both the necessary social climate and a history of somewhat similar rehabilitative efforts.

Temperance had been a recurrent theme in nineteenth-century America; in fact, several early organizations bore remarkable resemblances to the later AA. Altogether there were several strands in American social life which, when combined, channeled the temperance concept into its present organizational form: (1) the secret society—in the United States neither a criminal nor a subversive group; (2) the early American Christian Witness sects; and (3) the convergence of two important social movements: repeal and psychoanalysis—the exit of Volstead and the entrance of Freud onto the American scene.

As early as 1673, Increase Mather delivered a sermon entitled "Woe to Drunkards." While concern with alcoholism in this country never flagged afterward, it was not until the early nineteenth century that temperance movements started to spring up. At first they were not much different from other movements organized by proselytizers and crusaders. Historians record the meeting of a temperance group in the early years of the nineteenth century in Saratoga County, New York, followed in 1813 by the formation of the Massachusetts Society for the Suppression of Intemperance. In 1826, religious crusaders took the lead in forming the American Temperance Union; by 1833, when the delegates to an ATU convention changed the organization's name and made the United States Temperance Union a federation, the organization was said to have a half-million members—no mean number considering that the population of the country (including children) was then only about fifteen million. By the next year the claimed membership had doubled.[1]

In the 1840's, a total abstinence movement, in which people were urged to sign a pledge that they would cease to imbibe even the slightest amount of spirits, was introduced in Ireland by a Father Mathew. The pledge was a simple one, based not only on promising complete forbearance but on serving as an example of sobriety for others. The number of signatories reported was huge, and it was said that "distillers, brewers, and public houses went out of business." Father Mathew visited the United States in 1849–51, where he was honored; but with the Irish potato famine on the one hand, and, on the other, the leader's declining years leading to his death in 1856, the movement withered away.[2]

Contemporaneous with the Father Mathew movement were the Washingtonians, a thoroughly American temperance group whose history reads like an AA one hundred years before its time.[3] It was started by six drinkers who pledged to abstain henceforth. They then went on to take a further pledge, that each new abstainer would bring a drinker—and thus, it was hoped, a new convert to the cause—to the following meeting. Within a few years several Washingtonian groups were formed, bringing the total membership of pledgers to somewhere between 150,000 and 250,000. (These figures may have suffered from inflation—or intoxication—since all those who pledged were probably not sober.)

In the Washingtonian movement, unlike Father Mathew's, the former alcoholic went one step further than serving as a model of successful renunciation—he also became a proselytizing agent. As Raymond McCarthy says:

> Everywhere the pattern was the same. A former inebriate, telling his story in dramatic and moving fashion, was able to persuade hundreds in his audience to take the pledge and in turn become missionaries in the cause.[4]

These new reformer roles compelled the former drinkers to retain their sobriety: any slip would be a betrayal of both their comrades at large and those individuals whom they had taken under their wing.

One problem faced by the Washingtonians was how to

make their meetings interesting. They could not diminish the frequency because fewer meetings would only give the members greater opportunity to slip (or sip) away from the fold. A suggestion was made that each member relate his experiences as an alcoholic, explaining the depths of iniquity to which he had sunk, and praising his new freedom from the drive to drink. Once this suggestion was adopted, the format which AA came to follow a century later was born.

Like Father Mathew's movement, the Washingtonians gradually declined—in part, perhaps, because any movement built on a crusading fervor is bound to cool. Leaders were accused of being atheists, members of being secret drinkers. The group was also attacked by more orthodox temperance societies on the ground that it failed to advocate total prohibition; this attack, however, may have come simply because the Washingtonians were competition for the temperance societies.

Another group, in many ways just as close to AA, appeared right after the turn of the century, again in Ireland. Called by the unlikely name of Catch-My-Pal, its major theme was that each alcoholic would not only pledge total abstinence but would also work with other alcoholics—would support "the happy art of catching men." Pledging and proselytizing, abstaining and crusading were interwoven in Catch-My-Pal's philosophy; the work of the organization was conducted "on the theory that the reclaimed drunkard is the most effective medium through which to reach other victims of the drink habit."[5]

The story of the meeting between Bill W. and Dr. Bob in Akron, Ohio, is a familiar one. Bill had struggled for many years with alcoholism; everyone had given up on him. But finally, as he told Dr. Bob, he had come in contact with some people from Moral Rearmament (also known as the Oxford Group); through their assistance he had conquered the temptation to drink. Now a free man for the first time in his adult life, he offered to assist Dr. Bob first in overcoming his own alcoholism, then in going on to save other alcoholics.

Even stated so briefly, AA's origin was thus dependent not only on this chance meeting, not only on the strong temperance tradition both here and abroad, but as well on the activities of an organization—the Oxford Group—as yet almost completely overlooked (or at least underplayed) by AA's historians.

Officially, the organization has stated that, while certain of the Oxford Group's attitudes and tenets proved unsuitable to its purposes, it nevertheless did employ Oxford's basic principles—ones, AA adds, which were ancient and universal, the common property of mankind. "The early AA got its ideas of self-examination, acknowledgment of character defects, restitution for harm done, and working with others straight from the Oxford Groups," the official history states.[6]

The Oxford Group was founded by Frank N. Buchman, a Lutheran minister from Pennsylvania who had received a vision from God.[7] The group's name came from the work that Buchman did with Oxford students, but the use of "Oxford" was never authorized by the university. The movement that Buchman started called upon people to solve their problems by confessing their sins (he had spent a good deal of time listening to confessions of the erotic thoughts and practices of young college men) and surrendering their lives to God. Once a person surrendered, Buchman maintained, he would change.

The Oxford Group made six basic assumptions, several of which were germs of AA thought. Stated briefly, these were: (1) that men are sinners, (2) that they can be changed, (3) that confession is a prerequisite to change,

(4) that the changed soul has direct access to God, (5) that the Age of Miracles has returned, and (6) that people who have changed must change others.

Buchman made his appeal primarily to the upper class, perhaps out of snobbery, but also because, in an age of discontent, depression, and impending war, his viewpoint was basically conservative—if not frequently reactionary. Strikes were bad because they induced conflict, not love; what the hungry people needed was "to be changed." Unemployment would be taken care of by God. Buchman could even write that he thanked heaven "for a man like Adolf Hitler"[8] and that "the world needs the dictatorship of the spirit of God." As for social problems, "they could be solved within a God-controlled democracy, or perhaps I should say theocracy, and they could be solved through a God-controlled fascist dictatorship."[9] No wonder, then, that swastikas were seen at Oxford Group rallies.

Despite its individualism and reliance upon God, its refusal to give any consideration to the social context of human problems or to the responsibility of the social order for solving such problems—all of which made it, in the words of Hadley Cantril, "inevitably anti-democratic" —the Oxford Group did offer a prototype for AA. Particularly because AA concerned itself with a problem largely personal rather than one patently rooted in the social structure (unemployment, for example), it could adopt many of the Oxford Group's techniques without adopting its fascist biases. Alcoholics have, or believe that they have, a failing (the counterpart of the Oxford Group's sin) which they must confess; this confession in turn brings about a great catharsis, similar to that produced by religious confessions and psychoanalysis. AA, then, was born of the Oxford Group and Moral Rearmament, but AA was these movements made apolitical, stripped of their fascist implications (but not their conservatism), and applied to a specific social and personal problem.

The Oxford Group's confessional, at least when applied to alcoholism, is thus the Washingtonian movement all over again. But whereas the Washingtonians were concerned, on a conscious level, only with making their meetings interesting by confession, the Oxford Group saw confession as a surrender to God. For AA, the practice was an intertwining of both these goals. That the confessional had further roots for the lower class in American church and sectarian movements, in Congregationalism and revivalism, in the visible saints of Puritanism and of the Anabaptists, only made it easier for AA to work its appeal within the context of the American scene.

AA also originated the Twelve Steps, later to be followed by the Twelve Traditions. The steps themselves took over much that had been (and remains) in the Oxford movement; although adopted somewhat mechanically, they actually seem more suitable to AA than to the parent group. Held sacrosanct and untouchable, certainly unchangeable, by many members, these steps are formally referred to in official literature as the Twelve Suggested Steps of Alcoholics Anonymous:

1—We admitted we were powerless over alcohol—that our lives had become unmanageable.

2—Came to believe that a Power greater than ourselves could restore us to sanity.

3—Made a decision to turn our will and our lives over to the care of God *as we understood Him.*

4—Made a searching and fearless moral inventory of ourselves.

5—Admitted to God, to ourselves, and to another human being the exact nature of our wrongs.

6—Were entirely ready to have God remove all these defects of character.

7—Humbly asked Him to remove our short-comings.

8—Made a list of all persons we had harmed, and became willing to make amends to them all.

9—Made direct amends to such people wherever possible, except when to do so would injure them or others.

10—Continued to take personal inventory and when we were wrong, promptly admitted it.

11—Sought through prayer and meditation to improve our conscious contact with God *as we understand Him*, praying only for knowledge of His will for us and the power to carry that out.

12—Having had a spiritual awakening as the result of these steps, we tried to carry this message to alcoholics and to practice these principles in all our affairs.[10]

For several years after the meeting between Bob and Bill, a few AA groups struggled to survive. The movement was little known and could count only a dozen branches or clubs and several hundred members. Then an article appeared in the *Saturday Evening Post* in March 1941 describing the new organization in glowing terms.

In this article, the author Jack Alexander stated that doctors and staffs of institutions throughout the country were suggesting AA to their patients; that courts and probation officers were cooperating with the group; that scores of members were so dedicated that they sat up all night to help a drunk; and that 50 per cent of the alcoholics taken in hand recovered "almost immediately," while half of those remaining recovered after several relapses. It was nevertheless too early to state, Alexander said—thus stating it by implication—"that Alcoholics Anonymous [was] the definitive answer to alcoholism."

Since the publication of this article in 1941, the history of AA has been one of steady growth and expansion. Although it is stronger in some countries than others, and nonexistent in the communist world, today it is a worldwide organization. Its membership figures may not always be reliable because, strictly speaking, there are no members and no membership cards or dues, nor any lists that distinguish the belonger from the nonjoiner. Membership is determined solely by branch reports of attendance at meetings.

Today AA is found in prisons, in hospitals, in poor and rich sectors of cities, in small towns and large. There are AA branches in several American police departments, and others that cater especially to priests. The organization describes itself simply as "a fellowship of men and women who share their experience," and states that "the only requirement for membership is a desire to stop drinking."

AA meetings take on many forms, depending on the leadership, the socioeconomic and educational levels of the members, and the degree of interaction among them. I attended one meeting in Paris in which the seventh step (asking God to remove one's shortcomings) was discussed for several hours. Most of the remarks seemed to be heavily influenced by existentialism; the discussion hardly touched on alcoholism at all but centered rather on the belief in a deity. Insofar as there was no confessional, it was not typical of what seems to take place in American meetings.

The most common aspect of AA meetings, one which a visitor is most likely to encounter, particularly in the United States, and one which has had a considerable influence on other organizations—even on group therapy developments—is the confessional. At one such meeting I attended, there were about thirty people in the room when the leader called the group to order. He read the opening prayer, introduced the few visitors present (according to AA rule, we were introduced only by first name), then proceeded quickly to the guts of the meeting. Would Larry be willing to start? he asked. A man who seemed to be in his late thirties rose and walked to the front of the room. I later learned that many AA's are younger than their appearance indicates: alcohol and its related travails take an obvious toll.

Larry was a thin man, rather muscular, and had a wistful, almost smiling expression when he appeared before the group. Then his face became somber as he began:

My name is Larry and I am an alcoholic. I have been an alcoholic for as long as I can remember. I guess I took my first drink when I was twelve, when I was playing with some older kids and they had some wine. I thought I'd be a wise guy, a big shot, and show them that I could drink too. So I started then, and it seems like I didn't stop for twenty years.

I graduated from wine to whiskey, and when I was in high school and didn't have the money for a bottle, I stole it from my mother. After I'd been drinking, I had to come sneaking into my own house so my mother wouldn't see me and smell my breath.

When I was seventeen I got my driver's license, and a month later I had my first smashup. My girl friend was in the car with me, and before we left the party where we'd spent the evening, she said, Larry, you're stinking and I'm going to drive. I told her I was okay, and besides she didn't even have a license and no girl was going to drive me around. A half-hour later I had that car halfway

> up a tree—but, thank God, nobody was hurt. We climbed out of the car and she said, Larry, listen, say I was driving. Well, she took the rap for driving without a license, and when I called her the next day she wouldn't talk to me. But that was only the first time—and it wasn't the last—that a girl covered up for me because I couldn't hold my liquor.

So Larry went on, five minutes, ten, fifteen. He was expelled from college and lost one job after another because of the bottle; his first marriage ended in divorce, and he has never seen the child born afterward. By thirty his life was a shambles. He was ready to try anything: doctors, hospitals, psychiatrists, clergymen—anything if only he could control his drinking. He often thought of suicide as the only way out.

Then, one day, the girl he wanted to marry told him about Alcoholics Anonymous:

> So I figured they were a bunch of nuts. How were they going to help me if doctors couldn't? But she begged me to go. She said that if I'd give this a try and it worked, we could get married. So I figured I had nothing to lose.
>
> The first thing I learned in AA was that I was an alcoholic, and that an alcoholic can't control his liquor. He has to give it up. That was four years ago, and from the day I entered this room my life has changed completely. I've been able to hold down a job, and I don't have to worry that if I call in sick everyone will know that it's a hangover. I have a family, I have a car, and I'm on the way to having my health back. I owe all of this to AA, and to this room, and to the people I've met here, and to the support they gave me.

Any newcomer to AA meetings would hardly suspect that the group has heard this same story—albeit with slight changes, lapses, embellishments, and new turns of phrase—dozens of times. It is not that they regard any one story as novel; rather, they consciously await episodes and passages that are familiar to them. Larry's past becomes theirs; each time he narrates it, they relive it, managing to overlook the intermediary sorrows because, like children at the movies, they know there will be a happy ending.

The in-group solidarity developed within an organization by such shared experiences is further strengthened if the members have an argot of their own. This is the case with AA. Simon Dinitz mentions such AA argot as "nickel therapy," for "phoning an AA to avert a 'slip'" (the argot has since made its adjustment to inflation), and "the guy upstairs" for "God as you conceive of him."[11] There is sobriety insurance, defined as "behavior and thinking which guarantees continued sobriety, e.g. Twelfth Step Work."

One AA member, in that semi-jocular manner so often used to conceal serious import, confided that there is also a Thirteenth Step. As he put it, "It's the one you take when you ring the bell at the home of someone you're sponsoring—and when you know he's not in but his wife probably is." Then he quickly added: "You see, we're normal. Our organization is no different from the PTA and the Democratic and Republican clubs." The need to be just like everyone else is a very compelling one for those who in some way feel discredited as outsiders.

The organization's urge for solidarity—if not respectability—is also manifested in its auxiliary groups, Al-Anon and Alateen. These groups bring together close family members of alcoholics to give each other mutual support and reinforcement in handling the problem not, as in AA, of how to live *as* an alcoholic, but how to live *with* one. For the parent organization itself, the formation of Al-Anon (generally known among AA members as "the spouses of the souses") serves two other purposes: it broadens the field of AA's interest and influence, and it gives the organization an added weapon by which it keeps the alcoholic bound to the fellowship.[12]

The second AA auxiliary group, Alateen, is dedicated to counseling and advising the teen-age children of alcoholics. Whereas in Al-Anon the spouse is used as a mechanism for controlling the alcoholic, in Alateen any use of the child to reach or manage his parent is considered inherently dangerous because it challenges a basic American tenet: the subservience of the child to the respected parent. Furthermore, many Alateen members are themselves stigmatized by being offspring of alcoholics. That the problems of these children are often deeply psychological in nature, and may require expert professional assistance, has not deterred AA from launching what may be a unique, certainly a little-studied, phenomenon. Today Alateen groups are said to exist throughout the United States; the organization also claims groups in foreign countries, most notably in Western Europe.

One Alateen group in New York City was observed and its members interviewed. The group, which met in a church, consisted of twelve young people, seven boys and five girls. Eleven were white; the lone Negro was a girl. The meeting opened and closed with a prayer; in between, the group discussed the problem of being the child of an alcoholic (usually neither an AA member nor a dry alcoholic, but an active drinker).

This particular group expressed active and unanimous disdain for their parents' relatives. Either the parents had been rejected by their relatives, or, because of a special selectivity, only those children who had no sympathetic relatives to whom they themselves could turn had joined the Alateen group. In one case, no help was available because all the uncles and aunts of the child were themselves alcoholics. Taking up this problem, the leader (an AA sponsor) stated that inclination toward alcoholism can develop in a family. Then he seemed to realize that he was treading on dangerous ground; shortly thereafter, he assured the youngsters that they were not in danger of becoming alcoholics simply because their mother or father drank excessively. Then the subject was dropped.

On one level, Alateen educates a few young people to the problems of alcoholism. Its meetings provide an outlet for sounding off to a sympathetic audience. Undoubtedly this relieves some of the members' emotional pressure, possibly to a therapeutic degree. The exchange of experience among the young people, and the advice from the AA sponsor, combine to give the members some direction in coping with their alcoholic parents.

How successful is AA? This is an important question, one with considerable significance for the future of psychotherapy, particularly group therapy, and one which influences all those persons who would like to extend AA's methods, if only experimentally, to other rehabilitative groups. Unfortunately, however, such extensions are inhibited by the fact that many of AA's claims and assumptions are unproved, obviously self-serving, and of doubtful validity. They may be not only wrong but actually harmful. Some of these claims are: that alcoholism is a disease; that it is incurable but can be arrested; that AA has had a 50 per cent success rate with its members; and that only an alcoholic can understand—or help—another alcoholic.

To examine the broadest claim first—the success percentage—how can one accurately count the people (not to speak of the successes) in an organization which, in its own words, is composed of "men and women who *consider themselves*" members (italics added)? What are the standards for such membership? Must one attend a certain number of meetings before he can "consider himself" a member? How long does he have to remain sober? Is AA successful if a member only drinks less, not stops completely? Or if he only gets drunk on rare occasions, not, as he used to, often? What about a person who attends only one meeting? Is he listed in the branch reports on members? No AA study that I have seen has even considered these questions, let alone suggested answers for them.

A second AA concept as yet insufficiently proved is that alcoholism is a disease. In one sense, it is an ironical statement for an organization born in part of the Oxford movement, one which believed that all men were sinners and responsible for their sins. AA has now reversed that belief: man cannot be blamed or punished—nor should he blame or punish himself—for having succumbed to what was formerly regarded as a sin and is now regarded as an illness. The irony goes even further: Oxford asked the individual to define as sin those aspects of his life over which he had no responsibility (the socially caused ills), while AA now asks the individual to define as disease exactly that aspect of his life (alcoholism) for which he himself is primarily responsible.

Developed to replace the concept of alcoholism as a immoral and sinful practice, the disease theory of alcoholism is still debatable. In June 1968, the Supreme Court of the United States, perhaps for practical rather than scientific reasons, seemed to reject the disease concept when it ruled that habitual and chronic drunkards could still be subjected to arrest.[13]

The main argument with the AA position that alcoholism is a disease is twofold. First, it is asserted without proof or supporting theory. Second, it fails to admit—even consider—that alcoholism might be better described as a symptom rather than a disease.

When this latter suggestion is made to AA members, they generally look blank; unable—or unwilling—to understand the implications; they simply mumble something about splitting hairs. Unfortunately, professionals seem to be no more concerned than alcoholics; on several occasions they have told me that the difference is "only semantic." For AA, of course, the difference is absolutely basic.

If alcoholism were considered a symptom rather than a disease, there might be much more need for psychotherapy, much less for AA. Thus the organization has become, almost by nature and despite itself, anti-therapy. AA denounces without equivocation, both in publications and at meetings, all those who contend either that alcoholics are psychopathological or that they have behavioral disorders similar to those of manic depressives and compulsive obsessives. "What do you think we are," they say, "a bunch of nuts?" By such responses, AA members display not only their essential hostility toward, and their rejection of, persons suffering from mental illness, but, as well, their deep acceptance of their own stigmatized roles.

That the disease of alcoholism is arrested when one stops drinking is a cardinal tenet of AA belief. Certainly for many persons the conquest of the drinking habit does give greater fulfillment in life; that it does so for all, however, is not only open to doubt but unquestionably false. Loneliness, frustration, sexual torment, and other difficulties may actually be enhanced when one stops drinking.

An AA member who had been a model of sobriety for several years told me joyfully that his children can now bring their friends home without fear of finding him drunk; he boasted of his steady job and increasing income, his pleasure at owning a car. AA had saved his life, he said: now it's all peaches and cream. Until, as the discussion went on, he mentioned that he and his wife had not had a good sexual relationship since he gave up drinking.

"But it doesn't matter," he insisted. "It's worth it. She feels that way and I do too."

"What do you mean—a good sexual relationship?"

"Well, we pet and all that, but I just don't get hard. Finally I just turn over and go to sleep, and I feel bad for a while."

"And when you used to drink?"

"Well, we always used to have sex when I was a little bit drunk. Not dead drunk, just a little bit—and then when it was over, I used to get up and finish the bottle." The respondent laughed; he seemed to be enjoying the memory. Then he stopped himself: "But being a souse is a terrible life. If a guy has to give up something to stay on the wagon, so he has to. So what?"

Perhaps this man made a good choice; if he firmly believes so, his belief in itself is a strong argument in favor of his choice. That he should be marked up as a success, however, is open to some doubt. Fundamental to his present sexual difficulty is AA's position that alcoholism is a disease. In this man's case, it was not; his alcoholism was actually a symptom of an underlying problem which remains unresolved. The frequently heard statement that there is nothing wrong with an alcoholic but his drinking has here acted to prevent one man from obtaining the psychological help he so obviously requires.

For some, AA becomes a way of life and, as such, a social and psychological crutch. A bachelor in his forties told me that he attends two AA meetings every week—and two others of Schizophrenics Anonymous. "I got both diseases," he confessed. I couldn't help sensing that he felt somewhat proud—or at least lucky. Certainly he felt satisfaction, for what could this lonely soul do without his meetings? He has no relatives in the city; when I asked about friends, he replied, "Not any more. I used to have them when I drank, but not any more."

"Why not?"

"I mingled with people more when I drank. But not now."

"Then maybe drinking was good for you?" I was anxious to see how he would handle this question.

"No," he said firmly, "drinking is a disease. And when you have a disease, you have to do something for it." Then, lest he be led down a dangerous byway, he continued, "Drinking is the fourth greatest disease in America, judging by the number of people who are afflicted. There are five million alcoholics in this country." And so he continued, reciting the party line he'd so faithfully learned.

If the challenge to the disease concept of alcoholism leaves AA adamant, any challenge to that of the alcoholic's incurability is extremely anxiety-provoking. It is an untouchable tenet, to be accepted on faith. Nonetheless, the objective critic immediately asks: if alcoholism cannot be cured, then why go to AA? Because, comes the answer, it can be arrested there and brought under control. But it cannot be cured in the sense that no former compulsive drinker can ever trust himself to become a social drinker; one slip, even the slightest, says AA, and the entire downward spiral is set in motion. Thus, because alcoholism cannot be cured, there is no such thing as an ex-alcoholic; there are only alcoholics in control of their temptation. They are called dry or sober alcoholics, but never "ex." Like the watch-guard auxiliary, Al-Anon, incurability is a convenient weapon to hold over the former drinker.

AA's tenet, "once an alcoholic always an alcoholic," has been attacked by many persons, among them a professional who has worked extensively as a counselor to alcoholics, Arthur H. Cain.[14] "There are many recovered alcoholics, both in and out of Alcoholics Anonymous," he writes. Supporting Cain, AA sponsors who have been on the wagon for many years will, under friendly questioning, admit that they take a sip now and then. Sometimes, they say, they even smell liquor on the breath of very sober and very dried-out alcoholics at AA meetings.

In an article which appeared in a scientific journal generally favorable to AA positions, D. L. Davies insists that there are many cases of recovered alcoholics who are now able to drink normally.[15] Members, even leaders, of AA denounce Davies' article; according to Cain, however, careful discussion with these denouncers shows that they have never read it.[16] Their denunciations are those of true believers whose faith, not reason, has been challenged.

On a more official level, AA does have an answer to Davies: if these people drink normally today, then they were never alcoholics in the first place. This, of course, is *ex post facto* reasoning; it is one of those statements that deserves no place in science, if only because of its circularity. Furthermore, AA itself contradicts its denial that present social drinkers were ever alcoholics when it replies to the question, "How can I tell if I am really an alcoholic?" with the unequivocal answer, "Only you can make that decision." And again: "Only the individual himself can say whether or not alcohol, for him, has become an unmanageable problem."[17] Does the reformed alcoholic not also have the privilege of stating that he has again become a normal social drinker? According to AA, evidently not.

In a turn of phrase more clever than helpful, AA members regard themselves this way: "We're not *re*formed drunks; we're *in*formed drunks." *Reformed* might suggest *cured*, so the word is shied away from. But *informed* also has its dangers. Many members come to view the organization—and not without AA's approval—as a source of great knowledge and wisdom; after a few short meetings, the neophyte begins to glow with his own expertise, even as he had earlier admired that of the sponsors and the old-timers. This feeling of expertise may be ego-building to many alcoholics, but it can also be destructive. Professionals urge that AA leave research to the scientists, so that, in Cain's words, "scientists might get along with the business of objective research into the problem."[18]

Why AA's opposition to cure, its insistence that leaders and members are not *re*formed but *in*formed? Again, it seems to be a device—not necessarily a conspiracy or a conscious contrivance, rather a latent inherent function—by which the member is tied to the organization, and hence assists the survival of the group. If an alcoholic can never be certain that he is free from the danger of relapse, if he believes that he is likely always to require the protective arms of AA, then he will not only remain within the fold but he will continue to act as both example and sponsor. In much the same way, AA's motto, "Take it one day at a time," serves to bind the member to the organization. For this day—and this day alone—he refrains from drinking. That is all that he is capable of doing—except, of course, for attending those AA meetings which, it is implied, are the only thing that help him through his days.

Ritualism and cultism have grown strong in AA; even first names, which started as a protection, now continue as ritual. Included in the AA publication, *Alcoholics Anonymous Comes of Age*, is a photograph of the pot in which coffee was made at the first Akron meeting; one would think it was the Holy Grail. Along this line, AA feels that it has all the answers: "There's an aggregate of two thousand years of drinking experience in this meeting room," Cain quotes one person at an AA meeting as having stated.[19] And the member added, "If *we* don't understand alcoholism then nobody does." Cain describes this person as the "seer-and-pundit" type prevalent in AA. Perhaps more prevalent than he imagines: a few days after reading his description, I was startled to hear almost the same statement at an AA meeting. "If we don't understand alcoholism," the speaker shouted defensively, "then who the hell does?"

It is a short distance from this statement to the last of AA's major tenets: that only an alcoholic can understand (or help) a fellow alcoholic. Cain points out that, in this context, the word *understand* is a peculiar one: on the one hand it implies knowledge of what it is that makes the alcoholic tick—how he functions or fails to function; on the other hand, it implies empathy, the shared feelings of those who have experienced self-torture and self-destruction.[20] In terms of alcoholism, the first implication of *understand* is untenable: there is nothing about being an alcoholic *per se* that can give one a better grasp of the dynamics, the psychological nature, or the mechanism of the mind and mentality of another alcoholic. In fact, common alcoholism may well be a hindrance to understanding in that it biases the observer. But the second implication of *understand*—to reach out a helping hand—may be the major contribution that only a person who has lost control over sobriety, and then recovered it, can make.

The belief that "only an alcoholic can *help* another" thus gives importance, legitimacy, and permanence to AA; it makes many segments of American society dependent upon it. Should AA fail, where can the alcoholics (and those who look askance at their activities) turn? Nowhere, if the tenet is accepted. But these implications go further: if only an alcoholic can help another, then physicians, counselors, clergymen, and psychotherapists might just as well give up on them.

Responding to some of these criticisms of AA, Milton

A. Maxwell does not refute them; he simply denies that the attitudes criticized are widespread or universal.[21] In fact, he states, they represent minority views which are losing out in AA. Attitudes of AA members toward professionals and their services are spread across the board, Maxwell finds, "from hostility and ignorance to real appreciation and high regard." At the negative extreme, there is a general blacklisting of professionals: "Doctors, clergymen, social workers—none of them know anything about alcoholics." While this view is exactly the one which Cain and others have reported, for Maxwell it is an extreme statement, one created by that "articulate minority within AA who remain highly provincial—who feel that only an alcoholic can help another alcoholic—who oppose psychotherapy on the grounds that alcohol is the primary problem—and who strongly object to such valuable adjuncts as antabuse and tranquilizers."[22]

One can only read this last statement with amazement. Those speaking may be a minority, but—shades of Orwell —the fact is that it is they, and only they, who articulate what has become the official party line. Their views are based on the key tenet, "only an alcoholic can understand an alcoholic," one dictated by neither whim nor discontent with therapists, but by the simple need of the organization to develop a set of dogma to insure its survival.

This is not to say that an attempt at coexistence with the professional establishment as equal powers is not taking place. It is. Furthermore, as AA has become more affluent, gaining a preemptive position in the field, some investigators have detected a cleavage between its rank and file and its leadership, between its local groups and its national boards and committees. If there were not such a cleavage, sociologists would be surprised. According to Jerome Ellison, a consultant paid by AA to investigate the organization, its literature, written a quarter of a century ago, is woefully out of date.[23] New and fresh ideas are constantly being suggested from down below: "exciting, relevant, informed and up-to-the-minute experience," none of which finds its way into official AA publications. But "to publish such literature, it is felt," Ellison states, "would be to risk heresy." Sectarian, cultist, hero-worshiping, seeking to create traditions where they do not exist, able to point to tangible success, to display medallions and awards—all with romantic nostalgia for the good old days when AA started without a penny: these are the characteristics of a group that does not risk heresy.

At AA's national headquarters, Ellison found that he missed "the creative open-mindednesss, the open and stimulating swapping of ideas that made so many of the weekly neighborhood meetings memorable. . . . Committee politics took up half the working day; gossip was venomous."[24] One group of gossipers told him that a certain leader was a hypochondriac, another a homosexual; then he was informed that the accusers consisted of "a nymphomaniac, a schizophrenic, and a megalomaniac." Ellison quickly adds that he observed nothing to substantiate any of these charges. But one is still troubled by such pejorative stigmatization practiced by people who themselves have so recently been fighting against stigma, prejudice, and stereotyping.

Equally significant, Ellison found, was the ultraconservative policy of the nonalcoholic board of trustees; one member, Archibald Roosevelt, was associated with the John Birch Society. Racial segregation was also tolerated: there were no Negroes on either the headquarters staff or any national boards and committees.[25]

For Ellison, the character of AA results from "the shortsighted conservatism that affluence begets." But the source may be even more fundamental—and hence more ineradicable—than simple affluence. AA has found a niche for itself in our society; it has become a legitimate part of the American scene. Its affluence, durability, and success (or reports of its success) have brought about institutionalization. Gained at the price of great travail, sacrifice, and suffering, this institutionalization is not to be relinquished easily. Herein lies the source of AA's conservatism: the familiar urge to retain one's place in what has now become a very pleasant *status quo*. Nonetheless, while they all laugh and make merry in their prosperity, the whole scene may pass them by.

Despite all these factors, it does remain that AA inaugurated a movement to aid people whom many members of American society had renounced. Not only has the organization salvaged lost lives, it has also served as an impetus for the entire social movement of self-help groups. It is therefore all the more distressing that AA's sacrosanct attitude toward criticism endures, as the following extract from the proceedings of a scientific meeting indicates:

> In a famous national magazine in this country there was a sharp diatribe against AA. I feel that the diatribe was perpetrated by the author's own inability to come off his own dry drunk and he just put it into print—but that's another story.[26]

Indeed it is; it is the story of *argumentum ad hominem* —and, coming from a prominent sociologist, it is also the reduction of serious scientific controversy to character assassination.

AA is worth a better defense, or none at all.

3. Gamblers, addicts, illegitimates, and others: imitators and emulators

Without an original there can be no imitation.
—*Walter W. Grossmith*, The Diary of a Nobody

It was not long after AA showed its first signs of success that its formula was adopted by others. If inveterate drinkers could solve their problems by forming a fellowship, if they could accomplish miracles where churchmen and psychiatrists had failed, then why could not those who suffered from other afflictions, maladies, compulsions, and disorders meet with the same success?

Imitation has always been a basic factor in organizational life.[1] Any group's existence, let alone its publicity and alleged success, suggests to those in analogous situations the possibilities and advantages accruing from the formation of similar organizations. Although people are always prone to establish formal associations—social climate permitting—they are more likely to do so when successful precedents have been set.

Nevertheless, imitation has its dangers as well as its

advantages. While trailblazers may show the way and offer inspiration, they may also lead to a stifling of creativity. In organizational imitation there is often a mechanical and ill-planned transfer of attributes successful in one group to another to which they are most inapplicable.

The number of imitators of AA is not known. Most of them have been ephemeral, coming on a local scene for just a moment, often taken seriously only by their few members. Many are simply letterhead organizations founded by a couple of people with good intentions and lofty ambitions. One effort to compile a list of self-help groups some years ago yielded a brochure with some 415 listings. Few were of the AA type, however; most were unguided therapy clubs.[2]

Of all the efforts to emulate Alcoholics Anonymous, probably Gamblers Anonymous has been the most successful, if only because its groups have been the most enduring. This is not to say that the problem of gambling is as serious as that of alcoholism for American society. Not so many citizens feel that their lives have been severely and adversely affected, or made completely unmanageable, by a compulsion to gamble. Although thousands may be deep in debt to loan sharks, may have their families disrupted or unable to function because of cards or race-track betting, may even be enticed to embezzlement and other crimes to cover their gambling debts, such compulsive gamblers are relatively few when compared to the estimated five million Americans said to be malfunctioning because of an inability to control liquor.

It seems that the first effort to form an organization to control gambling took place in California, in January 1949. While California often crops up as the source of self-help movements, in this instance proximity to Las Vegas may have been a factor leading to the foundation of Gamblers Anonymous. In a 1950 article on gambling, Paul S.

Deland, an editor of the *Christian Science Monitor*, traced the short history of GA: "Fashioned somewhat after Alcoholics Anonymous, a group, suffering in the pocketbook from gambling, organized Gamblers Anonymous in California in January 1949." Deland went on to describe a social gathering at which men confessed to having lost tens of thousands of dollars:

> Before long there was a lively discussion, which resulted in the formation of a mutual-help group, with the purpose of encouraging people to cure themselves of the betting habit. From the original twenty-one, membership has now reached thousands in and outside of California.[3]

The group seems to have been primarily an upper socioeconomic one—at least if one judges from the amounts of the claimed losses.

Once its self-help mission was established, Gamblers Anonymous set itself two further tasks: those of exposing "the correlation of crime and criminals to the existence of race tracks," and of wiping out racing throughout the land. "Already," Deland wrote in this 1950 article, "they are establishing branches in other cities, and in due time they expect to put anti-racing bills on the ballot in New York, Florida, Illinois, and Maryland."

Thus, from its inception, GA's aims were quite different from AA's. GA was going to become a crusading, prohibitionist group, seeking not only to control the gambling of its own adherents but to outlaw the practice of public, and even private, gambling. Why this difference between the two organizations? In the first place, AA was organized just as the country was recovering from Prohibition; the crusader against legal traffic in alcohol was *persona non grata* on the American scene. What America wanted in the thirties was precisely what AA offered, or sought to offer:

the control of intoxication and the destruction of Skid Row, but, at the same time, the restoration of social drinking—a practice, it was now to be hoped, unsullied by staggering drunks, highway murderers, and illegal criminal traffic in alcohol. With GA, on the other hand, America had not just experienced a period of crime linked specifically to the prohibition of gambling; quite to the contrary, the country in 1949 was just coming to believe that *legalized* gambling was a major cause of crime.[4]

For all Deland's optimism, GA did not grow by leaps and bounds. Its crusading mission failed in California and never got away from the post in the other states proposed; finally this part of the GA program was scratched. Nevertheless, the same effort to combine self-help with social crusading was to be made in the future by other organizations, including groups of homosexuals, transsexuals, and illegitimates.

Once GA turned away from its prohibitionist and crusading orientation, away from its view of gambling as a *social* illness, it came to concentrate on an AA-type view of gambling as a *personal* illness. Already in psychoanalytic and related literature there had been sporadic mention of the so-called compulsive gambler.[5] Albert Morehead wrote:

> Temperamentally this type, and no less the businessman gambler and the percentage gambler, may be more receptive to dishonest schemes than the nongambler, but even this is not necessarily so. . . . Observation would make one believe that the habitual compulsive gambler is relatively rare, the occasional compulsive gambler quite common.[6]

What happened to GA after its inception in California? It is not clear whether it lingered for a while and then dissolved, or whether it simply continued on a small and modest scale. In 1957 a group calling itself Gamblers Anonymous—perhaps an independent second effort of the same name, perhaps a resuscitation of the organization Deland had mentioned—made its appearance. Whatever its origin, in an official pamphlet issued by the organization, it overlooks the earlier 1949 effort and in its stead states:

> The fellowship of Gamblers Anonymous is the outgrowth of a chance meeting between two men during the month of January in 1957. These men had a truly baffling history of trouble and misery due to an obsession to gamble. They began to meet regularly and as the months passed neither had returned to gambling.

The pamphlet then goes on to record that

> the first group meeting of Gamblers Anonymous was held on Friday, September 13, 1957, in Los Angeles, California. Since that time, the movement has grown steadily and groups are flourishing in many areas.[7]

One must regard even primary sources with skepticism, particularly when they are self-serving. Evident here in the GA pamphlet is the need to create a folklore in the chance meeting of two men. More than just an emulation of AA, this approach is a deliberate effort to project the hand of Providence into GA's founding, to make its history a tradition, and its steps a catechism.

Gamblers Anonymous is described in the pamphlet as a fellowship, one whose "only requirement for membership is a desire to stop gambling." GA boasts a "recovery program" substantially similar to the twelve steps of AA: it starts, "We admitted we were powerless over gambling

—that our lives had become unmanageable," then, as one would expect, goes on to state the need for a moral inventory, the belief in a power greater than oneself, and the request that this power remove one's shortcomings. Gambling, the pamphlet states, in words reminiscent of AA literature, is not only a disease but an incurable one; the only completely cured gambler, members are fond of saying, is a dead one.

Besides GA, only Neurotics Anonymous appears to have copied the format of AA more assiduously. A typical GA meeting opens with a prayer (but a rather secular one at that), after which the chairman recites the preamble and asks members to read the various steps of the recovery program. Following questions about compulsive gambling, the meeting moves to its focus, the narration of the members' life stories. Although now and then a member passes—the word is significant—when the chairman asks for his story, most frequently, he will cross to the front of the room and, following AA's anonymous format, will announce: "My name is John, and I am a compulsive gambler."

Now and then a member introduces a slight but generally disapproved variation: "My name is John, and I guess I'm a compulsive gambler." What does he mean, he *guesses*? The listeners are somewhat dismayed; when queried, the leader confesses, "I'd hoped you had missed that. But John *is* a compulsive gambler. No guessing—he *is*." There is no room for uncertainty in GA; one is either a compulsive gambler, or he isn't.

The average GA monologue lasts from eight to twelve minutes: it colorfully describes the depths to which the speaker had sunk in previous months or years, the roots of his gambling in early childhood or adolescence, the evil he has perpetrated on mother, wife, and children, and the constant unhappiness he has suffered. The degradation seems endless: one member stole from his brother with whom he owned a grocery store, and another from his son's piggy bank. Life for these men was a succession of lies, then new lies to cover old ones. Many had gone to prison; all had been involved with loan sharks.

Neither psychiatry nor divorce had stopped the head-long plunge toward self-destruction. Even a prison sentence had not restored sanity. The compulsion for gambling had continued unabated. "But then," a speaker says, "one day, sixteen months ago, for the first time I entered this room."

This room. One looks around. No crosses or stars of David, no prayer books or holy symbols. Just four bare walls and some seated men.

"I got hooked on numbers," the next speaker says. "I had such a miserable life. I loved to steal. I handled money from two jobs. At one time I had $28,000. Then I was penniless. I couldn't hold on to it. But I learned from this room that I gambled to lose."

"I am very grateful for this room," another speaker says. And still another: "I owe all of this to GA."

The dedication to the group, expressed through the transformation of the meeting room into a kind of holy place, is further strengthened by GA's constant use of bettor argot. Whenever a member speaks of *rolling bones* and *scores*, *jump shots* and *ice*, the others in the audience smile. This in-group language makes them feel that they are part of a fraternity or fellowship, each damned by a common failing and blessed by one another's mutual support. Mention the fear to answer the telephone because it might be a loan shark calling, and the smiles are ones of recognition: "He's talking about me," each listener seems to be thinking.

Upon joining GA, each new member is given a list of first names and telephone numbers of people whom he can call in case he feels he's slipping. Betting is not like drinking, however; the GA sponsors and reformed gamblers, men now in effective control of their compulsion, are unlikely to be able to stay the hand that's reaching for the wallet in the same way a dry alcoholic can stop the hand on the bottle. What they can do, however, is to serve as examples, as proof that reform is possible. Nonetheless, this example-role necessitates a strict control of their own behavior, stricter, say, than in AA. Since there are no tell-tale signs in GA—no heavy breath to be smelled—greater reliance is placed on the honor and integrity of the reformed gambler.

Branches of GA are maintained throughout the country, as well as in England; an Eastern Conclave was held in Rhode Island in the spring of 1968. Like AA, GA has a woman's auxiliary and a teen-age club; called Gam-Anon, the auxiliary also has its twelve steps, the first being an admission of powerlessness over the problems in the family.

One might finally ask what kind of people belong to GA. In a study of seventy-five compulsive gamblers, twenty-nine of whom belonged to GA, Joseph Scimecca found that, unlike other compulsives, GA members "are not isolated from the mainstream of American culture or from the realm of culturally prescribed behavior."[8] They show, he states, "a high degree of solidarity with their primary group of gamblers."

Alvin Scodel, a psychologist interested in inspirational groups, chose to study GA because he was himself a gambler.[9] In a West Coast group, about half of whose members were Jewish, Scodel found that their world was a taken-for-granted one maintained by clichés: everyone said that he was not only a compulsive gambler, but a compulsive loser. The latter claim is easy to believe: no gambler who is ahead is likely to attend GA meetings.

The group that Scodel studied called its confessionals "weather reports"; he describes them as simultaneously "cynical and platitudinous." He was particularly struck by the added status conferred on any person who had lost great sums or become extraordinarily degraded—a type of confession which, in my view, seems to be made less from shame than pride. As Scodel writes:

> . . . there is the man who claims not to have gambled in two years, but in eight months' time the losses he mentioned in his various weather reports climbed almost imperceptibly from $65,000 to $85,000.

Others boasted of their self-proclaimed ability "to con anybody out of anything."

This last statement makes the onlooker wary; how can he help but be skeptical of any organization of self-confessed con men? Are they putting each other on? Are they putting on the researcher? Most importantly: are they putting on themselves? One suspects the answers to these questions must be in the affirmative, especially insofar as reform is excluded. GA members are indeed people who have renounced gambling. Admit it or not, they are *ex*-gamblers.

Unlike the gamblers, whose organization seems to be on the road to permanence, the narcotic addicts' efforts to overcome their habit through anonymous groups have so far met with little success.[10] All Addicts Anonymous groups actually meeting under that name now seem to be limited to institutions. A valiant effort to form a permanent public organization has been made by a second group, Narcotics Anonymous. Although NA has helped some people, as one can judge from testimonials, the fact that it has few functioning branches necessarily restricts its scope.[11]

The failure to organize successfully and permanently may result in part from the fact that most addicts are loners. Their major contacts with other people have been made almost exclusively in pursuit of drugs or the money to obtain them. When they do decide to break the habit, they look to some strong authoritative agency, Lexington or another hospital, perhaps even a jail, to put them through the cold turkey. Furthermore, many addicts only want to be cleaned out so they can start again, but at a lower level. Recently, they have also been using one drug to assist them in going off another; while the practice may be self-defeating, the belief behind it is that the second drug will be less habit-forming, less harmful, and certainly easier to obtain.

Narcotics Anonymous was founded by a former addict who, inspired by AA, sought to adopt its outlook. Danny Carlsen had been attracted to an Addicts Anonymous group while in Lexington, but this organization functioned only under the close supervision of the hospital personnel. Carlsen began to think in terms of an outside, independent organization, one consisting of addicts who were clean and who wanted both to stay that way and to win over new converts. He chose the new Narcotics Anonymous name to avoid confusion with the initials AA.

In an autobiographical statement, Carlsen describes his own addiction and the events that led to the formation of NA. Although he recounts his years "of abject misery and slavery," he also reveals that his origin was upper middle- or possibly upper-class—that is, if one judges by the fact that his foster mother was a staff physician. He was introduced to narcotics, he claims, as a pain reliever during an illness. In 1949, he left Lexington, where he had first made contact with Addicts Anonymous; shortly thereafter he announced the purpose of his new organization:

> This is an informal group of addicts banded together to help one another renew our strength in remaining free of drugs. Our precepts are patterned after those of Alcoholics Anonymous to which all credit is given and precedence is acknowledged. We claim no originality.[12]

This new group advocated thirteen steps, starting with the admission that, while the use of narcotics had made life seem more tolerable, the drug itself had become an intolerable burden. Although it is clearly implied, it is nowhere explicitly stated that the person was powerless to resist drugs—the concept that figures so strongly in AA and GA. Yet, if the word *powerless* is meaningful in such contexts, it seems much more applicable to those fighting addiction than to those struggling against either alcohol or gambling.

The rest of NA's points continue in a familiar pattern: take a moral inventory, list the persons whom the penitent has hurt, and so forth. The thirteenth step, however, differs from the credo of AA and GA by the strength of its desperation and the affirmation of belief:

> *God Help Me!* These three words summarize the entire spirit of the twelve preceding steps. Without God I am lost. To find myself I must submit to Him as the source of my hope and my strength.[13]

Crusading for a cause that had now become all life to him, Carlsen obtained the assistance and cooperation of, among others, psychiatrists, psychologists, journalists, attorneys, and social workers. With them he formed the National Advisory Council on Narcotics, the sponsors of NA.

NA groups existed for many years. Located in churches and reform and treatment centers, these groups, like many other organizations of deviant people, seemed to gain a slightly stronger foothold in California than elsewhere. In 1963 two branches were operating in Newark, New Jersey. In a *Newark Evening News* write-up about them, one encounters almost every element of the well-established Alcoholics Anonymous: the small group of addicts who have hit rock bottom and want out; the premise that addicts and alcoholics have the same personality problems; and the decision to "do it one day at a time."[14] An addict who felt the need for a fix, the paper reports, could call his fellows in NA who would come to stay with him, if, that is—and this may have been NA's difficulty— he didn't call his best connection first.

NA was for addicts who were clean, or at least were not taking drugs at the time they attended meetings. Those who turned to NA said they had reached the end of their line; they attributed to the group their ability to refrain from further use of drugs. "They help me to stay straight and keep away from that first shot," one addict said; when asked to identify *they*, he named the twenty or thirty addicts who regularly attended meetings.[15]

Unlike many of the other anonymous groups, NA faced a number of special problems. One of them was the fear that addicts in intimate interaction would assist each other in slipping; another was that their fellowship would be penetrated by stool pigeons, undercover police agents, and others. Whether fear of police agents inhibited those who might otherwise have attended, or served to diminish the feeling of fellowship among the members, is not known; nevertheless, it can be speculated that such fears were factors that contributed to prevent the growth of the group.

To keep its members clean, NA also had its auxiliaries;

Carlsen himself organized a group, including parents and other relatives, of people interested in assisting the addicts.[16] These auxiliary groups were largely unsuccessful because most addicts do not maintain close family relationships, except for some whose wives are also addicts (and not infrequently prostitutes). As for penetration of NA by authorities, it is a fact that when meetings were held in the Salvation Army hall the police did make inquiries about the group.

When Carlsen died several years after founding the organization, the leadership fell to a woman, an ex-addict who had abstained from drugs for sixteen years. Although it was reported in 1957 that NA meetings were being held in fourteen cities in ten states and territories of the United States and in three foreign countries, that all in all twenty-four chapters or groups were functioning, the organization has declined since then.[17] Furthermore, as the use of narcotics spread, the efforts to salvage just a few people here and there began to seem futile.

Why did NA fail to catch on? Is it because once a man is addicted he is too far removed from the values of society to want to come back in? Is he, when he goes to Lexington, only seeking a fast cure so that he can return to narcotics and the world of escape and fantasy that it offers? Is the addict demoralized, or in such a psychological state that he needs more individual aid and therapy—or is this part of the folklore about addiction? Does cold turkey require the total institution, one in which, like prison, hospitals, or Synanon, the law is laid down and there is no opportunity for a slip?

Whatever the answer, responsible leaders in many sectors of American society are demanding rehabilitative efforts for addicts and ex-addicts. With the large number of addicts in the country today, ones who account, it is believed, for a considerable percentage of some forms of crime, perhaps the AA-NA model is worth trying again, if only out of desperation.

A few words about an anonymous organization that failed—one so ephemeral and unsuccessful that it is difficult even to speak of its having had form or structure. Like other deviant groups, it was formed out of a combination of despair and enthusiasm; nonetheless, it withered away before any real achievements could be recorded. It was called Illegitimates Anonymous, and the fact of its having failed may be instructive about organizations in general and deviance in particular.

When spoken vindictively, *bastard* ranks with racial epithets for its scornful quality; also like racial epithets, *bastard* is always directed against the most blameless of victims. Illegitimate children (many of whom are no longer children, and with less ambiguity should therefore be called illegitimate offspring) have always numbered among the outcasts of Western civilization. And they are not disappearing. One authority estimates that of the current American population of two hundred million, approximately seven million (or about 3.5 to 4 per cent of the population)[18] are what has been termed the "illys."

It has often been remarked that the child born out of wedlock is more highly stigmatized than his parents.[19] Thus, with seven million illegitimates in the country, and at a time when many other stigmatized persons who believed that they had been deprived of rights and dignity were making their hitherto muted voices heard, it was almost inevitable that an organization of illegitimates be formed.

In the fall of 1967, an advertisement appeared in the *Denver Post*. "Born out of wedlock?" the reader was asked. Those who could answer this question affirmatively were then asked a second one: "Why bear it alone? Contact: Illegitimates Anonymous." A Denver telephone number followed.

The attempt to organize Illegitimates Anonymous was motivated by what one person felt to be the disruptive impact on his life of being—and particularly of discovering—that he was a bastard. Thus he placed his ad in hopes of helping other persons cope with the fact of their illegitimate origins. (In the tradition of the other anonymous organizations, the founder of IA was known only by his first name.) Once the ad appeared, a few members joined and a few meetings were held. While the AA format was at first imitated at these meetings—which became less frequent as time went on—it was finally deemed unsuitable. Essentially, IA's members were concerned not with helping themselves but with changing the outlook of others. And, finally, the meetings became involved more with the organization's struggle to survive—to gain and hold members, to find issues over which to fight and ways to fight them—than with the matter of illegitimacy itself.

The organization lingered for about a year, but its failure was almost a foregone conclusion. Why?

If Illegitimates Anonymous was to succeed in its organizational aim, it had to convince the illegitimate that he had a severe problem; otherwise what would be the use of such an organization? Hence, IA had to focus on the stigmatizing forces in society even while it denounced those forces and sought to diminish their effect.

Sociologists in recent years have emphasized that deviance is to be understood in terms of the process by which the world of normals isolates certain people and labels them deviant.[20] But the degree to which this process causes human suffering is at least in part affected by the willingness of the individual—sometimes an entire group—actively to accept the definition of himself as deviant. With the illegitimate, then, there was not only the matter of the invisibility of his discrediting factor, but the question whether he had to be that much concerned about it in the first place. Is the stigmatization of illegitimacy as severely handicapping as IA maintained? To this question, IA adherents echoed AA's contention that only an alcoholic can understand an alcoholic. Thus, only one who had suffered the pangs of "the terrible discovery," who had felt the constant necessity of concealing his past, could know the inner turmoil of the person labeled bastard.

As an organization, IA was dependent on the illegitimate's belief first in his social condemnation, then in the need to overcome it. Thus the failure of IA derived precisely from its inability to convince illegitimates that illegitimacy was a serious problem. In this case the odd man didn't think he was odd, and stayed out.

To a varying degree, GA, NA, and IA dealt with social problems. Although Gamblers Anonymous was forced to abandon the social approach, both Narcotics and Illegitimates Anonymous were always concerned with their members' ability to function within, and to be accepted by, society. When one turns to the sufferers from obesity, however, the problem is almost entirely personal.

Fatties Anonymous was probably the first group to be modeled entirely after AA.[21] It was, in fact, sponsored by the early AA leadership who, while desiring to extend its influence in other directions, did not wish to offer the good name of Anonymous to anyone too highly stigmatized. Fatties were a pleasant, jovial sort of person to get involved with; unlike addicts or homosexuals, fat people would not be pilloried, only regarded with a sort of humorous acceptance. In the end, it would not be too stigmatizing if, through guilt by association, the alcoholics and the fatties were linked. "I would dislike to see AA paraphrased too often . . ." an AA leader stated. "But the fact is that overweight people can diet more cheerfully in groups than they can by themselves."[22]

There is some justification for the link between alcoholics and the obese. Both conditions can be considered the result of temptation, rather than a state of being; both are, in fact, oral. Furthermore, alcohol is a food and, except when it is used in place of other food, frequently a fattening one. Unless people make it such, however, obesity is seldom a deviant condition.

Thus, like IA, Fatties Anonymous and the numerous other groups concerned with obesity that have replaced the original have felt a need to increase the sense of personal distress and/or stigma. If, within the confines of his protective group, the obese person can be brought to see himself as a glutton (gluttony, let it be remembered, is one of the seven deadly sins), this stigmatized view may in turn motivate him to diet.

But many people not personally affected by obesity think the condition is a trivial, even an amusing one. What essentially they do is subsume two completely different conditions under the same label of obesity. One condition involves people upward of three hundred pounds (a little less if they are not tall); frequently nonfunctioning, these men and women are the fat people stared at on the street and resented when they make their way into a crowded subway (some find it difficult to get through the turnstile). The second condition of obesity relates to those who do not have quite the comely figure they would like to have. Though their extra weight is perhaps not good for their health, they can hardly be called stigmatized—unless, of course, they impose this definition on themselves.

Along this line, Hans Toch observes that our culture often views overweight persons not as amusing but "as sloppy, irresponsible, and ungainly. Worse, to some extent the fat person may subscribe to this evaluation of himself."[23] In this case, the organizations of the obese encounter a contradiction. If they attempt to convince the critical sector of society to be sympathetic to overweight persons, to discard the stereotypes that Toch describes, they may well impair the motivation of the individual to overcome his problem. As a result, more so than AA, these obesity groups tend to be entirely oriented toward the condition, not the social condemnation of it. Here, in the American tradition of activism, of every man a master of his own fate (and fat), people are told first that they have a problem, and second, that they, and they alone, can solve it. All it takes is willpower which in FA's case is obtained through mutual reinforcement—not, however, of the need for self-acceptance, but of the desire, willingness, and feeling of ability to change.

Once Fatties Anonymous was established, it was followed by TOPS (Take Off Pounds Sensibly), and an alumnus group, KOPS (Keep Off Pounds Sensibly); later came Overeaters Anonymous, Weight Watchers, and any number of other local and national efforts. Some of these organizations have become commercial enterprises; others have drifted far from self-help.

In contrast to FA and some of the other organizations of obese persons, TOPS maintains what Toch calls a lighthearted attitude; here one cannot help recognizing the stereotype of the jovial obese person. Even the names of the chapters reflect this spirit: Snack Snubbers, Pound Peelers, and Waistaways.[24]

The major theme of TOPS is competitive play. The members weigh in at every meeting; weight charts are kept; and prizes are given to those who have achieved the greatest losses. Anyone whose weight has actually increased is called a Pig, and must appear at the meeting wearing a pig-shaped label or bib. This latter attitude toward one who has slipped is quite in contrast to AA's. A lapsed alcoholic would never be stigmatized, scorned, or subjected to ridicule. But TOPS utilizes scorn precisely because it is never taken seriously enough to affect adversely the person scorned; on the other hand, it does motivate him to do better in the competition. This is a delicate balance, one which can work only when the problem is seen to be within the individual's control, and when any failure is not considered a deep tragedy.

The balance is also helped by a reward system. As Toch says, TOPS's rewards

> are sufficiently real to serve as incentives, but their symbolic or make-believe quality makes it possible to face failure with good humor. Inadequate weight loss leads to a mock reprimand and a not very serious stigma. Misfortune is further neutralized by being combined with the assurance of hope, the encouragement of interested friends, and a shared realization of the difficult nature of the enterprise. Moreover, the task is not prohibitive. It is not only physically impossible to be a perpetual pig, but an occasional weekly crown is a manageable attainment.[25]

What may be most disturbing about efforts of this sort is that they can represent an obsession with skinniness, one out of all proportion to obesity's natural health-impairment qualities. From my observation, the organizations involved with this problem do not seem to be attracting the four-hundred- and five-hundred-pound persons; in fact, few of them are seen at the meetings. For the most part, TOPS's members are only slightly overweight, if at all. That obesity does impair the health and functions of some persons is no doubt true; more frequently, however, this is what the organization would like its members to believe—not unlike the way in which Illegitimates Anonymous sought to convince its potential clientele that illegitimacy is extremely impairing. At any rate, the stories of those who lose one hundred pounds in a year, while authenticated, are atypical; most of TOPS's members would die of emaciation and starvation if their losses came near that figure.

Another weight-watching organization, Overeaters Anonymous, was formed in 1960. Deliberately modeled after AA, OA has simply crossed out the word *alcohol* from AA literature and substituted the word *food;* compulsive drinking becomes compulsive eating, and only you can decide if you're a compulsive overeater.[26] OA does stop short of imitating AA in at least one respect. Whereas the recovered drinker must stay away from all alcoholic beverages forever, the overeater is not similarly enjoined in regard to food.

As in AA, OA's members surrender themselves to a power greater than themselves. And while the theme may work, there is something absurd in an obese person feeling that a power greater than himself can, as OA maintains, restore him to sanity. The implication that compulsive overeating should be seen as a form of insanity is not only dangerous, but it may well illustrate the difficulties of an organization seeking to convince its would-be members that they must adhere to its rules and steps. Whatever value there may be in a group of alcoholics taking a moral inventory and making amends to all those persons whom they have harmed, the mechanical transfer of these steps to the obese renders the steps meaningless.

Collectively, the organizations that use the word *anonymous* in their title, and in some instances have adapted the AA format to their own needs, are referred to by loyal AA members as *the copycats*. Most such organizations have been formed by alcoholics who have been, and in some instances continue to be, adherents of AA. Listing these groups alphabetically—in what is a far more complete list than I have been able to locate elsewhere—one finds, in addition to Addicts, Alcoholics, Fatties, Gamblers, Illegitimates, Narcotics, and Overeaters, the following Anonymous groups:

Adults: an association of convicts whose innocent-sounding name conceals the nature of the group.

Business Failures: not located, but referred to by one writer.

Checks: a group of prisoners, all of whom have been convicted of check forgery.

Divorcees: mentioned on one occasion, but also not located.

Employment: a group said to have existed in Pittsburgh but whose nature is not clear.

Ex-convicts: one of many efforts to form organizations of former prisoners seeking to return to respectable society.

Neurotics: known both as NA and as NAIL, the full name representing Neurotics Anonymous International Liaison.

Priapics: a fictional group of people who pledge to abstain from sex in a world where sex is glorious and glorified.

Recidivists: a British group of ex-convicts, generally known by the initials RA.

Schizophrenics: a close emulator of AA.

Scrupulous: not really an organization—although it calls itself one—but a mailing list providing "mutual self-help for victims of scrupulosity, just as Alcoholics Anonymous does for the compulsive drinker."

Smokers: a group dedicated "to helping people understand and conquer the problem of tobacco addiction."

Suicides: a Johannesburg, South Africa, group working closely with the Suicide Prevention Centre Emergency.

Teen-agers: an organization of youths identified as delinquents. They later found it advisable to change their name to Youth.[27]

Indeed, Dr. Bob and Bill W. could never have dreamed, even in their most imaginative moments, that so many organizations, both "anonymous" and not, would be launched at least partially as a result of their own efforts.

4. Homosexuals:
the many masks of Mattachine

*Homosexuality . . . the term itself
is almost an anathema.*

Although it is only a few years since these words
were written by William Menninger, today it
would hardly be possible to find a statement
about homosexuality so dated. The term—as well as the
fact—is a household word today, a subject fit for both
newspapers and television programs, and a problem
openly discussed among high school students. Yet there
remains a modicum of truth to Menninger's statement, if
only because it is still difficult to find a term which, when
applied to a specific individual, is so completely stigmatizing—unless, of course, it be one of *homosexuality's* more
pejorative synonyms. Nonetheless, few subjects for so
long completely enshrouded in silence have so quickly become so widely discussed. It strains one's memory to recall that the word was literally banned from the pages of

the *New York Times* in the early 1950's, only to make its appearance there a few years later in the headlines.

Among associations of deviant people, the various homosexual organizations that collectively refer to themselves as "the homophile movement" are unique. No group so large in number (although size is a matter of dispute), so completely stigmatized, and placed into so disadvantaged a position remained so long unorganized in this organizational society. When one recalls that these deviants never wanted for educated and intellectual adherents, it is all the more puzzling that no homophile organization appeared in America until after the Second World War.[1]

Although it has been in use for about a decade, the word *homophile* does not appear in current English-language dictionaries; like *synanon*, it will no doubt find its way in before long. In one circle, *homophile* seems to be a euphemism for *homosexual;* in a second it is used to depict a wide range of affection and sentiment, with or without conscious erotic interest, between members of the same sex; and in a third it is used to refer to anyone engaged in the struggle, through formal organization, to alleviate the conditions of the homosexual in society. In this third connotation, a homophile may or may not be a homosexual himself (in America, he usually is), and a homosexual may or may not be a homophile (statistically, he usually is not). Furthermore, there is a tendency to speak of organizations, magazines, and movements as homophile, and bars and parties as gay (or homosexual).

Organizations somewhat similar to the American homophile groups, but with far more prestigious leadership and support, existed in Germany, led by Magnus Hirschfeld,[2] from the turn of the century to the rise of Hitler, and in England, led by Edward Carpenter,[3] also in the early part of the twentieth century. A very few, very weak efforts to develop such groups in the United States were made between the First and Second World Wars, but they met with little success. In those days, whenever Americans turned their attention toward sexual morality, it was to make dramatic appeals for birth control, for premarital sexual freedom (in the camouflaged form of companionate marriage), or for equal rights for women (including an attack on the double standard).

Sociological literature gives full explanation why voluntary associations are formed: when there is a gap in the services available to a portion of the populace, a corresponding need is felt to fill this vacuum. The literature is not quite so helpful in indicating why, when one cannot deny the existence of the vacuum, the need, and the manifold accompanying prerequisites, these organizations are *not* formed. At least insofar as homosexual groups are concerned, the answer may be too apparent to warrant articulation: namely, that while the social conditions conducive to the formation of any organization must be operative for a specific movement, at the same time society must not offer rewards (in the form, for example, of protection or freedom from punishment) for those who refrain from forming such organizations.

Thus several factors inhibited earlier organization among homosexuals; they were interactive, not independent, forces at work in society-at-large. Before the Second World War, an unfriendly attitude prevailed toward social change, or even discussion of social change, in the area of sex. Added to this was the anonymity, or the ease of concealment, which protected the homosexual —which encouraged him *not* to organize. Nor was there any established structure which could serve as the basis for an interchange of the undercurrent of ideas, concepts, viewpoints, and goals, which, in turn, would give rise to an organization. Furthermore, the leadership of any social movement, particularly if the constituents are themselves a disadvantaged minority, often comes from a few intellectually tolerant members of the majority. The anonymity so pervasively surrounding the homosexual, together with society's extremely negative attitude toward him, made suspect anyone who might come to his defense in a court of law or before a tribunal of public opinion. Finally, minorities who live in an atmosphere of contempt and hostility, who constantly feel the hatred of the majority directed upon them, turn much of this hatred inward.[4] This was often the case with homosexuals. They accepted society's verdict, and felt themselves vulnerable and unworthy—too vulnerable to expose themselves by organization, and, in their view, unworthy of the social acceptance for which any such organization would strive.

Despite all the foregoing, by the late 1960's scores of homophile organizations, a few national but for the most part local, were functioning openly. Many had formed more or less simultaneously, independently of each other, in various parts of the country. Newspapers and magazines, published all over the United States and Canada, constituted a homophile press within the homophile movement. At present there may be a few thousand people who belong to different homophile groups, people who can be counted as members, and perhaps an equal or slightly greater number who have been affiliated at one time or another over the years. In addition, there are thousands of regular readers or subscribers to the magazines.

How did all this come about? How did the homosexuals overcome such strong social and personal prejudice at last to form legal and public organizations? Obviously the social climate changed during and directly after the Second World War. If this climate did not actually produce the plethora of groups which comprise the homophile movement, at least it served as fertile soil in which such groups could thrive.

With its youthful marriages, its large numbers of families deprived of strong parental supervision, and its widespread fear of annihilation, the war served as a catalyst for the reevaluation of sexual mores among the youth of America. Sexual behavior could be, and was, discussed with increasing frequency and ever-greater candor. The newly liberal or permissive attitude toward the discussion of pregnancy, illegitimacy, venereal disease, and sexuality in general laid the foundations for homophile organization in essentially two ways: (1) it led to discussion of the "most unmentionable" of sexual activities, thereby bringing homosexuality into the open; and (2) it exposed to a few homosexuals the possibility of a liberal "pro-sexual" society, one whose tolerance might be extended even to themselves.

In addition to the new sexual freedom, the Second World War also increased geographic mobility. People traveled more frequently during the war, both in service and to find new and better work in the booming war economy. Homosexuals, like others, found themselves suddenly removed from their families—in their specific case, freed from possible family disapproval by distance alone. Among strangers, they were able more freely to seek out others like themselves. The increased urbanization brought about by the war also provided the homosexual with an atmosphere conveniently anonymous to his life and functions.

It was within this context that, in 1948, there burst forth on the country a veritable sexual "atom bomb." Dropped from the solemn halls of a scholarly enclave in a small Indiana town, this bomb, or the radiation from its explosion, affected almost every home in America within a few brief months. Attitudes toward sex would never be the same again.

Known popularly as the Kinsey Report,[5] this work must rank with the collected works of Sigmund Freud as among the most influential and controversial books on sex ever written. While the first volume of Kinsey deals with every type of male sexual outlet, including masturbation, animal contact, and premarital and extramarital relations, the figures on homosexuality attracted more attention and aroused more controversy than any other part of the book. Somehow, widespread masturbation, particularly among adolescents, and to a certain extent among adult males, was not a revelation that Americans were unprepared for; it was merely a practice which had seldom been acknowledged in print. Nor were the figures on male premarital and extramarital relations, though possibly higher than expected, particularly shocking: the conquering, even the promiscuous, male has always been somewhat of a hero in American society, particularly among his peers. But when Kinsey and his co-workers asserted that literally millions of American males were exclusively homosexual throughout their lives and that other millions were more homosexual than heterosexual, though not exclusively deviant, either throughout their lives or for a considerable period after the onset of adolescence, the country was truly amazed.

So was the homosexual himself. For the first time in his life he could feel his strength in numbers. If millions of men were homosexual, then would there not be a handful, a score, or a hundred who would be equipped to lead a social movement? Would such a movement not gain wide support among these leaderless people, and would it not be one difficult to suppress?

Shortly after the Kinsey volume appeared, there arose in many cities a number of discussion groups of homosexuals. They came on the scene spontaneously, usually with no connection with one another. In New York, a veterans' organization was already in existence. It sponsored parties, picnics, and discussions, and gave advice to members; it made little effort to conceal its homosexual orientation, except to use an innocent-sounding name, the Veterans Benevolent Association.[6]

Later, also in New York, a slightly more structured group was formed; called The League, it boasted a regular meeting place, with a library, officers, mailing list, and lectures.[7] It disbanded when some members gained the impression, probably an erroneous one, that it was under police investigation; however, some adherents had already become dissatisfied with the fear pervading the group, its unwillingness to proclaim its program to the public. In California, in the 1948 presidential campaign, there was a Bachelors-for-Wallace (Henry, not George);[8] it was followed by a Knights of the Clock,[9] and finally the Mattachine Society,[10] whose name comes from the court jester who told the truth while hiding behind his mask. The lesbians also formed an organization, protectively called the Daughters of Bilitis, after Pierre Louys's work glorifying lesbian love, *Les Chansons de Bilite* (*The Songs of Bilitis*).[11]

With the exception of the Veterans Benevolent Association and The League, which was so boxed in by its own fears that it was ineffective in changing social attitudes, most of the organizations thus far formed were instrumental or social-influence groups. That is, they were designed to benefit the members by organizing them to change, in some small way, what to them was a significant aspect of the social system. The VBA, on the other hand, was entirely expressive in character; its members derived benefits directly from belonging and from the interaction with other members.[12] Among the instrumental associations there was a fear that the two types of group could not mix, that they could not coexist under one name and within one organization. They resisted the idea that expressive functions could be used to tie the individual member closer to an organization which, at least on the leadership level, was performing its instrumental tasks. This resistance resulted from a fear that social functions would result in sexual importuning, arrests, scandal, and the like. Instrumental groups therefore attempted to project a public image of private puritanical morality.

One further type of organization, tangential to the homophile movement if not actually a part of it, appeared in America after the Second World War: the social work agencies. The first such group was started by the Quakers, who enlisted the aid of George W. Henry, a psychiatrist, and Alfred A. Gross, a social worker and theologian. Located in a municipal courthouse in Manhattan, the agency was mainly concerned with counseling people arrested for homosexual solicitation or activities in such public and semipublic places as streets, parks, and subway rest rooms. The agency had not been long in operation when a dispute between the Quakers and the leaders erupted. The result was that Henry and Gross broke all connection with their Quaker sponsors and formed the George W. Henry Foundation. Although Henry has since died, the organization still operates today. The Quakers for a short time also operated a similar agency under other leadership.[13]

Shortly after its foundation, the Mattachine Society was faced by a breakaway of some of its members. The organization had already run into difficulties when it took sides in a mayoralty election; weakened by reaction to that move, it was further enfeebled by a schism of members primarily concerned with publishing a journal. Appearing ultimately as *One*, the little magazine attracted some attention and has had a small degree of success.

Mattachine itself then became engaged in attempting to build a nationwide organization. The two groups, Mattachine and *One*, saw themselves essentially in terms of a division of labor, the former as organization, the latter as publisher. Though differences of policy did arise, they were often inflated beyond their intrinsic substance by the need of all people engaged in competitive struggles to locate areas that differentiate them from one another.

It was not long, however, before Mattachine itself was weakened by a series of internal schisms and scandals. In San Francisco, where the national office was tightly controlled by two persons, almost the entire membership rose up against the leadership. The revolt spread to Los Angeles, then to New York. For a time it was quelled by a compromise; then those in control used the journal *Interim* (supposedly published for members only, but often finding its way into the hands of outsiders) to disclose the identity and publish the photograph of a San Francisco attorney who, active in Mattachine under a pseudonym, was the leader of the opposition. Mass resignations followed, the Los Angeles and San Francisco chapters virtually dissolved, and the New York organization disaffiliated. For all practical purposes the national society had ceased to be.[14] The New York group later changed its name to the Mattachine Society, Inc., of New York (MSNY). From time to time, other organizations, independently of one another, have used Mattachine in their title.

In the decade or more that has passed since this last schism caused the dissolution of the national Mattachine effort, scores of new organizations have burgeoned in several cities. In a few instances, efforts have been made to affiliate them; most of these efforts have failed. Four groups in New York, Philadelphia, and Washington (two in New York), with some further meager contacts in Boston, attempted to form the East Coast Homophile Organizations (ECHO). It was a weak echo, however, one that dissolved after a short time into a cacophony of internal dissension. The National Coordinating Council of Homophile Organizations has been in existence for the last few years; it seems to serve largely as a center for correspondence. Most of the major organizations, however, have refused to adhere to it.

By 1969, there were approximately 150 known formal and structured voluntary associations, once in existence or presently operating, that could be considered part of the homophile movement. There were also any number of small clubs, entirely expressive in nature, on the periphery of the movement. Several have membership lists of only a dozen or even less; most are local and have no association with any national group except the National Coordinating Council. While a few meet in churches and have some institutionally accepted forms of public conduct, many meet clandestinely. Some openly enjoy social activities, although many shun or claim to shun anything that the respectable world might consider scandalous.

These homophile organizations have generally been ignored by the public, catered to by the mass media, tolerated by the police, largely approved of (but unsupported morally or financially) by most homosexuals, and applauded by the few social scientists who have taken note of their existence. And no wonder the applause: these organizations have undertaken the formidable task of acting as spokesmen for a leaderless underdog, a task which sociologists, often without first-hand information or a clear understanding of the nature and scope of the groups, always admire, especially when this struggle against injustice is assumed at such grave personal risk.

Erving Goffman was not specifically writing of homosexuals—but to no other category are his remarks so pointedly directed—when he mentioned persons with a particular stigma who sponsor a publication

> which gives voice to shared feelings, consolidating and stabilizing for the reader his sense of the realness of "his" group and his attachment to it. Here the ideology of the members is formulated—their complaints, their aspirations, their politics.[15]

Howard Becker speaks approvingly of deviants, specifically homosexuals, as being more organized,

> more willing to fight with conventional society than ever before . . . prouder of what they are and less willing to be treated as others want to treat them without having some voice in the matter.[16]

Edwin Schur, writing of the homophile organizations, notes that

> these groups appear to function for some homosexuals as a symbol of hope and reassurance of the worthiness of their cause, and to provide some solace to those isolated homosexuals who may have felt left out of homosexual life as well as heterosexual society.[17]

While all these comments may be considered "correct," they give only a partial picture of the organizations of sex deviants—and usually a favorable one. Underlying these sociologists' views is a sense of injustice and moral outrage, a sense of righteous indignation at the cruel social hostility directed against the socially harmless—and hence support for any measures that would make for retaliation and self-defense. Many sociologists seem to be ideologically predisposed to see usefulness and good in such organizations. In some instances, the predispositions may result from the fact that these organizations are a challenge to the world of respectability; in others, because they embrace the aspirations of the underdog.[18]

The type, character, size, structure, and area of influence of the various segments of the homophile movement, both in America and abroad, cover so wide a spectrum that it would be difficult to describe them all under one umbrella.

There are civil rights activist groups like the Mattachine Society of Washington, which takes cases to court and demands changes in the federal regulations governing employment, selective service, and security clearance.[19] But contrast this organization to one of male prostitutes which functioned for a time in San Francisco, meeting in a church and publishing a paper. Although it used a protective name, no effort was made to conceal the profession of its members.

Certainly one cannot characterize the homophile movement in a few words. In New York, the Mattachine Society holds aloof from national movements, while, for itself, it conducts lectures and sends speakers to universities; it projects a sober view of the homosexual both to itself and the public, and at the same time it goes into the discothèque business.[20] One, Inc., conducts a school and serious research, has amassed an excellent library, and continues to publish its journal, *One*. The Daughters of Bilitis, on a national scale a social-influence group, maintains local centers which are social clubs and where leaders conduct informal counseling; generally known by its initials, the DOB, it has a few honorary male members, whom it calls Sons of Bilitis, or SOB's. Behind the façade of humor there lurks self-revelation, the lesbian's hatred and resentment of males.

Some homophile organizations have truly lofty ideals

and prestigious personnel. Located in San Francisco, the Council on Religion and the Homosexual is supported by many churchmen, while another group by the same name functions in Dallas; the latter, one suspects, is and may remain a "paper" or "letterhead" organization. The ultimate in letterhead organizations came to light when a young man had cards printed for the Homosexual League of New York, ones which gained him entrance to newspapers, magazines, and radio stations; he seems, however, to have been the only member, and did not even have a letterhead.

One of the most prestigious groups, located in England, is called the Homosexual Law Reform Society. Brought about by a series of scandals and arrests preceding the inquiries of the Wolfenden Committee, this group has succeeded in many ways where its American counterparts have failed: it has gathered leading intellectuals to the cause, has openly espoused the repeal of anti-homosexual legislation without having the members of the committee labeled as or suspected of being homosexuals themselves, and has gained intellectual respectability and legitimacy both for the organization and its program. It is therefore all the more dismaying—yet characteristic of the homophile movement—to find that a group in Philadelphia (at one time known as the Mattachine Society of Philadelphia, later as the Janus Society) has also assumed the Homosexual Law Reform Society title, particularly since this organization has published *Drum*, a far from respectable and far from prestigious magazine.

But *Drum* and its parent organization have always scoffed at respectability—at the same time they have demanded it: while the magazine caters to the erotic, sadomasochistic tastes of its clientele, the organization insists that society confer dignity, equal rights, and freedom upon the homosexual. And why not? *Drum* sees itself as part of America's struggle against censorship; when it publishes pornography (which it indignantly denies is pornography), it proclaims that equality for the homosexual should mean that anything that goes in heterosexual publications (and there almost anything does go, or did until the *Eros* decision) should be permitted in homosexual journals as well. In fact, by a curious piece of irony, the very reverse of the commonsense notion that society should be more stringent with appeals to the abnormal than to the normal may eventually prevail in the United States: in one Supreme Court decision the right to publish lascivious material in homophile magazines was upheld on the grounds that these journals cater only to those already inclined to receive them and who are, therefore, already corrupted—or, one might say, incorruptible.[21]

Because of the fission that has marked the homophile movement, some will regard with dismay the inability of a force so weak, so fraught with dangers, and facing so formidable a task to heal the wounds within its own ranks. However, this disunity may be more functional than appears on the surface. The splinterized movement is able to divide its tasks by a sort of unplanned division of labor, leaving a place for the minister and the educator, the young male prostitute, the disturbed woman seeking companionship and solace, the boys out to have a good time, and the men looking for sex or a civil rights battle. It gives opportunities for people of diverse abilities to display their talents. More than that, it makes busy work of a legitimate and respectable kind: today there are national conferences of homophile organizations, in preparation for which Eastern, Western, and other regional conferences are held.

The formation of organizations fighting for the rights of homosexuals gave courage to many who were awaiting the opportunity to form purely social clubs. That such clubs might lead to sexual solicitation, even contacts—or what the square world would characterize as outrageous behavior—at first frightened many leaders who had sought to keep the original organizational goals unsullied. Nevertheless, since *One, Drum*, and other journals could openly be published, each more daring than the last, it seemed logical that clubs with purely expressive social aims could at last function.

Many such clubs exist today under a wide variety of names. In the smaller cities, they conceal their nature, seldom attempting to tackle the larger problem of public disapproval. Nonetheless, they admire the groups in the bigger cities able to do so. In at least one such club, the members, perhaps compelled by a need to reaffirm their masculinity, have assumed the trappings of the motorcycle craze; the façade of a motorbike club conceals the real nature of the bond between the members. Like the veteran's organization which became open both to veterans and their friends (among the members jocularly paraphrased as "veterans and their lovers"), clubs of the motorbike sort quickly put aside the requirement that members own bikes or even be involved with bike riding as a way of life, and recruited from among the larger reservoir of "the friends of riders."

It is not a long step from the leather-jacket uniform of the bike rider and the compulsive idealized demonstration of masculine strength, if not violence, that permeates the motorcycle cult, to the sadomasochistic homosexuality with which such clubs become involved. Leather is a sadistic fetish; thus the boots and belt as well as the jacket become sexual symbols; the chain, which was originally used to protect the bike against theft, becomes the symbol of enthrallment, of mastery over the slave, which is so popular a game with American homosexuals. Popular, but only as a game: although homosexual relations are characterized by psychic sadism and still more by psychic masochism, and while it is not unusual to find even physical maltreatment among these deviants, it usually stops short of maiming or disfigurement.

Along these lines, one club calls its publication *Black and Blue*. The cover is usually a rather artless drawing of what, in the homosexual vernacular, is called "rough trade," a strong, overmuscular young man, more titillating than obscene, whose crotch is bulging. The magazine itself contains a few matters concerning bike riding, some safety points, leather chain ads, and some club news.

Smaller groups, consisting of less than a dozen members, usually meet in a private home, but sometimes in a clubroom. They have no problem about what the members or even the organization can do because the organization *is* the meeting. At the weekly or bimonthly get-togethers, the members attend to their parliamentary procedures, their elections, their committees, and their correspondence with regional and national conferences. The meetings are lively and entertaining, and provide a feeling of having performed for the organization, even if there has been no lasting accomplishment. Participation is usually at a high level, as is frequently the case in small groups. Following business there may be a discussion or a social affair; either provides the satisfaction of belonging. Sometimes the discussions drift into unguided group therapy, as when a member brings up personal problems and others advise how they might be handled, but while the advice comes out of experience, it is often far from helpful.

The names of the homophile organizations are themselves a feast for the interested student. In Los Angeles, there is the Circle of Loving Companions, in Hartford the Institute of Social Ethics. Acronyms abound, with PRIDE,

ASK, ARC, and SAME, standing respectively for Personal Rights in Defense and Education, Association for Social Knowledge, Association for Responsible Citizenship, and Society Advocating Mutual Equality. Of the first, no one seemed to be sure, upon inquiry, what *Defense* represented ("I guess they needed a D," someone suggested). It could have meant the right either to serve in the armed forces or to be defended against police and courts in case of arrest. There are at least two, possibly more, Student Homophile League clubs on campuses; the Columbia University chapter made the front page of the *New York Times* when it was organized. Some groups claim hundreds of members, but the Demophile Center of Boston claims only one, who must be congratulated for his tenacity as well as his fidelity to truth in his resistance of exaggeration.[22]

A description of one group in this medley, even two or three, could hardly be representative of all that is going on in some universities, in several small cities and many larger ones, and in clubrooms, dance halls, and specialized publishing houses. But one turns first to Vanguard precisely because of its atypicality; it is unique not only on the homophile scene but in the entire spectrum of deviant people.

Vanguard is openly described by the National Planning Conference of Homophile Organizations as a "juvenile org." Let its Statement of Purpose speak for itself (with only the spelling corrected):

> Vanguard is an organization for the youth of the Tenderloin attempting to get for its citizens a sense of dignity and responsibility too long denied.
> We of Vanguard find our civil liberties imperiled by a hostile social order in which all difference

from the usual in behavior is attacked. We find our rights as human beings scorned and ridiculed. We are forced to accept an unwarranted guilt which is more the product of "society's" hypocrisy than scientific fact.

We have finally realized that we can only change these processes through the strength we develop through our own efforts. Vanguard is determined to change these conditions through organization and action.[23]

Perhaps the most important single factor about Vanguard is that is can exist. When society can permit the free organization of youthful homosexual prostitutes, either the limits of tolerance have become extremely wide, or else it has written off these people as hopeless—even at their youthful age—and thus allows them to live in a world controlled solely by their own norms. These norms are indicated by a little piece of doggerel titled "The Hustler" (the male prostitute's euphemism for himself), which appeared in a Vanguard publication under a picture of a teenage youth who looks as if he had just stepped out of John Rechy's *City of Night:*

> I'll go to bed for twenty,
>   All night for just ten more.
> Now don't get the idea
>   That I am just a whore.[24]

Banish the thought!

Vanguard was located at the Glide Church in San Francisco, the home of both an organization of transsexuals and the Council on Religion and the Homosexual, Inc. Many reverends are listed on a board of trustees of this council; among the civilians one recognizes several people, active in the homophile movement, who are avowed and self-labeled homosexuals. It is difficult to determine to what extent this church and the organizations it sponsors represent a united front, a false front, a real concern of the clergy with the downtrodden, or just a game of make-believe. Religion has always offered protection to those Americans who espouse otherwise unpopular causes. In this regard, the Council on Religion and the Homosexual is the epitome of respectability: its pamphlet, "A Brief of Injustices," is cogent and well-written; its arguments are strong and its polemic convincing.[25]

In contrast to Vanguard, the Mattachine Society of New York (MSNY) is one of the most influential groups of the homophile movement and, as such, is clearly a worthy subject for extended study.

The Society draws from a wide variety of adult age groups, but members in their thirties and forties predominate. It is made up largely of men who live in New York, a few in the environs, and a small but considerable portion elsewhere in the United States. A very high percentage of the current New York members have lived in the city only a short time. When studied not long ago, MSNY had three hundred members; since then, according to a leader of the group, no one has tabulated membership. Some join and pay a year's dues, then disappear after the first month or two; a few have remained on the list for several years.

MSNY has attracted very few Negroes, but many more white Protestants than one would expect from their percentage of the city population. In this respect, it seems that the membership is a reflection not of New York City's population as a whole but specifically of the New York homosexual population, one inflated by large numbers of geographically mobile people who drift away from small towns and families to the attractions of urban anonymity. There is considerable secularism and anti-religious sentiment among MSNY's members, but whether this sentiment is higher than in the American population of the same age groups, or simply in the American homosexual populace, one can only conjecture.

MSNY seems to be a group of middle socioeconomic status and, as such, the income of the members is surprisingly low; this may be a reflection of the inability of homosexuals to work in their own best economic interests. Nonetheless, the organization has not attracted drifters, school dropouts, or job-changers in search of an anchor. Nor does it count in its ranks the homosexual stereotypes: the hairdresser and the male nurse. It has few manual workers, skilled or unskilled, but it does have musicians, artists, actors, and interior decorators—the latter, however, in fewer numbers than the casual New York observer, impressed by folklore and unverified perceptions, might expect. In sum, MSNY is a small, educated, largely middle-class group. In some respects, it is characteristic of those one would expect to find in any instrumental voluntary association; in other respects, its composition can obviously be traced to certain aspects of the homosexual's life.

Although it is one of the taken-for-granted tenets of this sort of group's catechisms that homosexuality is neither an illness nor a disturbance, a considerable minority of MSNY's members do not share this view. One-third of the members replied affirmatively to the question whether homosexuality should be seen as a disturbance, illness, neurosis, or symptom of an underlying neurotic difficulty. Furthermore, just under half the members stated the belief that the average homosexual is more disturbed than the average heterosexual (although few saw themselves as being in the "more disturbed" category). More than two-fifths of the members have been in therapy, a proportion that reaches one-half when considering only members under thirty.

It is one of the great tasks of a group of this type, in fighting for the homosexual's acceptance by the public and himself, that it must put forth a set of beliefs that will assist the organization's goals, regardless of scientific evidence and empirical observation. The homophile movement, in handling this problem of ideology, must project an image of the homosexual consistent with the one that, it is felt, will further the aims of the movement—even if this image is inconsistent with the knowledge that members of homophile organizations obtain from everyday experiences.

To accomplish this aim, the group offers a set of enticements to members, particularly in the form of appeals to group pride and psychological needs. While many homosexuals, including members of Mattachine and several of its leaders, may consider themselves and other homosexuals disturbed, the organization, on the other hand, seeks to bolster its adherents' feelings that they are "as good as anybody else"—which means "as *well* as anybody else." Although the individual member, even the officer, may be leading a life which he himself considers licentious, the organization encourages and attracts members by making them feel that their lives are replete with the purest type of love.

Hostility is therefore generated toward any scientific evidence antagonistic not only to the group's goals but to its ideology. To impugn the motives and to ridicule the findings of scientists producing adverse evidence becomes another of the group's aims. Furthermore, self-protection demands that MSNY must make constant denials that it is a propagandist for homosexuality, at the same time that it must refute the idea that homosexuality is any kind of an illness or neurosis, even an inferior or less desirable way of life. These aims largely determine how the homophile movement structures reality.

If, for example, people are to have civil rights, if they are to be accepted into the family of man and treated with dignity therein, then some believe that this goal will be achieved only to the extent that the people accepted are— or appear to be—normal (although nonconformist). In a society whose traditions and pretensions (no matter how frequently they may be flouted) are essentially puritanical, one must be pure and loyal in love, with the emphasis on romance and not on the physical aspects of sex. Thus, even the word *homophile* is a euphemism for the harsher *homosexual*. And, like many euphemisms, its origin lies in ideology: it removes the concept of sexuality from the relationship, and suggests people whose love, not their libido, is directed toward their same kind.

According to this projected image, the homosexual is "just like" everybody else, except that his "love object" happens to be of the same sex. His relationships with partners, it is maintained, are long-lasting and monogamous, at least as much so as those between husbands and wives (and everyone "knows," in the homosexual's view of the world, that every husband cheats, that suburbia is replete with wife-swapping, and that the only thing that holds a marriage together is either legal and social pressure or children). As *One* says, "That within heterosexual families there exists a warm, pink cloud of understanding is just so much fantasy. It just isn't so."[26]

With the image of heterosexual romantic love before him (which he admires and ridicules, imitates and denigrates), the homosexual describes his relationship to a sex partner in terms of love. Sometimes, however, the most successful residential units he establishes take on forms that depart quite radically from the world he is seeking to emulate. In such units, there may be mutual affection without sex; or, on the other hand, considerable sexual activity devoid of any semblance of affection. There is often, in fact, a sharing of sex partners; or a two-way pretense in which each partner seeks to conceal from the other his many "extramarital" relationships.

It is almost impossible for an observer to fail to note the divergence between the homosexual's romantic fantasies and his life experience. On the one hand, he projects (particularly through the homophile movement) an image of romantic love; on the other, he shares knowledge of an extraordinary amount of male prostitution and compulsive searching for partners (or *cruising*, as this activity is called). Homosexual pornography has a wide market; sexual interest in strangers, particularly in adolescent strangers, knows hardly any bounds. Homophile organizations are constantly involved with aiding people apprehended for sexual solicitation (or even sexual performance) in men's rooms. Every homosexual is aware of the ubiquity of casual relationships, ones that last a few minutes or at most one night, of the hunger for love that meets constant frustrations, and of the fleeting nature of relationships that start with great promise and vows of fidelity.

In a bulletin issued by the New York Mattachine Society, discriminatory practices against homosexuals are briefly summarized, then explained in a simple phrase: "All this because he loves." In the same bulletin, the following description of the organization is given:

> The Mattachine Society, Inc., of New York, a nonprofit, volunteer organization, is entirely dedicated to the complete understanding and full acceptance of homosexuality as a way of life—and love.[27]

The use of the word *love* and the avoidance of the word *sex* in these two passages are significant. Not unlike all other sectors of the homophile movement, MSNY is engaged in an effort to project a view of men whose bonds of affection and loyalty are similar to those that tied Damon to Pythias or that inspired Plato to write of Greek lovers dying for each other as heroes on the battlefield. Yet this view is in sharp contradiction to the experience and knowledge of members. While the group calls for change in legal sanctions against homosexuals, it also admits that "fully half of the solicitation cases [in the New York courts] occur in the subway toilets."[28] There is, however, no effort to reconcile this information with the themes of romance and love.

The homophile organizations also seek to project an image of men who are "all male," people whose sexual proclivities in no way diminish their masculinity. The effeminate homosexuals—characterized pejoratively with such expressions as "the swish" and "the screaming queen"— are discouraged from participation in the organizations. This image of masculinity is part of the search for acceptance; the public is not beseeched to extend a hand of sympathy to homosexuals as they are, but is shown a section of homosexual life that might accelerate understanding. Along this line, note the description of the Mattachine members who picketed the White House:

> The pickets (10 men, 3 women) were well groomed and neatly dressed (suits, white shirts, ties for the men; dresses for the women), carried carefully lettered signs, and, in general, made a good appearance which was noted.[29]

Appearances aside, many authorities see the homosexual as a deeply disturbed person. No one has expressed this view more strongly than Albert Ellis, who states that, in addition to himself,

> practically all other psychotherapists insist that males and females who desire *only* members of their own sex as sexual partners are wrong or emotionally disturbed.[30]

Although some of these people, Ellis contends, are "reasonably integrated individuals," whom he would classify as among the "normal neurotics of our society," most are maladjusted, self-defeating, short-range hedonists, generally anxious, and have "various other symptoms of emotional illness." He contends further that they are obsessive-compulsive and disordered in their lives, that they think negatively a good deal of the time, are often depressed and extremely defensive, and that they have exceptionally low opinions of themselves.

Although this view is echoed by many well-known persons in the professional world, a few reports to the contrary have appeared. The best-publicized has been that of Evelyn Hooker, who took a small group of homosexuals, chosen by Mattachine in San Francisco, gave them projective tests along with a group of heterosexuals. The researcher found that the two populations were about equally well adjusted.[31]

With such backing, the homophile movement insists that, to the extent that homosexuals are disturbed, they are no more so than other people. The organization both denies disturbance on the one hand and blames it on a socially hostile atmosphere on the other. It denounces the concept of sickness or pathology in homosexuals as one which gives aid and comfort to their persecutors. MSNY has made this plain:

> In the absence of valid evidence to the contrary, the Mattachine Society of New York maintains that homosexuality is not a sickness, disturbance, or other pathology in any sense, but is merely a preference, orientation, or propensity.[32]

One of the ablest leaders of the homophile movement has urged the organizations to take the position that until and unless clearly valid, positive evidence shows otherwise, homosexuality, *per se*, is neither a sickness, a defect, a disturbance, nor malfunction of any sort.[33]

This leader (a Ph.D. in one of the physical sciences who has had no specific academic training in medicine or in the behavioral sciences) has also stated that "if our movement is to succeed, we must be prepared to take bold, positive positions on relevant controversial matters, not negative, wishy-washy neutral ones."[34] In this view, one does not take "bold, positive positions on controversial matters" because the evidence is in, but simply because failure to do so will harm the movement. It would be difficult to find a more explicit admission that organizational needs for survival and growth dictate an ideological restructuring of reality.

If, as the homophile groups do, one takes the position that homosexuality is neither a disturbance nor a sickness, then the next logical position is that homosexuality is not subject to cure. Anyone who suggests cure, according to Mattachine leaders, must be a charlatan or a quack. Of Bieber, one of the best-known psychoanalysts who has published claims that some homosexuals have been reoriented in their sexual interests, *One* writes that his work is "risible," and that he represents "present-day psychoanalysis at its most obvious and grotesque." Particularly risible, *One* found, is this sentence from Bieber:

> Homosexuals do not *choose* homosexuality. The ... adaptation is a substitutive alternative brought about by the inhibiting fears accompanying heterosexuality.[35]

Ellis has compiled a long list of people who have reported cures; such lists are either ignored by Mattachine

leaders or denounced as lies. The entire idea of cure is ir-
relevant, writes one leader, who then further remarks that
he does not see "the NAACP and CORE worrying about
which chromosome and gene produces a black skin, or
about the possibility of bleaching a Negro." Nor, he states,
is the B'nai B'rith Anti-Defamation League interested "in
the possibility of abolishing anti-semitism by converting
Jews to Christians."[36]

The manner in which the homophiles ridicule the concept of cure is illustrated by an article that appeared in
The Ladder, the organ of the Daughters of Bilitis, under
the title, "The Causes and Cures of Heterosexuality." The
writer weaves a fantasy, reporting excerpts from a sym-
posium at a state university in which learned speakers
declare that many people are alarmed

> at what seems to them a rapid increase in hetero-
> sexuality. . . . Some of us [are] coming to realize
> that heterosexuality is an illness and is to be
> treated, not punished.

One doctor, discussing the etiology of heterosexuality,
found himself "embarrassed at the paucity of knowledge
in the field."[37]

While the antagonistic attitude to cure is often stated as
strongly as the foregoing at meetings and in conversation,
it is seldom made so explicit in writing, if only because
many homophile organizations, to gain legitimacy, attempt to utilize therapists who would not condone so outright an attack on their profession. Nevertheless, the an-
tagonism to cure or change is so strong that the leadership
of Mattachine proposed to the board of directors that it,
MSNY, investigate so-called therapists who promise "mir-
acle cures," and determine what fees they charge and what
their motives are.[38]

In both these areas (hostility toward the view of homosexuality as a sickness, and hostility toward cure), the defensiveness of homophile organizations is understandable. If the public considers homosexuals unchangeable, homophile leaders believe, then it is more likely that social hostility will be alleviated. If, on the other hand, the public accepts the possibility of change, then it will continue to hold homosexuals personally responsible for continuing on their deviant path.

Within the homophile organizations, members sneer at anyone who expresses an interest in changing. They remark pessimistically that such a person will soon be back in the fold. Nobody changes—*but nobody*—they assert. But they do not find this belief at all inconsistent with their frequent citation of persons who change from heterosexual to homosexual, often in their twenties, sometimes later. Talking about his roommate, one active member said, "He didn't find out about himself until he was out of the Army and was about twenty-five years old." The choice of words is particularly revelatory: "to find out" about oneself, as if homosexuality were always there, just waiting to be discovered. A woman active in the Daughters of Bilitis related that she had been married and had had a child when the marriage "went bad" and ended in divorce. Shortly thereafter, and for the first time in her life, she became consciously aware of sexual interest in another woman. She was then past thirty. She has now been living an exclusively lesbian way of life for several years, yet firmly denies that any lesbian in her circle, herself included, can ever change. Similarly, Mattachine members frequently state that "every man has something of the homosexual in him." Needless to say, one never hears a member assert the corollary.

Once a member denies that homosexuality is an illness or a changeable condition, he is next led to the conclusion that, as a way of life, it is just as desirable as the normative one. "Homosexuality," states a bulletin of MSNY, "is a propensity that is on a par with and not different in kind from heterosexuality."[39]

Another MSNY publication goes so far as to suggest that it might be a good idea to teach young people what an excellent way of life homosexuality is:

> Sex education was urged as part of the educational program in New York City schools recently by Dr. Mary Calderone, specialist in Public Health. She urged that sex be taught from kindergarten through high school in order to correct conflicting views on the subject. Among these views is the propriety of monogamy and sex within marriage while sex outside marriage is regarded as being "fun" and the thing to do. Such education was viewed as engendering greater responsibility through knowledge on the part of teen-agers.
>
> The idea is commendable. The plan's value diminishes, however, when one considers that such education would enforce an exclusive method of sexual behavior as being proper and all others as being improper upon young minds. This could only increase the confusion and difficulties of those who find other sexual behavior preferable. The concept is also subject to the individual prejudices and quirks of those who might be teaching the subject.[40]

In conversation, an even stronger position is taken. One officer of MSNY maintains that homosexuality is preferable because a person can be free. "I feel sorry," he told me, "for anyone caught in a snatch-trap."

As a corollary, the fact that homosexuality is often shown to be an undesirable way of life is dismissed as unworthy of serious consideration:

As the folklore of homosexuality would have it, homosexuals are inclined toward the use of narcotics and alcohol as crutches for their psyches. These same folklorists see us as unstable, bad risks and of course seducers of the young (preferably below the age of four).[41]

One prominent member of the Mattachine Society, a minister, suggests that "the Church should recognize that homosexuality is a built-in safety valve on the human population explosion problem."[42]

When Irving Bieber wrote an article in the *New York Times* on the early recognition of homosexual tendencies in children and the measures that can be taken to prevent them,[43] a writer for Mattachine denounced the "avowed ignorance" of the analyst. Bieber was offering advice to parents, the writer stated, on the basis of "platitudes, half-truths, ignorance, and unprofessional bias." The writer made Mattachine's position clear:

> Heaven help Dr. Bieber, the editors of the *New York Times*, and all abusers of behavioral science who use the prestige of their professions to perpetuate a sexual orthodoxy which has for centuries made large numbers of people abjectly miserable if these people should ever fail to adequately suppress the fact that large numbers of homosexuals not only enjoy their proclivities, but function as well as anyone can be expected to under the circumstances in which homosexuals must now live. Let these people devote their energies toward making all forms of harmless eroticism acceptable.[44]

Homophile organizations have often stated that they are not seeking to spread homosexuality. At the same time, however, they assure the public that, in the area of sexual behavior, the deviant way is equivalent to the accepted one; society is urged not to educate its youth in a one-sided prejudiced manner.

Despite its denials—and its intentions—these organizations thus become proselytizing agents for homosexuality. When confronted with such a charge, however, the leaders reply, "No one was ever converted to homosexuality." A glib statement, unsupported by the evidence. In the first place, it is known that, particularly for the adolescent, sexuality of any type is a learning process. The work on sex offenders from the Institute for Sex Research indicates that many institutionalized youths had themselves been seduced into homosexuality by older men.[45] In a Polish study, as reported by the U.S. Department of Health, Education and Welfare, "the authors concluded that seduction plays an important role in causing environmental homosexuality."[46]

What is not yet known is the effect on ambivalent young people of propaganda that maintains that the "gay" life is "just as good" or "on a par" with any other.[47] Youths striving to find the sexual way are in a stage that may be called ambisexual or even pansexual. It is entirely possible that they can be influenced away from the normative path. To this Mattachine members privately shrug their shoulders. "So what?" they ask. "Why make a value judgment? Why isn't our way just as good?"

Whether exclusive or near-exclusive homosexuality, even in the most sexually permissive society, can be as fulfilling to the individual as its reverse is open to doubt. Whether it can ever be, or should be, placed on a par with heterosexuality, without endangering the continued existence of the family, is more than questionable. Nevertheless, the stance of many spokesmen for the homophile movement is readily explicable. People trapped in any way of life require reinforcement of the value system that they are compelled to assume in order to gain self-acceptance. This value system is reinforced when one is assured that his condition is not an illness, that it is inescapable and incurable, that those who pretend to change or to have changed are exploiters and frauds, and that, when all is said and done, the condemned way is just as good as any other. In this manner, the homophile movement has developed an ideology which in turn becomes a mechanism for reconciling apparently contradictory views.

A dissident minority within the movement has suggested that homosexuals recognize their condition not only as a handicap but as a pathology. As such, homosexuality seems to be more deeply rooted in life patterns than is alcoholism, less easy to eradicate, more completely (and probably more irrationally) stigmatized, and, while perhaps not so difficult for a functioning individual to live with, certainly more difficult for him to abandon. This view—homosexuality as pathology—in no sense justifies the attitudes of a hostile society; hence the purposes for which the homophile movement has been established continue to give it a reason for being.

In England, the Wolfenden committee proposed that homosexuality, whatever may be the justification for considering it a sin, should not be considered a crime.[48] Like many other sociologists, Edwin Schur states that homosexuality, when committed by consenting adults, is a crime without a victim, and for this reason the onus of criminality should be lifted.[49] Both these views can be formulated in a statement of the homosexual condition as an undesirable handicap that does not make those afflicted undesirable.

In this view, homosexuality is not an "equally good" way of life; it is not "on a par" with heterosexuality any more than blindness, claustrophobia, and epilepsy are on a par with the absence of these states. Although it is pathological to be blind, and more desirable to be sighted, to those who cannot be the latter, it is obvious, only human sympathy and acceptance should be extended. Blindness is undesirable, but a blind person is not himself an undesirable. Then why cannot this same attitude be extended to homosexuals?

Many members and leaders of homophile organizations (although, it is stressed, not all) privately express agreement with this view. Then why not openly articulate it? When asked this question, a leader of Mattachine replied:

> You can't get people to join an organization when you tell them that they're sick. That's not what they want to hear. They hear that all the time. They want to come to Mattachine to be told that they're not sick—even if they are.

The contradictions in the homophile movement are likely to prevent it from becoming other than isolated and cultist, sinking deeper into untenable ideological distortion as it proclaims only that which its members want to hear and which they need (or feel they need) to believe. The short-range gains may well be encouraging; but, while the movement may help to correct some abuses and offer some support to individuals in distress, while it may exert some small pressure on governmental and private bodies, in the long-range view it is doomed to failure. As it's constituted now, it must continue at war both with itself and the world of science. Its ideology has led it into a *cul de sac* where, despite itself, it has become a proselytizer for sexual deviation. As such, the homophile movement cannot be successful in reorienting the public's attitude toward, or its image of, the homosexual in society.

Indeed, the mattachines wear many masks.

5. Transvestites and transsexuals: boys will be girls

For spirits when they please
Can either sex assume, or both; so soft
And uncompounded is their essence pure.
—*John Milton*, Paradise Lost

Historians describe the Chevalier d'Eon as a political adventurer; for most of the contemporary world he would not even be a footnote in history were it not for the fact that he was also a female impersonator who lent his name to the phenomenon of cross-dressing. Once called *eonism* for him, it is now more frequently known as *transvestism*.[1] Few deviations from normative behavior elicit so much ridicule as does transvestism. But of those few, transsexualism is one: as opposed to transvestism—the effort *to masquerade* as a member of the other sex—transsexualism is the effort *to become* a member of the other sex. More formally, transsexualism is defined as the complete identification, on a mental or psychic level, with one sex, while having the physical organs of the other.[2] Perhaps the most lucid de-

This chapter was written in collaboration with George L. Kirkham.

scription of this condition has been provided by Jan Waldiner:

> Transsexuals not only want to dress like the opposite sex, they abhor the signs of their anatomic sex, especially their genitals, and they want to have their bodies altered to resemble that of the other sex. They are often convinced that nature has made a mistake in their case, that they really belong to the other sex, that their bodies have developed along the wrong lines.[3]

From biblical days to the present—but perhaps more so recently—society has been concerned with cross-dressing. "The woman shall not wear that which pertaineth unto a man, neither shall a man put on a woman's garment: for all that do so are abominations unto the Lord thy God" (Deuteronomy XXII, 5). Today, the first part of this warning is almost impossible to violate: there are few, if any, men's garments which a woman cannot appropriate free of any charge of masquerading. However, despite what Charles Winick has called "the beige epoch"— a process of blurring the lines that separate the sexes[4]—a man still cannot appropriate a woman's finery without being labeled deviant.

Transvestites and transsexuals constitute a curious, probably a small, and certainly a little-known group of people (and usually, it may be added, people who anatomically are clearly men). The lines that define their characteristics are not at all well drawn. While psychoanalytic literature has occasionally been punctuated by an article on the case history of a transvestite, in general no large number of these deviants has been studied. Replies to a questionnaire in one of the transvestite journals, an occasional autobiography of perhaps doubtful validity, and a quantity of folklore and rumors: such is the literature on transvestism. Thus when an authority writes, even with the qualification that his estimate is very rough, that some 1 to 3 per cent of the population may be transvestites,[5] one can only reply with disbelief and the suggestion that his figure is probably fifty or one hundred times too high.

Transvestism (or, as it is sometimes called, transvestitism) has often been defined simply as the urge to put on the clothing of the opposite sex.[6] This desire may be sporadic or permanent; some transvestites wish to cross-dress (or, to use their own expression, *to dress*) only when alone or in the presence of another transvestite; others may not be satisfied unless they can walk the streets in full masquerade; while a third group may want to wear only the underclothes of the chosen sex beneath the outer apparel of the ascribed one. Spokesmen for transvestites insist that dressing is only one part of their story and that transvestites have a so-called feminine counterpart of their personality that seeks expression in numerous ways.

The male transvestite has not been prone either to form organizations or to fight for the right to dress. For one thing, he has sought to retain his identification as a male, and has emphasized his heterosexuality even to the point of showing scorn for the homosexual. The scorn is reciprocated. At the same time they ridicule the transvestite's dressing, homosexuals question his sexual normality by suggesting that he is probably only a "closet queen," or at best a latent homosexual.

In his own world, the transvestite calls himself a TV, probably obtaining considerable satisfaction from this in-group language which serves as an argot between himself and an insider, and which others hearing the word do not comprehend. To the marginal world of transsexuals, male prostitutes, and the occasional transvestites that mingle with them, the transvestite is known as a transie.

A few transvestites have become female impersonators; as such, they have legitimated their deviance, often to the point that, within a specific sphere, it may cease to be considered deviant. In such cases, it is legal to cross-dress; impersonation becomes a public service in that it offers entertainment at the same time that, privately, such entertainment fulfills the impersonator's need to display himself publicly and receive the catcalls and hoots of the scornful watchers.

Thus far there have been some very small signs of organization among the TV's. To join hands with Mattachine or other such organizations would be totally unacceptable; transvestites cannot identify with the homophile movement. Because so many have families and hold down jobs, dressing only when alone or with one or two others, it would be both a jeopardy to their status and an act without rational goal to form a pressure group to fight for changes in legal and social attitudes. As a result, few transvestites feel a strong need for such change. Most of them are content if they can find a handful of others for the purely expressive and personally gratifying purpose of group dressing.

Although there are no formal transvestite organizations, there are two transvestite publications which have assumed certain organizational functions. *Transvestia* has been published in California for several years; its editor Virginia Prince is probably the best-known and most articulate, as well as the most defensively polemical, of American transvestites. While all the other members of the editorial staff have women's names on the masthead, Virginia Prince and at least one other are known to be men. Obviously, cross-dressing is not enough for transvestites; they like to assume other accouterments of the opposite sex, such as their names.

The second transvestite journal, *Turnabout*, is published in New York, and has on several occasions exhorted transvestites to form a pressure group to "help combat the creeping cancer of conformism and anti-thinkism which has contaminated our body politic."[7] *Turnabout* discusses legal difficulties and court struggles, and urges transvestites to band together to fight for their rights; despite such pleas, however, the instrumental groups that have punctuated the homophile scene have not yet made their appearance among the TV's.

While *Transvestia's* subscribers have formed an organization, it seems to function only on an expressive level, giving members the opportunity to meet one another and to dress in semipublic. The organization calls itself FPE or Phi Pi Epsilon (a Greek-letter fraternity, members state, which they more often call a sorority). The letters are also said to stand for Foundation for Personality Expression and Full Personality Expression.[8] The F and P further represent FemmePersonator, an unhyphenated word coined by Virginia Prince to describe the individual who "personates" or brings to life his feminine side. Another word coined by Prince is "femiphilia"—love of the feminine—which he would like to substitute for the rather disrespectable transvestism; this word not only has the F and P so useful as symbols, but, he says, involves "an awareness of the feminine personality," as opposed to the cruder definition of transvestism: "putting on feminine clothes for erotic, masquerade, masochistic, or fetishistic reasons."

FPE has been the subject of one rather lengthy study by H. Taylor Buckner;[9] while little can be gleaned from it about the organization, it does offer a great deal about some members. FPE is said to have functioning chapters in about a half-dozen or a dozen cities of the United States, as well as affiliates in Sweden and England (the British affiliate is called the Beaumont Society, after the Chevalier d'Eon de Beaumont). Chapters issue bulletins, and the national society publishes *Femme Forum* as a sort of internal organ.

Any organization of transvestites, and especially a social one, provides them with one of the few opportunities to dress without subjecting themselves to ridicule and the possibility of arrest. Hence FPE has parties or social gatherings, called Hose and Heels meetings, described by Buckner as "a way for many people who had never been outside, dressed, before to get in touch with others, to reassure others of their real feelings by bringing and wearing a pair of women's shoes, and being reassured in turn by the others doing the same thing, a much less traumatic experience than appearing, perhaps for the first time before others, in full dress."[10] The Los Angeles Hose and Heels Club was formed in the early 1960's, had about fifteen transvestites at its first meeting, and in February 1962 became the Alpha Chapter of FPE.

FPE seems to function on two levels. First, it provides an opportunity for the transvestites to see each other dressed, and, secondly, it holds forums, arranges radio and television programs, and invites "outsiders" to learn about the transvestite phenomenon. The Los Angeles group, by far the most active, arranged a seminar for police, lawyers, judges, doctors, marriage counselors, and probation officers—in the words of Virginia Prince, "in short, anyone who is in need of the information." In the opinion of most professionals these people would seem to include mainly transvestites, and mainly professionals in the opinion of most transvestites. There is a very real possibility that groups of this sort may seek to propagandize the professional world through their real motivation of displaying themselves in front of others.

Like other deviant groups, the TV's are both proud and defensive of their deviance. Transvestism, they maintain, is even an advantage in life: "As a TV, you can mix the best of both worlds: have a family, a rewarding job (usually much higher paying than a GG [genetic—or real—girl]) and the pleasures of hobbies that give vent to both sides of your expression."[11] And, like members of other deviant groups, the TV's pillory psychiatry:

> The urologist pronounced me perfect, somewhat small, and the psychiatrist rambled around through the chasm of his Freudian background and came up with a zero. This is par for the course, but let's not condemn psychiatry. They can only learn so much from a textbook.[12]

In many ways the disturbance of the transvestite is less severe than that of the transsexual (or TS). Like the TV, the transsexual denies his homosexuality, but he does so by a different method. Instead of suppressing his sexual interest in the same sex, he redefines himself as a member of the opposite sex. Thus, having sex with a man is not an abnormal act for the transsexual because he is, in his self-view, a woman. What does he do about his genitals? They can eventually be removed; in the meantime they are conceptualized as abnormal growths or deformities.

The transsexuals have made a greater effort toward organization than the transvestites; that they have done so is the result of several factors: first, they have a goal (sexual change) which they feel organization will help them to achieve; secondly, they have less to lose (family connections primarily) by exposing their deviance; and, thirdly, they have certain personality traits which, in their highly stigmatizing effect, encourage organizational structure.

Whether or not California is the national—perhaps even the world—capital for voluntary associations of sexual deviants, its designation as such is rendered additional justification by the emergence in San Francisco of COG, probably the first formal organization of self-defined transsexuals in the world. Although COG may originally have been an acronym for Change Our Gender (this is not certain), it is now said to represent Change: Our Goal (a curious name if one removes the punctuation). But since *cog* is defined as a protrusion, the members in choosing these initials may have inadvertently emphasized the one feature of their persons that they reject.

The distinguishing characteristic of the organization is its members' shared wish to join the opposite sex through organic transformation (which they believe possible by hormone treatment and genital surgery). Pending such an operation, which is unlikely in the foreseeable future for any of them, they live as members of the opposite sex.

The members of COG—most are Caucasian, lower class, unemployed, and range in age from eighteen to fifty—evince the anomalous psychosexual aberration which Harry Benjamin has labeled "the transsexual phenomenon."[13] In transsexualism, or transsexuality, "body and mind are not in harmony; the psychological sex clashes with the anatomical one."[14] This description assumes the existence of psychological sex as an entity of its own, a view of reality which the transsexuals find useful, but one not without its opponents in the professional world.

By definition, therefore, the transsexual members of COG are not content with the mere approximation of femininity which the transvestite achieves through cross-dressing, and which, for him, is usually a sporadic episode. Rather, transsexuals constantly beseech members of the medical profession, in the colorful language of one writer, to "do the unspeakable to their unmentionables,"[15] to castrate them and reconstruct an artificial vagina by means of so-called "sex reassignment surgery." That such surgery actually does cause a sex change, or sex reassignment, is a matter of dispute; nonetheless, its certain (but future) success is the basis of the transsexual's taken-for-granted world.[16]

Transsexuals may be divided into two groups: those who have had sex reassignment surgery performed, and those who desire it. The former generally prefer not to mingle with the latter. Convinced (or hoping to convince themselves) that there is no difference between a man-made and a "God-given" vagina, they view themselves as real girls who can share nothing with men who only wish to become women. These girls are as real as their mothers, suffering only from the inability to bear children. Their suitors, lovers, and husbands are real men, not (Heaven forbid!) homosexuals; to reinforce this attitude, they generally scorn "pansies" and "queers."

The second transsexual category—those who desire sex reassignment surgery—is harder to define. It consists of people (for the moment, call them homosexuals) who live in the fantasy world of attempting to accept, and of forcing the acceptance of, the view that they are members of the other sex. They are convinced that both anatomical and psychological gender exist; what *really* defines a person's sex, they maintain, is how that person feels or what he believes. In addition to this conviction that they are what others do not take them to be, the transsexuals also look forward to, long for, and confidently expect, the apocalypse: the day of The Operation. They will be transformed. It is this group of people, not those who have had the surgery, who constitute the membership of COG.

Since transsexualism itself is so uncommon, it is remarkable that COG came about at all. It was the well-publicized success of the ex-GI, George Jorgensen, first in securing a "sexual conversion operation" in Denmark in 1952, then in living a presumably happy and adjusted life as Christine Jorgensen, that originally emboldened several San Francisco transsexuals. In the years that followed, they pursued quixotic individual attempts to induce local hospitals to perform sex reassignment surgery on them. Without exception, they encountered steadfast medical opposition to the surgery on both ethical and legal grounds.[17] By the middle 1960's, however, several breaches in the wall did occur. First it was announced that such operations were being conducted at Johns Hopkins; then, almost at the same time, a very favorable book about transsexuals was written by Harry Benjamin, a physician who spends a considerable part of the year in San Francisco.[18]

Largely as a result of Benjamin's work, the hitherto isolated transsexuals in San Francisco became acquainted with one another; in the fall of 1967 a few of them sought to bring about through organization what their individual efforts had so far failed to produce. These goals included a better attitude from society; freedom from fear of harassment; and the legal right to assume the roles, activities, and privileges of the other sex despite the lack of anatomical transformation. Other more personal goals were the exchange of advice on how to function as a transsexual; where to shop; how to find a lawyer and doctor; how to protect oneself against those who prey on deviants; and—most manifest of all the goals—how to obtain surgery on a convenient and inexpensive basis.[19]

If organizations of deviants are epidemic, spreading by imitation, they can also be considered endemic, spreading within a given area. In San Francisco this has been particularly true of formal groups of sex deviants—specifically the homophile organizations about which the transsexuals have always been quite well informed. These organizations have achieved a good measure of peaceful coexistence between their members and the police department. Furthermore, whether out of curiosity or a genuine interest in serving public needs, the news and mass media have opened up hitherto inaccessible channels: doors are no longer closed to homophiles at public agencies. In short, the representatives of the "square world" have publicized homophile causes, and to this extent may have helped them overcome the difficult problems of living in a hostile environment. It was against this successful background that COG organized, disclosing its hope of winning from society a recognition of the legitimacy of its members' goals first to choose their own gender, then to obtain surgery to reinforce that choice.

From the outset these transsexuals were convinced (principally as a result of their own individual failures to obtain conversion surgery) that some degree of organized effort to educate the public to an "enlightened" understanding of transsexualism had to precede any attempt actually to obtain the desired operation. It was felt that if only the public (and thereby the medical community) could be made to grasp the "true nature" of the transsexual's condition, to realize that he is not a deviant but someone with an easily remediable physical deformity, then the long-sought surgery would become a reality.

With conversion surgery on a nationwide basis established as its primary goal, and with a grandiose conception of the San Francisco group as the headquarters for other groups across the country, COG began to grow. In addition to obtaining new members, the organization took on most of the trappings of a typical voluntary association of deviants. While stating that they sought to make the public knowledgeable about, as they define it, the true nature of transsexualism (a formidable undertaking which no group either so small or so unprofessional could seriously expect to carry out), COG members performed quite another task for themselves: they obtained expertise of a type acceptable to their own view of reality and then proceeded to reinforce that view through mutual contact, interaction, and the organizational process.

COG provided yet another advantage for its members. Paramount to the function of any deviant group is the provision of a means whereby the member can escape the all-pervasive element of stigma. For these formerly isolated transsexuals, desperately seeking to mitigate the onerous stigmata which attach to those who repudiate the sex role dictated by their biology and ascribed by their culture, COG offered escape from a grossly unacceptable self-image. In the case of the transsexual, this self-image is doubly unacceptable: on the one hand, he suffers from being labeled homosexual, and on the other from being ultraeffeminate.

To some extent, transsexualism can reduce the negative self-image by convincing the individual that he is not a homosexual because he is not a male; he is not really seeking a sex *change* operation, but *corrective* surgery. Nonetheless, the stigma simply of *being* a transsexual remains. Like many of the other organizations of deviants, COG seeks to handle this problem not by demanding that the individual relinquish his deviant behavior but rather by convincing him that he can reform the norms of society.

The strength of COG's desire to escape stigmatization is revealed by its highly defensive reaction to any view of its members as deviant, or to any labeling of them as psychotic, schizophrenic, or even sick. Transsexuals generally deny any suggestion that they might be less well-balanced than the average person. But it is not at all infrequent to hear one transsexual refer to another as "sick, sick, sick."

In fact, the transsexuals are constantly faced with the problem of explaining the presence in their midst of individuals who are clearly either neurotic or psychotic. That people with less severe problems than the transsexuals are capable of erecting elaborate defenses to rationalize what their peers consider weird world-views has long been known to students of human behavior.[20] Perhaps because their vision of reality is in one important respect so incongruent with that of the people around them, the transsexuals have become particularly adept at this game. Their obviously disturbed members, they point out, are but living proof of the damage which society can do to otherwise normal people by subjecting them to continual persecution. When individual members of COG do admit, or are faced with undeniable evidence, that they have long histories of bizarre behavior, male prostitution, alcoholism, confinement in mental hospitals, and even voluntary participation in psychotherapy (which is always defined as an utter failure), they carefully point out that such apparent indices of emotional instability are merely the by-products of society's unrelenting harassment.

Edwin Lemert has applied the term "secondary deviance" to the deviance that results from, and the psychological damage caused by, one's being labeled deviant.[21] What the COG members (and for that matter many sociologists) do not seem to be willing to face is the quite apparent imbalance in a personality that pursues a line of behavior leading to such severe social flagellation.[22] For this, too, COG has a ready answer: its members do not choose to be transsexuals; they simply are. They were probably, they maintain, born that way; at least the condition goes back so far into early childhood, if not infancy, that choice was impossible. Hence, they are not deliberately exposing themselves to public scorn.

At the time COG was enjoying its greatest success as an organization (it has since declined), there were seventeen registered members, none of whom had had a "sex change" operation. Most of them were taking hormones, using electrolysis to remove facial hair, and seeking in other ways to resemble members of the opposite sex. Among the seventeen, only one was a female (i.e., an anatomic or born female, a "real girl").[23] The view that sex change surgery is far more practical for the biological male than for the female, who might well have her breasts removed but could not effect any other important change, was objected to by this female transsexual as short-sighted: "In this age of heart and kidney transplants, who knows but that we will be having penis and testicle transplants, and organs will be left to a needy woman by a generous donor."

In their belief that sex reassignment surgery can be nothing but successful in creating a happy, well-adjusted person, the membership of COG is further united by its thorough rejection of any psychogenic explanation of transsexualism, or any psychotherapeutic solution to its problem.[24] Psychotherapy, transsexuals maintain, offers no hope for curing the dissonance between biological sex and gender identity. Members regard psychiatrists and psychologists as necessary evils to be endured only in order to obtain the operation. Like members of many other deviant organizations, they suspect psychiatrists of being exploiters. Here they draw upon and generalize from their own experience; they quote freely those authorities who state that psychotherapy is hopeless in cases of transsexualism. If any person troubled with gender identity was ever helped by therapy, they say, then he was not a transsexual in the first place, just a TV.

If psychotherapy's uselessness is one pillar of the transsexual's value system, a second is an adamant insistence that the etiology of the condition is entirely physical. Quite understandably, the transsexual cites only literature which supports such an explanation. Of contrary literature, he is either unaware, or readily able to dismiss it as the scribblings of the ignorant. Paramount among the works approved is *The Transsexual Phenomenon* by Harry Benjamin, a physician who has been active in work toward sexual liberalization in Europe and America for half a century.

In fact, the Benjamin book is an almost official eschatology of COG; its presence at meetings is as predictable as that of the Gideon Bible in American hotel rooms. Because of his sympathetic espousal of sex reassignment surgery, Benjamin is regarded by COG members as the final authority on the subject. His book provides the principal theoretical rationale for COG's advocacy of surgery; its frequent references to people whose lives were aided, if not saved (Benjamin does all but say that transsexuals after the operation "live happily ever after"), buoys the spirits of all those who know that they too will one day have their problem neatly solved. Suffice it to say that for any member of COG seriously to challenge any tenet of *The Transsexual Phenomenon* would be tantamount to heresy.

Nonetheless, it is difficult to assay the level of the members' emotional commitment to sex reassignment surgery, if only because the operation is so remote for most of them. While all COG members assert their determination to proceed with transsexual surgery "at any cost"—even if so doing, as stated in a warning frequently made to them, results in an incapacity ever again to experience sexual gratification—the distant quality of the goal serves to insulate them from any real confrontation with it. Though it would be impossible to predict that any of the group's members would not actually undergo the operation if it were available, it is perhaps significant that COG members speak often of imagined dangers surrounding the surgery, not infrequently citing the case of someone thought to have been maimed for life by it. Whenever such surgery is under attack by outsiders, however, COG members defend it; in this effort, they are supported by the statements of selectively chosen individuals who maintain that such an operation "is now, in essence, a relatively simple one."[25]

But the incontrovertible fact remains that no COG member has ever even come close to obtaining conversion surgery. While they all know that this type of operation is being performed at Johns Hopkins in Baltimore, they are anxious not to know how rare it is. There is always the hope that, in this respect, America will become more liberal. Until that time, they react to the relative unavailability of conversion surgery in the United States by mutually supporting fantasies of leaving for Casablanca, or some other faraway spot where the operation may be obtained, as soon as they have enough money. But while they talk of these trips and operations which, together, would cost some $3,000 to $6,000 per person, they are for the most part living in hand-to-mouth poverty, several of them "hustling" for the rent money. In fact, most COG members are unable to produce the $25 currently required by the Legal Aid Society to change their names to conform to the desired gender. Is it not possible, then, that their willingness to fight for the operation may well be due to the extreme unlikelihood that they will ever have to undergo it?

At present the members of COG seem relatively content with the less substantive, certainly not so irreversible, but still symbolic "chemical castration" provided by estrogen treatment.[26] Small prescription bottles of estrogen tablets are invariably brought to group meetings where, in addition to fostering the conviction that community acceptance of organic sex change is feasible (otherwise why would a society that bans so many drugs permit these to be freely sold?), they provide a source of gratifying competition with those members who either are not receiving the drugs or have been taking them for a shorter period of time.

This competition is a sort of race toward ultrafemininity, the determination of who can pass as, and who can acquire the most traits of, a woman (and these two goals may not be entirely congruent). As a result, members strive to adopt the cultural accouterments of womanhood, particularly those of a conventional nature. Members do not imitate those women who, completely heterosexual and assured of their image as women, wear trousers and short hair. These women in pants could never be mistaken for transsexuals. COG members, on the other hand, are not so much feminine as effeminate.

When "dressed," COG members run the gamut from those who closely approximate the normal apparel and behavior of women to those who at most achieve a bizarre, somewhat pathetic, caricature of femininity. The latter commonly overdress, and may easily be "read"—the in-group term for public recognition as a male, or, in the minds of the members, recognition as a transsexual. One cannot really speak of recognizing a person as a male if he does not accept that definition of himself.

In judging their degree of success in being accepted as women, however, one must always beware of put-ons. To be able under the most trying conditions to be accepted as a woman is the transsexual's ultimate achievement; hence, he is prone to exaggerate his successes. A good example of such a put-on is the case of Agnes, studied by Harold Garfinkel and his associates.[27] Agnes said she lived with a girl friend who did not know her anatomic gender; modest girls, they undressed in the bathroom. Even Agnes's boy friend was not privy to the secret. What necking they did was of a highly respectable nature; as for any exploration below the waist . . . well, Agnes was just not that kind of girl! When she visited home, her brother brought a male friend to the house, who showed considerable interest in Agnes, but relatively little in a female cousin, a real girl, who was also there. Sounds good, but the denouement of the case history was that Agnes had told Garfinkel and his associates many lies, all stimulated by the desire to prove how much she needed the transsexual operation. Once the basic story of how she became a female "trapped" in a male body was exposed, what further details could be believed? Are all stories of transsexuals' successes in the normal world equally exaggerated?

The ability to navigate successfully as a woman on a daily basis becomes a source of considerable personal satisfaction for the transsexual, as the story of Agnes so vividly illustrates. Regularly to carry off the masquerade without eliciting either recognition by the public or an arrest by the police—to walk the streets, use the facilities of ladies' rooms, particularly to work undetected as a woman—all this yields a positive evaluation from one's peers. This is not to deny, however, that transsexuals may feel an inner need to be apprehended. If so, this need results not so much from psychic masochism—the desire to be punished—but, as with so many criminals, from the desire to have one's achievement known.

The need for apprehension may go far—but not too far. Members of COG dread arrest and incarceration, both of which inevitably result in a brutal confrontation with one's real and unacceptable sexual nature.[28] In prison, a transsexual is not a woman. He is a man, and a queen at that. The experience of being booked, fingerprinted, and photographed; of having one's feminine clothing and possessions confiscated and laughed at; of being required to submit to the indignity of a haircut; and last of being placed in the "tank" where one will certainly be ridiculed by both the guards and prisoners—all these things represent for the transsexual Goffman's "mortification process" with a real vengeance.[29]

As for their individual sex lives, COG members generally relegate (or say they do) overt sexual activity to that time when they can experience orgasm "as a woman." How many of them have therefore repressed, sublimated, or deflected their present erotic interests is difficult to know: for the transsexual being (or acting as) a woman is to be "good" and "pure"—not to behave like an ordinary slut. Here, too, there may be a put-on; only a combination of depth interviews, what has recently been called "unobtrusive measures" (for example, obtaining venereal disease records from hospitals and physicians),[30] and participant observation by persons who can identify with COG (an unlikely prospect), can reveal whether the transsexuals' is, as they state, primarily a nonerotic life. The COG members certainly gossip about one another, making accusations of promiscuity; but whether these accusations reveal the truth or simply competitive scorn is not at this time known. Many members seem to have been involved at one time or another—several at the present time—in prostitution.[31] Nonetheless, even prostitution can be rationalized as one of the few possible occupations in a society which has closed the doors of ordinary wage-earning to transsexuals. Furthermore, prostitution inflates the egos of those transsexuals who can pretend that their johns are real men who can't read them (they tell these men that they are menstruating, but will perform fellatio).

Those transsexuals who deny having an active sex life nevertheless accept those others who elect to have sex with men while still genitally male themselves. Such behavior is regarded as entirely a matter of individual choice, mostly because it can be rationalized as "real heterosexual activity between a normal male and a female with a deformity." Even Benjamin has referred to one transsexual who had a "perfectly normal boyfriend."[32] If this statement can be made by a scientist, it is easy to see that any transsexual would accept it.

A few members of COG have developed pseudo-heterosexual liaisons with other men which they describe as conventional marriages. They maintain that their relationships are as filled with love, romance, affection, and stability as any heterosexual union. Not a remarkable recommendation, for these same transsexuals are extremely cynical of ordinary heterosexual unions which, they say, are replete with hate, not love, and are most accurately depicted by Tennessee Williams and Edward Albee. In the transsexuals' vision of the world, no marriage would endure were it not for children and the law.

The suggestion that normalcy in any relationship between a COG member and a male is impossible, that the partner is and must be a homosexual, and that, even with conversion surgery, a transsexual can at most become a castrated male with an artificial vagina, produces only anxious and highly philosophical rationalizations about "true womanhood" not being reducible to the biological functions of menstruation and childbearing.[33]

COG seeks to make the transsexual's real or supposed indifference toward obtaining sexual gratification, his complete lack of interest in legalizing erotic activities between members of the same sex, and his view of his own sexual activity (if any) as heterosexual, his threefold means of escaping stigmatization as a pervert, degenerate, or "drag queen." This practice makes COG unique in the subculture of sexually deviant groups: transsexuals, it maintains, are not deviants. Though tolerant of other groups such as Mattachine and the Daughters of Bilitis,

COG draws an increasingly sharp line of demarcation between transsexuals on the one hand and such psychosexually disturbed persons as homosexuals and transvestites on the other. While homosexuality, in this view of pathologies, is seen as a permanent condition, transsexualism is simply an organic problem capable of surgical correction.

This self-defensiveness of groups like COG often leads "square" society to charge them with proselytizing. At first glance, it seems difficult to imagine how anyone could be recruited into transsexualism. COG itself indignantly denies proselytizing by simply denying the possibility. But some members betray the reverse. At one meeting a member suggested, "Let's go down to the Tenderloin and round up those hustling drag queens and show them they're really transsexuals." Certainly any small organization can always use a few more members to keep the group going. The frequent references by COG members to "latent" transsexuals bespeak their anxiety to convince the world that it would be better off if only some people would recognize and admit what they really are—in this case, transsexual. Here, of course, COG denies proselytizing: since transsexualism is the true, but unrecognized, state, COG is only bringing into the open that which has always existed beneath the surface.

Whatever precedents exist for groups of sexual deviants to interact with police departments primarily in terms of conflict and survival,[34] this is clearly not the case with COG. Perhaps nowhere is the militancy of contemporary groups of deviants better illustrated than in COG's unusual and essentially successful relationship with the San Francisco police. Commensurate with Howard Becker's description of today's deviant as "more self-conscious, more organized, more willing to fight with conventional society than ever before,"[35] COG's members have been emboldened to enlist police aid in reaching their goals. The police, in turn, seem to have found in COG a mechanism for furthering their own aims.

COG has actively sought the support and cooperation of the police through the establishment of what can be described as a highly symbiotic relationship, one mutually beneficial although not mutually dependent. The creation of this anomalous liaison between the polar extremes of deviant and nondeviant, lawbreaker and law-enforcer, has been made possible by the official San Francisco police policy of nonharassment. The department is actually willing to aid groups of deviants in their quest for recognition and acceptance by the community if, in return, it can better control the deviants and dissuade them from engaging in any form of criminal conduct. It is a tenuous relationship because it is not rooted in firmly held community values; a single incident elevated into a scandal, or a campaign by a candidate seeking to arouse the public against degenerates and those who cooperate with them, might cause a rupture at any time. In the instance of COG, this symbiotic contract, though never written or explicitly stated, has encouraged cooperation between two groups having traditionally antithetical goals and interests.

Thus, the police could and did react with considerable enthusiasm to a proposed COG membership drive aimed at recruiting "latent" transsexuals from the city's unorganized mass of sexual deviants. The police cannot be expected to see any possible danger in reinforcing a new self-image (of a female trapped in a male body) on a person who has hitherto defined himself as a homosexual. These psychodynamic problems of personality change, which have explosive potential for an individual's relation to society, are nonetheless simply beyond the scope of police competence. The latter's only concern is that such isolated deviants are often involved in sporadic criminality, ranging from relatively innocuous offenses such as prostitution and petty larceny to the more serious crimes of armed robbery, narcotics traffic, and drunk-rolling. Furthermore, the sexual deviant's involvement in crime is one not only of perpetrator, but of victim: he must be protected against himself even more than society must be protected against him.

The police therefore consider COG a potentially valuable ally in controlling crimes committed *by and against* San Francisco's sexual deviants. Through the Police Community Relations Division, an officer has been assigned to work with COG, to attend the group's meetings, where he functions both as a sergeant at arms and an informal counselor on matters pertaining to the group's relationship with the law, police, and courts. Though this police officer easily melts into the primary group structure as an amiable friend and benefactor, utterly shunning authoritarian tactics or any manifestation of his official status, he nonetheless wields great influence over the entire group, particularly as the final arbiter on matters disputed among members. He may also serve the transsexuals' psychological need to have a "real man" around, one whose uniform, occupation, and status almost symbolize masculinity. His presence no doubt assuages some members' fears that their meeting will be broken into by a bunch of hoodlums out "to get the queers."

Of far greater importance than the provision of practical assistance for the members of COG is the fact that the police department, through its officer's presence at and participation in the group's meetings, symbolically accepts the individual deviant as "she" is. By its use of the disputed pronoun, by its presence at meetings where members are "dressed," and by its cooperation with those members in their efforts to obtain "the unspeakable"—its unquestioning acceptance of the group goal of sex reassignment surgery—the police extend an aura of community legitimacy to COG.

Illustrative of the increasingly cooperative stance of the department toward COG is the fact that it has assured for them what is tantamount to immunity from harassment and persecution under a long-standing body of statutes which technically permit officers to arrest transsexuals on any of a multiplicity of charges, ranging from dressing as females to merely disturbing the peace. Quite naturally, this protection extends to deviants in no way associated with COG, to transvestites and homosexuals, but it is COG's outstanding achievement to have attained this immunity as an organization. Furthermore, COG members are more likely than others to be free from fear of molestation by authorities if for no other reason than that they are known to them in a special status (i.e., as members of an organization), a status which it is in the interests of the police to preserve in order to exploit.

The major legal concessions which the police department has extended to COG were crystallized at an official Police Community Relations meeting attended by several members of COG, ranking police officials, and representatives of the medical community and local public assistance agencies.[36] Essentially, the police agreed not to arrest transsexuals either for dressing as females or for using ladies' rooms unless forced to make the arrest on the complaint of a private citizen.[37] One police captain went so far as to suggest that through the Center for Special Problems, "a card might be prepared for transsexuals who are being treated which would give some sort of legal background and they would appear to have the right to issue this type of card."[38] Such a card would then permit dressing in public with impunity.

While this card would not represent a police order, nor would it have the force of law of a judicial decision or legislative act, this suggestion nevertheless expresses a re-markably tolerant position for a police officer. One must be wary, however, that his own liberalism may not be shared by his fellow officers, and that it might have been aggrandized by the setting at which it was articulated. Nevertheless, it is obvious that the proposed issuance of a "transsexual identification card" would represent a major step for COG members in their efforts to be identi-fied as nonconformists rather than deviants. Another offi-cer expressed sympathy with this goal when, in referring to "sexual deviates," added that he prefers "to use the term sexual variants when talking about transsexuals."

Those members of COG who eschew criminality, and whose public appearances are discreet enough not to of-fend the sensibilities of private citizens, are told that they need not fear arrest or incarceration.[39] And yet arrests of some COG members do occur, partly due to the failure of the police department effectively to disseminate its policy to line officers. The latter often display only thinly veiled hostility toward individuals whom they regard as degen-erates. Furthermore, some members of COG persist in criminality and in inviting arrest. Sometimes it seems that they are daring the community, seeing how far they can go, how much will be tolerated.

In addition to having secured a high degree of cooper-ation from the police department, COG has likewise at-tracted increasingly sympathetic attention from social workers and community agencies; it has even sparked the interest of local news media.[40] Such accomplishments in public relations are attributable in part to the group's ability to project an image of middle-class respectability in all aspects of life other than gender orientation. They also serve the normal world both by permitting it to iso-late the transsexual as an outsider, and by reinforcing the world-view of normal people that there are two, and only two sexes, and that everyone except the most outlandish belongs to one or the other.

Of the first ability, the image of middle-class respectability: The casual visitor to a COG meeting, whether researcher, minister, or social worker, suddenly finds himself surrounded by people who seem warm, affable, and sincere, who seem to shun any involvement in crime, who never use obscene language (how unladylike this would be!), and who give blood to the Red Cross (Freudians might consider this the symbolic act of people who want to, but cannot, menstruate). COG projects the image of people who want to live and let live, who seek only to pursue what might be termed a conventional life free of persecution. These transsexuals appear to be as far removed from deviant stereotypes as the hometown PTA. As a representative of the Center for Special Problems says:

> These [are] human beings very much like every other human being except for the fact that they have something which is commonly referred to as a gender identification disturbance.[41]

The occasional visitor to COG meetings is therefore easily lulled by the group's appearance of sophistication and respectability into the tacit belief that he is, indeed, sitting in a room of clubwomen rather than transsexuals. One person studying the group stated that, after in-depth communication with them, "it soon becomes impossible for you to think of them as anything but women." That one begins to use the pronoun *she*, to speak of someone as *Miss* instead of *Mister*, is true; though it starts with difficulty, it soon comes with ease. In the long run, it is impossible not to use the feminine pronoun when one constantly hears a person referred to as *she*, and when slipping into *he* and *him* would inhibit continued interaction with the group. But despite the language one adopts and the very real interconnection between the words one uses and the mental images they convey, it is also very possible to think of the transsexuals as other than women; in fact, it may be impossible to think of them as women, but quite possible to think of them as men trying to be women. One is seduced into watching the drama; then, as he becomes involved in it, begins to believe in it, and to forget that the roles are not real, only special masks that everyone knows are masks.[42]

However effectively the pathology which is responsible for COG's very existence is obscured during the initial exposure, further contact with the group only demonstrates the great disparity between the ideal qualities which it projects to the community and its inherent characteristics. Behind COG's militancy and activism, reflected in its increasing contact with police and other local agencies, its publication and distribution of a biweekly news bulletin, and its drives to recruit new members, internal conflict and divisiveness are found.

COG is constantly plagued by bickering between individual members; factionalism lies beneath the surface of meetings conducted within the decorous context of parliamentary rules of order. That there are periodic virulent eruptions of open discord, marked by irate resignations from office and angry exits from the meeting room, is not surprising. Any such outburst is a manifestation of neurotic interaction and frustration at the group's inability both to solve the basic problems of the individual members and to succeed in its larger, one might say overwhelming, goals. Such outbursts lead to skullduggery, competitiveness, and fission, all fed by a paranoia that seems both to inhere in the transsexual's condition and to be aggravated by the very real persecution that he encounters in life.[43]

These long-smoldering tensions have finally culminated

in a schism led by two dissident members of COG. Announcing their resignation, they have formed a rival group, the California Association of Trans-Sexuals.[44] The self-hatred and the self-mockery of an organization that would deliberately adopt the initials COG, when the "cog" is the one thing about themselves that they claim to reject, is only surpassed by the decision of a group of transsexuals to call themselves CATS. They betray their genuine feelings toward the female sex in adopting a name whose acronym is overwhelmingly derisive of women.

In addition to the threat of internal dissension, one now made manifest, COG is also menaced by apathy: attendance at weekly meetings sometimes consists of only a few, and usually less than half, of the members. It is possible that the threat from CATS may for a time create greater cohesion in the remaining group; if this occurs at all, however, it is hardly likely to endure. In the meantime, the same members seldom appear from week to week, while matters requiring a vote must frequently be put off for want of a quorum. The editor of COG's weekly news publication, after several impassioned and unsuccessful pleas for help, finally resigned and announced the cessation of publication due to a total absence of contributing articles. The long-proposed drive for new members seems unable to generate sufficient interest among the existing members to become a reality, while the blood-donor program faces termination because of its inability to maintain a level of even one donor per month.

Organizations of deviants such as COG, though attempting to project an image of respectability, and displaying a nominal commitment to such lofty ideals as "enlightenment of the community," are at the same time plagued by their members' hostility toward the "square world" that has so long rejected them. COG numbers a considerable percentage of rebels and nonconformists; it finds itself in the paradoxical position of pretending to be "straight" in every respect except gender disorientation while, actually, its members nihilistically reject many of the attitudes and values of society. These members manifest their hostility in occasional vitriolic outbursts against society itself, then against society's representatives. Police, psychiatrists, doctors, and judges are all potential scapegoats, not to mention researchers who do not become true believers. Any member of the community who has demonstrated an unwillingness to accept the legitimacy of COG and its goals—particularly those "squares" who are overtly re-jective—runs the ironic risk of being denounced both as a fraud and as a latent transsexual.

What is the future of groups of people with gender dis-orientation? It seems likely that, in this age of deviant organizations when the odd man is in, COG, perhaps even CATS, as well as the somewhat less formal organizations of transvestites, will all continue to exist despite both the remoteness and unrealistic nature of their goals, and the almost inevitable conflict and divisiveness within their structure. For the individual transsexual and transvestite, these groups represent the only tangible hope for securing a redefinition of themselves as nondeviant.

To what extent there may have been an increase in the desire to change one's sex because of the creation of the word *transsexual* and the favorable image projected around the sex-change possibility is something that should be of great concern to social scientists. Is transsexualism nothing more than a self-fulfilling prophecy? When one student asked a COG member, "What makes you think that you are a transsexual and not just a homosexual?" he received the reply: "I'm not looking forward to being a homosexual all my life. I want to have the operation. I want to be a woman."[45] Could such a want exist, so strongly as to structure one's entire life pattern, if it were not encouraged by the belief that it is a possibility? If people were told by authorities that they could become Jesus Christ by believing, and that some believers have actually been transformed into Jesus, would our mental institutions suddenly be overpopulated with hundreds of thousands of new Christs? Or would they form an organization to project this view of reality?

It has been stated that the COG consensus is that it's better "to try it as a woman than as a feminine man."[46] If such a consensus exists, could it be because the possibility of trying it as a woman had been implanted in the members' minds? Behavior, as Edwin H. Sutherland has pointed out in his work on deviants and criminals, is learned; certainly, then, the attitudes which motivate and direct behavior must also be learned—and if they are learned, it's because they are taught.

As for society, the interest in these groups, particularly on the part of the mass media, may represent a function which normal society requires. In publicizing transvestites and transsexuals, society may be not only catering to the interests of the curious but drawing the boundary lines between normative and punishable behavior. While, from a humanitarian stance, it may be relaxing its legal punishment, it may at the same time be heightening social scorn by placing in the limelight of publicity a group open to ridicule. It was Emile Durkheim who pointed out this social function of deviance, one that is best fulfilled when the deviance is well publicized.[47]

"The deviant act," writes Kai Erikson, in a passage restating Durkheim's position, "creates a sense of mutuality among the people of a community by supplying the focus for group feeling."[48] And again:

> The excitement generated by the crime [or, one can read here, the deviant act] . . . quickens the tempo of interaction in the group and creates a climate in which the private sentiments of many separate persons are fused together into a common sense of morality.

COG, like *Transvestia* and *Turnabout*, like Mattachine and the entire homophile movement, brings to the fore the problem of how much deviation from sex-role identification can be tolerated, even—or particularly—in "the beige epoch," this age of blurred sex roles. Stated differently: how can society develop the utmost possible sympathy for transsexuals and transvestites, the fullest degree of tolerance, and the greatest reduction of the stigmatizing process, without endangering the process by which young children grow up making a strong and secure sex-role identification with their anatomic sex? Or, stated simply, can transsexualism be discouraged without transsexuals being maltreated?

6. Synanon:
repent, repent, and nepenthe

> *The remedy is worse than the disease.*
> —*Francis Bacon*, Of Seditions and Troubles

Some authorities contend that there are a quarter-million drug addicts in the United States. So far, however, efforts to control the traffic and cure the addicts have been discouraging.[1]

The self-help, AA model (Narcotics Anonymous) has been able to reach a few.[2] Lexington has "cleaned out" many addicts; while some remain clean, others drift back to narcotics, how many no one is certain.[3] Some young users, as they have matured, have thrown off the habit by self-discipline, determination, suffering, and temporary substitutes. New York State is presently experimenting with methadone, a "maintenance drug," said to be addictive itself.[4] And, finally, some sociologists and psychologists are calling for the legal, inexpensive dispensing of drugs to addicts under a system modeled after the British, in which, while persons are discouraged from using narcotics, those who are addicted are permitted to obtain the necessary dosage.

The search for a solution to the problem of addiction, for a method of protecting both society against the depredations attributed to addicts and the addicts themselves against the deleterious effects attributed to the drugs, has thus led in many directions, but none more curious, more unexpected, and more controversial than Synanon.

In many respects, Synanon does not at present qualify as a self-help movement. Nevertheless, it did evolve directly from AA; in fact, it originated not in order to apply AA techniques to the treatment of addicts, but rather to search for a new manner of solving the alcohol problem itself. Later, however, the alcoholics dropped out of Synanon while the few addict members remained; it then evolved as a self-help movement, run by and for people trying to kick the drug habit. Ironically, it was (and is) dominated by a former alcoholic who has never been addicted, thus contradicting the AA-type slogan that "only an addict can help an addict."

While the mystique of the reformed addict acting as model and therapist for the present victim of addiction still dominates Synanon, and constitutes the image projected to society, the organization has actually taken on wider dimensions. Once addict treatment was established, Synanon made an effort to rehabilitate felons of all types, two-time and many-time losers; it also worked in prisons with people who had never been addicts. Finally, it branched out to still a newer stage, working with people in the square world whose hang-ups made them dissatisfied with themselves and society.

Synanon differs from the other organizations under study here in one other important respect: it is much more a total institution than a voluntary association. Not that entry and exit are anything other than voluntary—they are not; but whereas AA becomes a way of life, Synanon becomes life itself. One comes to Synanon and one stays (except for the newly affiliated squares): Synanon is where one lives. Though a person may eventually return to the world "out there," it is hardly a likely goal, certainly one that is disdained and discouraged. Synanon is like a mental institution, a prison, or a nineteenth-century American utopian community in that one's entire life is lived within its walls. Like monks and nuns, the members give themselves over to the place. But the keys to the doors are always in their hands. They can go out, they can split; but they are warned that leaving is the road to H (which is heroin) and hence the road to Hell.

Synanon is dominated by the figure of Chuck Dederich. Every story that comes out of the group, from both adulators and critics, describes Dederich as power-hungry; he himself readily admits being a megalomaniac, although he sees no danger in a therapeutic movement run by such a person. Dederich started on the road to Synanon as an alcoholic; twice divorced, he was a man unable to form good relationships—in fact, it seems, a drifter. At the first AA meeting he attended, he insisted on dominating the group; speaking loudly and long, he ended by asserting his leadership. It was a position not earned but grabbed. AA, or at least his branch, became his thing; it gave him a reason for existence. From that point on, he drew to himself a separate group of alcoholics, carved out his own small AA group, and began to develop and practice a new type of rehabilitation therapy which came to be known as "attack therapy." Tell the alcoholic what a worthless, sniveling, lying louse he is, Dederich proposed (and did). Don't let him take a moral inventory; tell him he's lying and copping out and putting on when he does. We'll make the moral inventory for him, Dederich decided—and we'll make it ruthless.

A half-dozen alcoholics used to meet in these talk-outs, called gut sessions; later a few addicts drifted into them as well. At these sessions, everyone denounced everyone else and himself; they laid themselves bare, stripped themselves of all dignity, all semblance of humanity. It was catharsis in the raw.

Having found a small clubroom, a storefront near a California beach, the group started to live there. Anyone who wanted to straighten out could come in and empty his pockets (usually of not more than a few pennies), then join the sessions and empty his soul. They scrounged for food, got day-old loaves of bread from local bakers, and managed to eat, but not well. It was a hovel but a home, a Salvation Army whose converts acted as the leaders, a mental hospital run by the inmates.

The story of how one of Synanon's early members, Jesse, a Negro, found the group in its first stages of non-affluence is described by Guy Endore.[5] Jesse was walking down to Ocean Park, looking for the address that his parole officer had given him. Finally he came to an old store; inside, some white people were sitting on chairs that didn't match, around a table that was ready to fall apart.

"I guess the total membership at that time," Jesse told the writer, "must have been no more than fourteen, probably less." Jesse was invited to sit down and talk over his problems, but the group never got around to a real discussion.

> It seemed like the moment I opened my mouth those white people shouted at me: "Shut up! Move in, and when you get some of that street garbage out of your head, then we'll listen to what you have to say."

Endore also describes how a man named Reid came to find Synanon.[6] One day, after years of addiction, Reid was staggering along Olympic Boulevard, resting at every bench and looking for a dealer. As he sat on one bench, he could read three letters, TLC, painted above the corner door of a store.

> And while he was watching he saw that door open and a colored man and a young girl, with their arms about each other's waists, walk out and take a bit of a stroll, up and down. From the open door came the sound of music, hi-fi accompanied by bongo drums. The two strollers took only a minute or two and then returned to the inside, closing the door behind them.

Although Reid did not know it then—and most of the present Synanon adherents might be surprised to learn it now—TLC stood for Tender Loving Care. Reid watched the people going in and out; the place looked very much like a beer joint, one sufficiently low class to suggest that he might be able to make his connection there. And so he entered. What he must have found inside is summed up by the reaction of still another early visitor:

> The spirit of this little group! The sense of dedication. The tremendous vitality and purpose of these former felons, these former drunks and prostitutes and dope addicts, all crowded into a couple of rooms. They impressed me as being completely visionary, and yet at the same time hardheaded and real.[7]

This was Synanon at its inception, in 1958. Having retreated from the world in which they had not been able to make it, these many-time losers found with each other, particularly with their leader, a way to survive. Ordered to vacate the Ocean Park storefront, Synanon made its new home in a respectable part of Santa Monica. There was opposition from the members to moving out of the slums into the world of respectability, but Dederich insisted that the organization was growing out of its diapers, that its members had to learn to live like other people. Language would have to be cleaned up now, and, while the group would remain interracial, it would be tolerant and understanding of any prejudiced whites, knowing, as Dederich pointed out, that "it's not the fault of the average American that he's prejudiced."

Synanon moved to its new quarters, a castle in comparison to its old storefront. With the rent set at five hundred dollars a month, the organization had to depend increasingly on rich sponsors in the square world. At this point, the second stage in Synanon's history was reached: it had a new home and a new, single mission. Interest in alcoholics had almost completely withered away; Synanon was tackling more or less exclusively the problem of addict rehabilitation.

Despite their efforts to adapt to the new surroundings, the group ran into considerable difficulty in Santa Monica. Steps were taken to oust them from their quarters on the grounds that they had violated the zoning law. During the course of this struggle, Synanon found new allies and made many new friends. Its fight to stay in Santa Monica was eventually won, but not before Chuck Dederich served twenty-five days in jail, a term brief enough to permit him to retain control of the organization, and long enough both to make him a martyr and to validate his status as a former jailbird, one which helped him overcome the fact that he had never been an addict.

Once at Santa Monica, Synanon developed its technique of all or none. Either one moves in, bag and baggage, or one stays away. Joining means becoming a part of the group, surrendering oneself entirely to it—not merely in a moral or spiritual sense, but physically. If there is a family on the outside, either it moves in or is left behind. To come for an hour or two a day, to attend the seminars (called *synanons*, supposedly from the malapropism of an early member), to be subjected to the special therapy, and then leave—even if one promises to stay clean—is forbidden. A doctor, addicted and anxious to break the habit, was turned away from Synanon because he sought admittance on a part-time basis. In this way, the organization has put into practice the theory of total control of a person's life as a necessity for the group's effectiveness. The neophyte must be stripped of his former self, a process that cannot be carried out if he walks away freely after each session.

Synanon works through group sessions or synanons which take place three times a week. The groups are small, numbering seven to ten persons, attendance is compulsory, and a synanist (or synanonist) or staff member is in charge. Unprofessional and untrained (except for the training he receives at Synanon which presumably makes him a professional, at least within the organization), the synanist leads a session in which verbal "haircuts" are given. Stress is laid on direct confrontation: everyone has to tell the truth, spill his guts, attack his fellows at the same time as he lays himself open to attack.

An addict is not coddled at Synanon; for him there is no TLC. Instead he is told that he is anything but a human being; he is made to feel completely worthless. This technique stands in contrast to the many forms of active-directive therapy currently in use, in which the subject is told that the root of his problem is his *lack* of feeling of self-worth; he is made to believe that he is a worthwhile human being, and that his problem stems, at least in part, from his failure to accept that judgment.[8] At Synanon, the very reverse takes place: the subject's self-contempt and self-hate are developed. When Reid asked to be readmitted

to Synanon, Dederich took one look at him and said,
"What is it? Oh, put it on a couch. There's a bare possibility that there may be something human inside all this
garbage."⁹ The use of the pronoun was not accidental, but
it is frightening.

Once the addict is admitted, therapy gets under way.
The newcomer begins at the bottom of the line cleaning
out toilets; then he climbs to washing dishes. At each point
those above him kick him in the face lest he think himself
too uppity or seem to want to climb too fast. All the while,
he is attending the weekly gut sessions.

These synanons have been described by Lewis Yablonsky in a detailed but uncritical book. At one point he offers
a verbatim account of part of a synanon that probed the
problem of prejudice. In many ways it was atypical, particularly in the nature of the problem with which it dealt;
but Yablonsky states that it reveals "some of the dynamics
of the direct-confrontation approach to underlying feelings in a synanon session."¹⁰ The session involved about
ten people, two of whom, Wilbur and Pete, were Negroes,
the rest whites.

> PETE: I want to ask Wilbur something. Wilbur,
> what did you react to so much in synanon the
> other night?
>
> WILBUR: Oh, I got triggered off. We had a syn-
> anon and talked about prejudice.
>
> PETE: You're not prejudiced are you?
>
> WILBUR: Yeah, I'm prejudiced.
>
> NANCY: [Sarcastically] Oh, Wilbur, are you
> really prejudiced . . . really?
>
> WILBUR: [Jokingly] As bad as I hate to say it and
> as much as it hurts me, I'm prejudiced, and I got
> triggered off and I started yelling and screaming.
>
> PETE: What triggered you, Wilbur?

WILBUR: When Danny called me a black nigger I got very, very mad—and I just blew.

PETE: I hear you went around the room and said fuck you to every white face in the room. How do you feel about the white faces in this room?

WILBUR: Well right now—when I'm not prejudiced—I like everyone in this room. I don't have any hostility right now towards anyone in this room. But I imagine if they start throwing hostility at me, I probably would react.

HERB: If people don't try to communicate with you everything is hunky-dunky. But if people start communicating with you, then you have hostility for them.

WILBUR: I don't think that's true. I like to communicate with people. You know, communicating is communicating. I don't feel anything about talking to a person, which means communicating. But hostility, I react to hostility. What I think is hostility, I meet with hostility.

PETE: You mean to tell me nobody in this room brings your prejudice out in you.

WILBUR: No, not just like this. If someone starts talking about prejudice and calls me a black nigger, where I'll feel something, then watch, you'll see.

PETE: What about this sucker right here that goes around the house all day spewing his prejudice shit out of his mouth all the time. [Pete refers to Don, accusing him of spreading anti-Negro prejudice in Synanon.]

NANCY: Yes, Don always is dropping his prejudice around the building.

WILBUR: I've never heard it.

PETE: You've never heard it? Call him a black

nigger, Don, like you do other people everyday of the week.

NANCY: Like you do everybody else, when they're trying to eat dinner.

GEORGE: Yeah, you always talk about these spick [Spanish] meals!

DON: Yeah, well, I don't like spicks, but I didn't say anything at dinner.

WILBUR: Well, you see, that triggers me, hearing about this son-of-a-bitch and what he does all the time.

PETE: [To Don, sarcastically] You say you don't like spicks. How do you feel about niggers?

DON: Well, I don't dig them like I dig Jewish guys, you know. [Don is Jewish.]

PETE: Who's talking about Jewish guys, sucker?

DON: I'm prejudiced, all right. I'm prejudiced like Wilbur.

PETE: I asked you a question. Why don't you answer it?

DON: Hey, listen, I don't want to scream in synanon. Wilbur has a bigger prejudice problem than I do.

WILBUR: No, look, I get mine out in synanon. No one can tell you that they hear me around the floor talking the shit that I talk in synanon. I talk about my prejudice in synanons, and I'm talking to a mother-fuckin' white face like you. You see, I call you a mother-fucker, but I do it in synanons.

DON: So what does that prove—what does that prove?

WILBUR: That proves you ain't got no goddamn guts.

NANCY: Don, you can do the right thing in here by spewing your prejudice garbage in a synanon, where more people can look at it with you. Get it out here and now. Then maybe you won't be spreading it all over the house.

PETE: You gutless mother-fucker, you won't call him [Wilbur] anything to his face. You'd rather go behind his back and call him something. Why don't you call it to his face?

DON: We've spoken about my prejudice already in synanons.

PETE: Tell it to him now.

. DON: I'm not going to tell it to him again. I told him how I feel about him.

PETE: How do you feel about him, then?

DON: I can't see a colored guy doing executive work or in charge of me.

JACK: What did you tell Sherry [a Negro woman] the other night? You know, all colored broads ain't supposed to do nothing but clean up, you know?

DON: When did I tell her this?

JACK: In synanon the other—

DON: Oh, you say a lot of things to trigger the guys.

JACK: That's how you feel. Man, why not admit it? Get it out. You might feel better!

GEORGE: This is how you feel. You know you've had this all your life. All colored women coming and cleaning your house and so forth, once a week or every other week, you know? And this is the conditioning you've had.

PETE: You fat, ignorant slob. That's exactly what you are. And you don't have any guts, man—not a gut in your whole fuckin' body . . . You're the biggest asshole in the house and the biggest coward.

DON: [Trying to act unprovoked] Right.

PETE: I could probably get up and spit in your face right now and all you'd do is wipe it off.

DON: Go ahead and try it.

PETE: You fuckin' coward.

DON: Go ahead and try it.

[Here the "no-physical-violence" rule is tested. It permits Don and Pete to express their real feelings, without the possibility of physical retaliation.]

PETE: What do you think of me right now?

DON: What am I supposed to do, get mad at you, man?

PETE: I'm mad at your crazy ass right now. You know what you are to me right now?

DON: What?

PETE: You're exactly like them suckers down in Birmingham last week that turned dogs loose on people to do what they couldn't do. That's exactly what you are to me right now. You're like that prejudiced mother-fucker, Governor ———.

DON: That's good; that means you respect me, you're afraid of me.

PETE: Yeah, I respect you all right.

DON: Definitely.

HERB: Do you think anybody in here respects you, Don? Forget about the prejudice—do you think anybody in here respects you?

DON: No.

HERB: Now they put you down all the time and ridicule you.

DON: They can't down me all the time.

HERB: *This is the world, Don, this is the world!*

DON: Herby, I'm in a world of my own. Jack here goes to the other extreme with his prejudice. [Jack is Jewish, and Don accuses him of getting

"too close" to Negroes. He implies that Jack's frat-
ernizing is reverse prejudice.]

JACK: My bed's in his [Wilbur's] house and it
don't bother me, but a Jew prick like you [Don]
bothers me more than a black guy like Wilbur, see?

WILBUR: It's all right for you if you have to feel
this way, Don. No one is indicting you for your
feelings.

DON: Then what's all this bullshit about?

WILBUR: What I'm indicting you for is taking
these feelings out everyday in the building and
spreading all this goddamn garbage and hate into
our house. Dump that prejudice garbage here in a
synanon, where you can get some help and change,
and maybe you'll understand it better, and maybe I
will too. Let's use the synanon to handle these vi-
cious prejudice feelings. Maybe we can work the
problem out here together.[11]

Some of the elements of attack therapy are illustrated
in this brief passage. A member having a problem or characteristic that is considered undesirable—in this case
prejudice—is provoked, castigated, and made to feel utterly reprehensible because of it. Every pejorative, every
demeaning term in the vocabulary, is applied to him—and
in his presence. As a sinner (in this instance, a man spreading his prejudice in Synanon), he is worthless. But while
being put down—and one might say put all the way down
—for being prejudiced, he is nonetheless urged to bring
his prejudices to the group sessions, the synanons, where
they can be examined, understood, and worked out.

But, from just this brief example, it seems the synanons
can also work the other way around. It may also be cathartic to do the attacking, to participate in putting down the
other(s) when one has been himself a lowly person in the

outside world. Thus, is the function of the synanons not only to get the garbage out of the attackee's system by subjecting him to relentless provocation and abuse, but to purge the attackers' systems of hostility by permitting them to indulge in this merciless sadism toward another?

Organizations like Synanon tend to discredit the motives of all those who do not accept their way of looking at the world. Thus, professionals are (in this view) afraid of the organization because it represents a threat to them, never because it may counter a theory of therapy in which they believe. Researchers visit Synanon only to slum (unless, of course, they turn out to like the place). According to one leader of Synanon, the enemies of the organization are:

> The people who don't bother to visit us, ever. The people who don't like us, in front, because we're ex-criminals and ex-addicts. And because at Synanon we refuse to draw any distinction between black and white. Who hate us because we refuse to believe that there is some special therapeutic value in sorting out mankind according to sex and locking them up in separate buildings. The people who want to stop us because we don't care what special brand of politics or religion you may have. . . . People who are just waiting for their chance to smash us. Just waiting. . . .[12]

Nonetheless, Synanon has many admirers. Of the three books written about it, all are adulatory; they are worth studying primarily because of their unintentional revelations about the organization, its leader, and its methods. Lewis Yablonsky, a professor of sociology, is more a special pleader than an observer; but his work is filled with valuable descriptions of the group's history, organizational structure, techniques, and underlying theory. Guy

Endore's book is anecdotal; although the stories he quotes are frequently contradictory, they do offer many insights into Synanon. Daniel Casriel, a physician, was one of the first to befriend Synanon, and his book was written before he became critical of it; later, he became associated with Daytop Lodge, a group in some ways modeled after Synanon.[13]

The jacket of Endore's book describes the author as a close friend of Synanon since its inception, one who tells his story "with an undisguised pride and enthusiasm." This may make for good reading, but not for good history or social commentary. However, one can read between the lines, for instance in this statement that Endore quotes:

> This place is really a more powerful fix than heroin. You get hooked here. I don't know about you, but I'm hooked. I'm really hooked.[14]

That Dederich has always considered the organization and its members subject to his private manipulation is clear from almost all the literature about Synanon. From the start, according to Endore, Dederich knew that

> dope addicts were nothing but little children, nasty little brats arrested in their development. Kids crying for their little white lollypop powder so that they could shoot it up their veins.[15]

And again: "They'd grow up some day, his prostitutes and his dope addicts." The possessive pronoun here is particularly important; these are people whom Dederich owns and controls. Endore takes seriously a jocular reference to Dederich and the group as "Fatso and his trained seals." In fact, he carries it to a disturbing conclusion: "They'd grow up [these prostitutes and addicts] and then they'd regret that they had let this golden opportunity to become one of Chuck's trained seals slip by them."[16]

Chuck's trained seals. In the words of one man who later broke with him, Chuck had a "power of life and death" over people that made him "a kind of god." This ex-Synanonist asked Endore:

> Don't you see that the more people he got into Synanon the more he could become the great father-figure? That's why he never wanted anyone to leave—unless they dared to stand out against his ideas. Then from being the man who never wanted anyone to leave, he would become the angry god who expelled you from paradise! Plunged you back into hell.[17]

This particular man felt that he had to get out of Synanon and back to the real world. Endore's investigation of his story reveals that Synanon is far from a paradise. It is a home filled with gossip, in which everyone, including the highest leaders, maintained that the splittee (a Negro) had conducted a synanon in the library that had developed into an orgy, had had epileptic seizures under conditions embarrassing to the group, had had a fixation on every white girl in the house (even one going cold turkey), and finally that he had raped one of the white inmates. Such a story reads like Stalin's apologists writing about a Trotskyite!

Of the father-figure himself, one adherent states that "Chuck is my god, and Synanon is my religion." Other worshipers, more modest ones, deny that Dederich is God, only Jesus. Others describe him as "a modern Socrates," engaged in "a total war against stupidity," of which "the present war against drug addiction is of course only one tiny segment."

All the writers on Synanon describe Dederich's scorn for the addict, a scorn directed not at his habit but at him as a person. For Dederich, addicts are "dope fiends" and

Synanon is the tunnel back—"back into the human race." But if Synanon is a tunnel back, does this mean that Dederich and the members accept the verdict of those who have expelled addicts from humanity?

In a critique that appeared soon after Yablonsky's book, Robert Martinson sought the secret of Synanon's amazing growth in the face of adversity.[18] He found in "the encapsulation of the hopeless and powerless addict into a small total community" a source of the energy and power of the organization. He points out that Synanon is searching for total control of the member's energies and identity; such control means cutting off all ties with the outside world—with mothers and lovers "who have already demonstrated their inability to help the person."[19] But when do people start through the tunnel on the way back? Martinson inquires. Actually, Synanon is so hostile to the outside world that members build up little will to get out. Perhaps what Synanon has done is modify the AA-type statement, "once an addict always an addict," to "once an addict to narcotics, always an addict to Synanon." It is a convenient modification, one similar to AA's statement that alcoholism cannot be cured, and one which performs the same function: to keep the individual tied to the organization, thus preserving its present state and insuring its further growth.

For Edgar Z. Friedenberg, Synanon is an exercise in brainwashing, a charge readily accepted—but defended—by many of Dederich's followers. But Friedenberg finds here a grave danger both to Synanonists and society:

> How uniform in design and operation the apparatus of "gut-level" indoctrination has always been, wherever and whenever it has been installed: the Church into which the supplicant Luther was received; the Maoist struggle session as

> Robert Jay Lifton has described it in *Thought-Reform and the Psychology of Totalism;* the Marine boot camp; the Zen master and his group of disciples. All these make the most of the dubious proposition that their neophyte comes to them as a petitioner to be tested, minimizing the social pressures that drive him to their door by treating these pressures as legitimate aspects of social reality that the neophyte has failed to meet. All of them isolate the recruit from contact with the outside world for several weeks, until his old identity has been smashed and a new prosthesis molded to fit the demands of the organization. And, most important, all of them depend heavily on institutionalized devices for mobilizing and focusing group hostility against any remnant of his old self that a member might have preserved, and reinforce that hostility with well-staged rituals of public humiliation. What is new in Synanon is chiefly the therapeutic cant in which all these procedures are discussed and justified.[20]

That Synanon sets out to destroy the individual is undeniable. One newcomer is told that he is a "whining, sniveling brat," another that he will be told when to talk; there is, however, hope that this ukase will last only "for a while." Perhaps when the neophyte has completely assumed the group's outlook he will be trusted to talk without waiting for permission. By then, of course, he will have learned the party line.

Today Synanon is seeking to extend its influence by entering the field of rehabilitation of felons who have never been and are not now addicts. Even further, Endore has stated that Synanon would like to undertake a complete reform of our sick society. Synanon now sees itself as a "social movement of immense significance." This lofty goal would not be possible to dream of without money, and that the organization now has.

With Synanon affluent, Dederich is no longer the ex-alcoholic but "the ultimate executive." There is a bronze bust of him at Santa Monica, and Synanon itself has become a little empire that extends from coast to coast. "We're not much different from other corporations, General Motors for instance," Peter Collier quotes Dederich, in a highly critical *Ramparts* study, as saying. "But they just lack the philosophical base that leads to satisfaction for the workers."[21] For workers one might substitute "proles"; as in General Motors, those at the top get the greatest rewards, and not only ones of spiritual satisfaction. One addict, still on drugs and bitter because he could not afford to pay the fee that would gain him entry to Synanon, told Collier, "I don't give a damn whether it calls itself a social movement or the French Revolution. It's just the country club of junkie places."

More and more, Synanon's new entrants come from middle-income, and even upper-income, families. Many of them are Jewish, few are Negro. The prime requirement for those who seek admission is the entrance fee. On this topic, Collier quotes a report from the New Jersey Narcotic Commission:

> In June, she [the mother] took her son [a barbiturate user] to the Westport House of Synanon. She was informed that her son would die unless accepted at Synanon. She was told that he would not be accepted at Synanon unless an entrance fee of $1000 was paid. Four money order certificates were presented to the Commission in the amount of $250 each. There was also produced a

receipt signed by the chairman of Synanon Foundation for $1000. The boy stayed exactly 27 hours at Synanon. Despite repeated requests, no portion of the money was returned. This woman does time work in the garment industry and is the sole support for herself and her son. In 1964 her total earnings were $1349.[22]

Although Synanon discourages quitting, almost half its members depart within the first six months. But the ex-member leaves his entrance fee behind, and Synanon is all the richer for his absence. The organization also obtains funds from square society now that it has formed a coalescing group with respectable people. Not surprisingly, this has been far from a difficult task. Synanon has never even criticized society for leading people to narcotics; it has simply denounced those who have been led. In fact, it has read them out of the human race, at least until such time as they have submitted to the rigors of the organization. "Of all the interesting lessons to be learned from Mr. Yablonsky's work," writes Friedenberg, "the most important and perpetually timely is simply this: *No democracy can afford to have outcasts.*"[23]

Synanon, however, does more than acquiesce in the maintenance of this outcast status. It defends and even propagates it, demanding, for example, that union cards be taken away from musicians who are addicted. Hatred and contempt for the addict exude from every page of its literature. But just as surely as "no democracy can afford to have outcasts," neither can it afford to allow such addicts to be brainwashed into accepting their outcast status. In fact, some people would even suggest that we can more easily afford the tragedy of addiction.

And addiction remains just that, a great human tragedy. Synanon has introduced a new effort to overcome the narcotic habit; if much of that method must be discarded (even to the point of conceding that being completely dehumanized may be worse than being an addict), its total institutionalization and attack therapy may be basically a good idea. If the now-forgotten Tender Loving Care of Synanon's early days is combined with both the rebuilding of self-confidence and self-worth (without first destroying it) and an attack on addict stigmatization, the Synanon movement may well bring us new and necessary answers.

7. Convicts and ex-convicts: using the skeletons to open the closets

You can wipe out the sin, but not its memory.
—*Russian proverb*

Throughout the United States today, hundreds of thousands of people are attempting virtually the impossible: to change their biographies. They live with skeletons in their closets, in this case the stigma of being ex-convicts. Most of these people are white; but because convicts comprise a larger percentage of America's black population, the black ex-convict is an important factor in the Negro's struggle against poverty and squalor, and hence in his efforts toward unification and equalization with white society. Most ex-convicts are male, and their violations were major; the females, on the other hand, for the greater part were prostitutes, shoplifters, or, in more recent years, narcotics offenders.

The prison is often called a revolving door. How many

This chapter was written in collaboration with William C. Kuehn.

of those who leave are going to come back and how many of those who enter have been there before are matters of dispute. One authority, Daniel Glaser, suggests that the parole system works for about two-thirds of released convicts.[1] However, there are many complications in arriving at an accurate estimate (Glaser discusses them), which lead others to find his figures overly optimistic.[2] For one thing, Glaser's work deals only with federal prisoners, for whom recidivism may well be lower than for state prisoners. At any rate, authorities agree that parole leaves much to be desired, and that too little has been done to make it possible for the ex-convict who has paid his debt thereafter to hold his head high.

To this end, some criminologists are now suggesting (and many are opposing) the use of ex-convicts as therapists in self-help groups. Nowhere is the belief that self-help organizations can be fruitful among ex-convicts more explicitly supported by a corrections official than in this statement by George Saleebey, chief of the Division of Delinquency Prevention Services of the California Department of the Youth Authority:

> Encouragement should be provided ex-offenders to organize themselves into self-help groups in much the same manner that Alcoholics Anonymous, Narcotics Anonymous, Parents Without Partners, etc., have organized. While a few of the pioneering attempts to do this have resulted in dismal failure and have had more negative than positive value, these groups can have a profound influence upon their members if there is good leadership and proper guidance and direction plus community interest.[3]

The suggestion that the AA technique be applied to convicts preparing to leave prison, and to ex-convicts struggling to remain out of prison, has been put forward on several occasions. AA itself has worked with prisoners, utilizing a sort of self-help missionary approach in which alcoholism is viewed as the key to the problem that led to the prisoner's downfall.

Prisons themselves are conducive to group therapy efforts, not only because they maintain insufficient personnel for individual therapy, but also because prisoners accept group therapy as a sort of bull session that breaks the monotony and gives them an opportunity to talk, gripe, interact, and undergo catharsis. One large inmate group, known as SIG (Self-Improvement Group), organized by the Catholic chaplain at the federal penitentiary at MacNeil Island, Washington, is described by Glaser:

> It is essentially a discussion club on problems of the prisoners in achieving a self-sufficient non-criminal life, emphasizing self-analysis, but featuring one or more outside speakers at most of its meetings. Speakers come mainly from service or professional organizations in the Seattle-Tacoma area and have included police officials as well as businessmen, clergymen, educators, and others. The organization has its own newspaper circulating both in the prison and to outside cooperating organizations and individuals.[4]

In addition to the efforts of AA and such groups as SIG, the Black Muslims have developed a distinctive form of in-prison group therapy[5] which penologists have frequently lauded as being remarkably successful. Epileptic prisoners have formed a special organization of their own in Leavenworth,[6] and another group of prisoners, all of whom had been convicted of forgery, at one time had an organization called Checks Anonymous. Many penologists and criminologists have described, analyzed, and generally sought to encourage what has been variously described as inmate therapy or prison-*guided* group interaction.[7]

On the other hand, efforts to form organizations of *ex*-convicts have met with one serious obstacle. It is the tradition in American corrections and parole work that a discharged prisoner on parole is forbidden from associating with known criminals—which means, among others, with ex-convicts. So that, while many officials countenance the self-help movement *in prison*, they oppose its continuation outside.

Donald Cressey, long associated with the theory of differential association—that people learn to be criminals in association with those who have rejected the norms of society—has made an eloquent plea for the use of ex-convicts in the rehabilitation of their fellows.[8] These people, he believes, offer not only empathy and understanding but the example that the ex-convict can make it in the straight world. Furthermore, as sponsors they become missionaries and reformers, taking on the attitudes and values that go with that status, and hence permanently reforming themselves in order to serve as an example to others.

Although efforts to form "go-straight" or, in Yablonsky's words, "anti-criminal" societies have been numerous, most such groups that continue can claim only small success.

Many of these groups have originated among youthful offenders. One of the first was formed in Denver, under the supervision of a judge. Called the Friday Nighters Club, its aim was to apply the principles of group therapy to juveniles on probation. To avoid any stigma, the word probation itself was not mentioned in the organization's name. The group was kept informal, and met in the judge's chambers; envious youths not admitted are said to have inquired whether they had to break a law to be eligible.[9]

A few years later, a group of young people in Detroit formed a self-help club within a "training school" for delinquent boys.[10] The youths elected their own chairman and in many ways modeled their group after AA. The name Delinquents Anonymous was at first suggested, but rejected in favor of Teen-Agers Anonymous. The switch to the latter name, according to Albert Eglash,

> indicated their awareness of stigma. To be stigmatized is to be set apart as different from others. The goal of this program is to enable people whose behavior has set them apart to rejoin their peers.

Subsequently the name was changed to Youth Anonymous; the young adults, it was said, had become sensitive to the negative connotations of being identified as teenagers. Youth Anonymous was not an independent venture in that it was started in a correctional institution; attendance and participation were not entirely voluntary. Yet it did enjoy a self-help type of orientation in that it operated on AA principles. Short-lived as it was, Youth Anonymous served several functions: it formalized the effort to organize voluntary associations of delinquents; it imparted the "anonymous" structure to what had hitherto been vaguely defined as "youth work" in houses of correction; and, finally, it was self-help and not help-us directed.

A group of New York ghetto youngsters, several of whom, having spent time in prisons and reform schools, seemed to be starting the revolving door career, have recently organized themselves into the Real Great Society. They have gone on speaking tours and held dances, always showing other youth how well they can function as straight young people. They have also started a small business, received a grant from the Vincent Astor Foundation, and launched the Real University of the Streets which, among others, offers classes in computer programming, ballet, chess, Spanish, and karate.[11]

In 1957, a self-help movement started among the adult prisoners at La Crosse, Wisconsin. Initiated by a man on probation who had been jailed twenty-seven times, it was called Adults Anonymous and, as the name suggests, was modeled after AA. The use of the word *adults*, rather than *prisoners* or *convicts* or even *recidivists*, suggests that the stigmatizing characteristic had to be concealed from the world.[12]

Meetings of Adults Anonymous were held in the county jail; about eight men sat around a table discussing their Twelve Steps. Whatever success the group may have had in jail, it seems not to have held its members once they were freed. "After discharge," one writer reports, "few men make any further contact. An exception are those men who consider themselves alcoholics; some of these have continued to attend Alcoholics Anonymous meetings." Nevertheless, one should not too quickly conclude that the out-of-prison effort failed; more accurately, it never really started. And one can readily understand the reluctance of the ex-inmate to return voluntarily, even for the purpose of reforming and aiding others, to the walls whence he had so recently departed.

Gamblers Anonymous, AA, and many other self-help groups have ex-convicts among their members; the organizations help these people find relief from the stigma of having served time, but their focus naturally centers on quite another problem. Thus, while it is not unusual to find people openly mentioning their prison records at meetings of Gamblers Anonymous, the organization makes no special efforts to gain insight into the problems of the ex-convict.

In England, there is an ex-convict group which operates

under the name of the RA Fellowship Trust, the initials representing Recidivists Anonymous. Like Adults Anonymous, RA had its inception in prison.[13] At Wandsworth Prison a group of inmates banded together "with the aim of assisting one another in their efforts to reintegrate themselves into the community." As their work continued, both at Wandsworth and at Chelmsford, contacts were made with employers, local authorities, and private individuals who were prepared to help prisoners upon discharge.

So far, the main activity of the group has been the foundation of the RA House in London, somewhat similar to the American halfway house, except that it was established and is run by ex-convicts themselves. After holding meetings in prison, where it prepares people for discharge, RA then welcomes them when they are released. Those who come to the RA House do so willingly; most stay five or six months, but a few remain only one. Occasionally, an ex-convict lives at the RA House for several years.

There are failures at RA. Of the seventy-three men who have come to the RA House, twelve have returned to prison; of this dozen, five received short sentences and were later freed. Thus, on the surface, it would seem that seven were failures, five partial failures, and sixty-one successes—in all a higher proportion of success than one would expect to find in a cross-section of former English prisoners. But the real measure of RA's success can only come from a follow-up study of the sixty-one who have remained free men. Have they abandoned their criminal pursuits? Are they employed? How well are they handling the problem of being discharged prisoners? A comparison of them with a control group of other former prisoners, who have served an equal amount of time for similar crimes, but who have never been exposed to the aid extended by

RA, would be ideal. To date, however, no such research has been undertaken; one can only accept RA's figures—but with the realization that they have not been compiled by a neutral investigator.

In Canada, the John Howard Society, named after one of the heroes of the history of prison reform, has been working with groups of ex-convicts for a number of years. Several JHS groups, despite their close association with the parent organization, have become sufficiently independent to be considered self-help. This is not to deny that there is an element of guidance to their work, but the self-help orientation is clearly evident and seems to be growing in significance.[14]

The Johoso Club (the name comes from the first two letters of John, Howard, and Society) was organized when several ex-inmates requested the Hamilton staff of the Society to initiate such a group. In a report which estimated that eighty men had attended Johoso meetings at one time or another during a one-year period, the reporting officials could count only three "slips," or recidivists. The figure of eighty is misleading, however, for many members stay only a few weeks. The hard, activist core of Johoso consists of about fifteen members who meet weekly with a few volunteers and staff members to fulfill the group's original purpose of providing "an opportunity for ex-inmates on release to find understanding, companionship and an evening of social entertainment."

Variations of the Johoso Club are found in several other John Howard branches. The London, Ontario, branch reports that its group, which consists only of ex-offenders and members of their families, has

> relieved loneliness and offered understanding and support to the recently released; has provided the opportunity to "do something worth while" for

others and has offered "interaction without fears" with "square johns."

While the group does not conceal from the public the fact that its members are men with prison records, in the tradition of the anonymous societies only their first names are revealed. In Toronto, a John Howard group calling itself The Confreres among its other activities meets men as they step off the bus from prison—a task that any philanthropic organization of businessmen might have done, but somehow did not. In Alberta, one John Howard group functions under the name of Add-Can (for Addicts-Canada); a second is called Dead Numbers (the numbers by which the members were once identified are dead, and they are once again persons known by names).

In general, these Canadian groups tend to have small memberships ranging from eight to fifteen members. They emphasize open, frank discussion of problems, and the concomitant development of trust among members. Some groups work on vocational study plans, while others have devoted considerable energy to the organization and direction of criminal addicts, a project which is reported to have achieved some success.

Attempts to form groups of ex-convicts, and to employ the ex-convict as a bridge to reach and teach the present inmate, have been made in several parts of the United States. Probably the most prominent single supporter of this work has been Billy Sands, himself a convicted felon who has told his story in two books.[15] Today Sands is conducting what amounts to a one-man rehabilitation campaign among prisoners.

Called Seventh Step, the movement has enlisted the aid of several of America's foremost penologists as supporters and consultants—perhaps none more notable than the former warden of San Quentin, Clinton Duffy. However, it still meets a great deal of opposition from the professional community at large. Sands attributes such opposition to his challenge to their vested interest:

> Most of the penologists who still oppose us do so because they see the Seventh Step movement as a threat to their way of life. They are right. They try to justify their position by saying that our work is experimental. The Seventh Step program has been continuously successful since its inception. The experiment has ended, but the work continues.[16]

Sands's conclusion about the vested interests of penologists may well be correct; but this same charge—vested interests—could also be made against him. Like most other self-help groups, Seventh Step turns its back on psychiatrists, psychologists, and social workers, although it adds that it "respect[s] members of these professions." The fact is that any self-help movement feels threatened by the offer of help from others, help which, if successful, may remove the need for the organization. Sands himself has explained why Seventh Step meetings are better off without professionals:

> Convicts may listen politely to educated free men, but they do not answer back. They are not polite at Seventh Step meetings, and they do answer back —because they are deeply involved. The movement is their own.[17]

Essentially, Seventh Step has become a movement of prisoners to better themselves by group work and contact with dedicated outsiders, and thus to gain an early release. Once released, they often have jobs and other aid awaiting them. But as a movement of people struggling to help each other live with a past that will not die—as a rehabilitation program for ex-convicts—it has done, and is doing, little.

Among efforts to form ex-convict groups, The Inn in Hartford, Connecticut, while not entirely successful, has resulted in a good deal of private rehabilitation work by a former offender, Robert Glazier.[18] At first employed by Community Service and the Greater Hartford Council of Churches, Glazier became involved with two related problems, narcotics addiction and the status of the ex-convict. He quickly found that the addicts, who shied away from discussions, needed therapy, while the ex-convicts needed jobs. Perhaps the one thing that none of them needed was a meeting. Given on the one hand the difficulties of administering therapy to addicted losers, and, on the other, the reluctance of the ex-convicts who had jobs to retain close ties to the group, The Inn's basis of organization could not be firmly established.

Leaving the addicts to professional therapists, Glazier turned all his attention to the ex-convicts. As he says:

> When these guys come out, they are introverted. People don't realize that a released prisoner is more afraid of society than society is of him. What these guys need most when they get out is bread, a little cash. The prison gives them ten or fifteen dollars and a suit of clothes that you can spot as prison-manufactured a mile away. Then they can't get a job because they're not bondable.

Having switched from meetings to one-to-one relationships, Glazier then undertook a one-man crusade to find employment for these ex-convicts.

Along the same lines, a group of former convicts in Washington, D.C., operates Bonabond, an agency whose primary purpose is "to aid former offenders from whom prospective employers demand a fidelity bond as a condition of employment."[19] The group was initiated by a social worker who borrowed organizational ideas from many sources: "A little from the Boy Scouts, a little from Alcoholics Anonymous, and a little from fraternity life." The director of Bonabond is an alumnus of Sing Sing, his assistants alumni not only of that institution but of Dannemora and the Lexington center for the rehabilitation of addicts. Some describe the group as a sort of Addicts Anonymous, run by a former pusher. The members meet once a week for self-help discussion, as well as run a youth project, picnics, and socials. Bonabond claims to have 375 ex-convicts who can be considered members; although at last report it admitted that twenty had had difficulties with the law (a low percentage if a sufficiently long period of "keeping clean" is covered), not a single claim had yet been filed against a bond. On these grounds alone Bonabond must be viewed as successful.

Like this Washington organization, the Fortune Society in New York was initiated by a man who has never seen the inside of a prison, but it is directed almost entirely by former offenders.[20] As opposed to Bonabond, however, the Fortune Society is oriented toward education of the public, rather than help for members. An outgrowth of an off-Broadway play about prison life (and more or less specifically about homosexuality in prison), *Fortune and Men's Eyes*, the group describes itself in simple terms:

> The Fortune Society has as its basic purpose to create a greater public awareness of the prison system in America today, and to help realize the problems and complexities confronting the inmates during their incarceration and when they rejoin society.
>
> The Fortune Society does this by sending out

teams of speakers (ex-convicts) to talk to school groups, church and community groups, and tell the public how they are affected by what happens inside our prisons. The Fortune Society also arranges for radio and television programs in which the ex-convict can express his views about the conditions that exist in the prisons.[21]

Thus it may be seen that many different types of voluntary associations have been operating among and for convicts and ex-convicts in the United States, Canada, and England. One of the most interesting of these organizations is the Boston-based Self Development Group, Inc., usually known as SDG.[22]

SDG is an outgrowth of an experiment which began in the summer of 1961 at the Massachusetts Correctional Institution at Concord. Under the direction of Timothy Leary, then of Harvard University (later becoming world famous as a result of his activities in the psychedelic drug movement), a research team administered the drug psilocybin to a selected group of Concord's three hundred male inmates.[23] Starting with just a handful of subjects, the Leary team eventually gave the drug to more than thirty prisoners. It was hoped that the psilocybin would release the inhibitions and expand the horizons of the inmates, enabling them to take a searching look at themselves and their past lives. After taking it, the subjects in the experiment met in small groups to discuss what they had perceived and felt. Some reported "profound religious experiences," while others stated that they had been able to look at their past and to realize that that mode of life and its consequences were not what they hoped to enjoy in the future. While not disputing the powerful effects of hallucinogens, one must at the same time treat statements like the latter with some skepticism: the prisoners could have easily put on the professors to obtain their approval and, possibly, to gain allies in the quest for early release.

Leary has recently described his experience at Concord:

> The first psychedelic session in the prison was well planned. The first thing we did was to tell the prisoners as much as we could about the psychedelic experience. We brought in books for them to read, reports by other subjects, articles which described the terrors as well as the ecstasies of the experience. We spent most of the time describing our own experiences and answering groping questions. We made it very clear to the prisoners that this was nothing *we* were doing to them. There was no doctor-patient game going here. We would take the drugs along with them. We were doing nothing to them that we wouldn't willingly, happily have done to ourselves.[24]

Thus the experiment started, with five prisoners and three Harvard psychologists meeting for a trip. The first was followed by many others, good trips and bad. The group setting, particularly the presence of the Harvard men, seems to have acted as a great force in restructuring the inmates' thinking. For the majority of them, this was the first time in their adult lives that they had come to trust anyone who, in a professional position, advocated any form of rehabilitation. As one of the leaders of SDG said, "We were hit so hard by Dr. Tim as to how our lives were wasted. We *had* to get together to help each other make changes in our lives."

Leary was proposing that the group (inmates and Harvard experimenters) form themselves into a clan-type family. This would produce emotional involvement, not rehabilitation in which the professional was detached.

Our strategy was exactly opposite to the detached professional approach. The aim was to build a network of friends who would help each other. To construct a group that could perform some of the functions of the tribe. If a middle-class person gets in trouble he is typically rescued by middle-class know-how which bails him out, gets him a lawyer, talks middle-class jargon to the officials, gets him a job, provides him with a middle-class home to return to.

Our plan was to use the resources of our group (including middle-class know-how) to weave a web of protection for the convicts.[25]

There are probably few settings, except perhaps that of the mental hospital, where the chasm between the superior and the subordinate is so great as in prison; even the turnkey—no less a Harvard professor—is part of that vast collectivity of men who walk out free at the end of the workday. Here at Concord was a team of free men sharing experiences with the inmates, in a sense fusing into one group.

While Leary's work with the inmates came to an end, he did inspire them to continue the group—or, some would say, provoke them. In one of their final meetings, Leary told them that in all the years he had been coming to Concord he had never seen one convict who "gave a damn about another." The founders of SDG regard Leary's words as crucial ones. The statement—the insult—that convicts are completely self-centered went counter to much of the folklore by which they live. In their own world of the damned, convicts like to believe that there is a firm bond of honor and loyalty to those damned with them. Thus the Leary statement provoked intense anxiety.

If a convict did not care about his fellows, then what was he but a man without a friend?

Regarding Leary's charge as a challenge, the Concord convicts sought to meet it by continuing their group and dedicating it to aiding all those, themselves included, incarcerated in American prisons. Furthermore, these inmates realized that they had disclosed not only their thoughts but their greatest failings and weaknesses to each other. While some people shun those who have penetrated their secret selves, others, as in the case of the Concord convicts, seek them out to band together in common protection.

When Leary's team departed from Concord in the spring of 1963, they left behind two distinct and quite different impressions of their work. On the positive side was the core of enlightened and dedicated inmates who saw in the Leary episode a structure which would enable them to help themselves and other convicts, as well as men recently released. On the negative side was the staff of Concord and other corrections professionals around the state. Most of these people felt that the Harvard experiment had been little more than a "pot party." They refused to attribute any beneficial results to it. In fact, this feeling (which may, as Sands points out in his defense of Seventh Step, derive from the threat to the professionals) still pervaded the minds of many corrections officials several years later—reinforced no doubt by Leary's subsequent activities. Thus they dismiss SDG's efforts as the outgrowth of a worthless and sensational experiment, one which in its turn can produce nothing of value. Although this attitude has inhibited the growth and development of SDG, it has not stifled the group's initiative and determination.

A few weeks after Leary left Concord, two convicts who became co-founders of SDG, James Kerrigan and Donald Painten, approached the prison superintendent to convince him of the group's value and to seek permission to meet on a formal weekly schedule. Greeted with a great deal of suspicion and skepticism, their request was denied. However, informal meetings had been going on in the prison yard for some months; gathered in clusters, the prisoners, for brief and rather surreptitious moments, convened their "meetings." It was under these conditions that the men continued to formulate plans for gaining recognition for their group. They sent letters to influential people in the community who might be able to aid their cause. Among those responding were Robert F. Kennedy, Richard Cardinal Cushing, Miriam Van Waters (former superintendent of the Massachusetts Correctional Institution at Framingham), and many members of the Boston academic community. The group also wrote to the State Commissioner of Corrections, explaining their plight and inviting him to come to Concord to meet with them.

Meanwhile, the group—or what might be described as the remains of the old one and the embryo of the new—had gained the confidence of a psychologist connected with the Division of Legal Medicine at Concord. He permitted the prisoners to meet with him under the auspices of the division. The relationship thus established was conducive to the revitalization that the inmates sought. But movements of this sort often exist at the mercy of personnel; in this instance, the psychologist soon left Concord, and the man who replaced him sought to run the group in a manner which the prisoners considered authoritarian. The focus of decision-making came to lie in the outsider, not in the prison community itself. All the group's carefully thought-out structure and methodology seemed to be on the verge of destruction; it was doubtful if the group could survive, or would want to survive, under such conditions. Shortly after their disillusionment set in, however, the commissioner of corrections accepted their invitation. Favorably impressed, he gave SDG permission to meet independently in the prison, pending official approval from the State House. That approval was granted in June 1964.

At this point, the group consisted of ten men who met by themselves, supervised only by a prison guard who was to remain silent but report any disturbing events to the superintendent. Since that time, the guard requirement has been relaxed. In July 1964 SDG obtained permission to form a second group under the auspices of the first; the original was known as "the center group" and the newly formed one as "binary group one." The binary consisted of ten Concord prisoners chosen by the men of the center. Since then, other binary groups have been formed both at Concord Prison and Concord Farm.

With the release of several SDG members from prison, and the impending release of more, many expressed the desire to establish a follow-up organization in the community. The concept of an outside ex-convict group thus came entirely from the prisoners; it was neither initiated, sponsored, nor encouraged by the officials. Whether this lack of interest was due to the officials' limited imagination, to their consideration of such an association as a threat to their vested interests, or to their suspicion of danger in the association of parolees with one another, it is difficult to say. Perhaps every factor was at work. On the other hand, one should not overestimate the extent of information which the officials had on this new SDG project. Isolating the project from all circumstances in which it was begun, it appears to have been a momentous event in the history of Massachusetts correction; back in context, however, it could well have been lost in the routine paper work, research, and many other duties facing prison and parole personnel.

At any rate, the appeal of an outside SDG organization was immediately strong. Prisoners on discharge are stigmatized as ex-cons; they have little money, few respectable connections, and relatively no prospect of satisfactory employment. But if SDG could continue among ex-convicts, the stigma might be turned from punishment to reward; the members (and particularly the leaders) might gain power, however small, and funds, either from a foundation or the anti-poverty movement.

Nonetheless, the newly released prisoners expected profound difficulties in receiving permission to continue their SDG work outside. Believing that, as prisoners, they had developed outstanding abilities for organization, manipulation, and, one might add, conspiracy, they decided to meet the challenge head-on. The regulation prohibiting the assembly of parolees, or for that matter, even conversation between them, had to be circumvented. They appealed to the chairman of the Parole Board who, along with the commissioner of corrections, visited the prison to meet with the group awaiting release. A few months later, in October of 1965, permission was granted for the outside meetings. Although rather strict regulations were established, at least the men could, legally and officially, meet. The biggest setback at this point came from the failure to notify many individual parole officers of the decision; as a result some of these officers prevented parolees under their jurisdiction from attending the meetings.

By the fall of 1967, SDG existed outside prison, and had a paid official, John Anthony, as executive director. Anthony, a former prisoner, was contacted by officials from the Suffolk County House of Correction at Deer Island and asked to set up a regular schedule of SDG meetings at that institution. This invitation can be seen both as a tribute to SDG and its generally favorable reputation, and at the same time a recognition of the meager success of more traditional methods of prisoner rehabilitation, both before and after release.

After the establishment of the Deer Island meetings, SDG set up an outside "central group" in early 1968 to direct its various programs and to rule on any possible changes in policy. This central group has essentially the same position and function as the original one, except that it is located in the community, not in prison, and can be viewed as a sort of board of directors or executive committee. SDG has also expanded its scope to include working with a group of delinquent and so-called predelinquent youths in South Boston, an activity that many regard with considerable fear, unsure as they are of the effects that association with ex-convicts may have on these youngsters. As reformers, are they themselves reformed; or, as former offenders, will they slip and serve as a corruptive influence? It is still too early to tell. To date, the youth branch holds meetings once a week, with at least one SDG staff member present. In addition, staff members spend time with the boys during the day, talking with them and directing their recreational program.

In a sense, the projected goals of SDG may be said to be grandiose. AA caught on, and Billy Sands became a national figure. Why can't SDG get programs working in every penal institution, first in Massachusetts and eventually in the whole country? Why, at the same time, can't it work with people in Boston and later elsewhere, who have problems other than that of being ex-convicts? Although their program is designed primarily for the rehabilitation of criminals and ex-criminals, SDG leaders are not modest in their ambitions. In moments of enthusiasm, they state their readiness and willingness to attack any of society's problems in order "to make the world a better place for everyone." But many will look askance at this task being undertaken by ex-convicts.

Within prison, SDG is a voluntary organization which recruits its members through personal contacts and educational programs. The official criteria for membership are quite simple: "A desire to stay out of prison and a willingness to help others do the same."[26] No dues are collected nor funds solicited from any of the members. All that is asked of and expected from them is that they make what the leaders call "a meaningful contribution" to the group by attendance and discussion at meetings.

Like AA and other self-help groups, SDG has its "points" or "steps." The seven points of SDG are the central theme of group discussions, and they read very much like the programs of other groups of stigmatized and deviant people:

> 1. Trying to solve personal problems in an honest setting assisted by others of a similar purpose.
> 2. Learning to relate with each other and the world as reasonable, responsible persons.
> 3. Building a useful life structured on faith in God, in self, and in the ideals of the group.
> 4. Earning social respect and respecting society in return on the basis of mutual commitment to the objectives of the community.
> 5. Living as a power of example towards helping others in trouble.
> 6. Reviving commitment to SDG every day in compliance with the principles of the program.
> 7. Keeping SDG independent of ineffectual programs, yet open to assistance from any person or group who can help it in attaining its goals.[27]

It is interesting to note that nowhere in these steps are the words prisoner or offender, inmate or ex-inmate mentioned. Either SDG wants to avoid its stigma in hopes that it will go away, or, more probably, the seven points are based on the hope that SDG will one day expand, losing its original base and becoming the source of a great national movement.

At the same time that most voluntary associations seek new members, they also suffer from the inability to hold those already in the fold. Few associations are highly restrictive, enjoying a greater demand for entrance than they are able or willing to fulfill. These are usually status-conferring organizations, and it seems that SDG is one of them—at least so far as status within communities of prisoners and ex-prisoners is concerned.[28] Since the various SDG groups are limited to ten members each, it is sometimes necessary for the would-be member to wait. Openings within prison SDG groups are created only by parole, resignation, or expulsion.

When an inmate indicates that he would like to join SDG, he is interviewed by one of the leaders to determine if, in the leader's view, he is sincere in his desire to change his life pattern of crime and what amounts to, or is at least defined as, self-punishment. Once he passes this test and is declared eligible, the inmate is voted on by the members of the group he wishes to join. But even the leader's recommendation and the group's affirmative vote do not guarantee membership. Finally to attain the status of member, the inmate must attend at least twelve consecutive meetings. In explaining this rule, John Anthony has stated, "The initiate must attend twelve meetings before he can ask anything of the group. Up until that point he must give to the group, but not ask anything from it or expect anything from it." Belonging, then, is seen as having an advantage, and one must first prove his worth to enjoy it. Like other organizations, the group finds its prestige enhanced to the extent that it is made difficult to penetrate.

Nor is one safe even when the final vote has been taken and the twelve meetings attended. SDG figures for January 1967 show that one out of three members left the group, and not all voluntarily. If at any time the members feel that a fellow is not sincerely trying to help himself, or that he has become a detrimental influence on the body as a whole, he may be expelled. The wording of the charge is vague—in a court of law it would surely fail the test of specificity—but voluntary associations do set their own standards. However, though a person has been expelled and forbidden to attend meetings, he is not yet a lost soul. On the contrary, individual members continue to meet with him and encourage him to prepare for reinstatement. Many SDG members who were either expelled or who voluntarily left the group have been invited to return after such individual consultation. Since the January 1967 tabulation, the rate of departures seems to have decreased.

The membership of SDG varies significantly from the general Concord prison population in a number of respects; in others, it is an accurate reflection of that population.[29] For example, the type of offense committed by the SDG member does not differ significantly from those of the prisoners as a whole. On the other hand, the membership of SDG is significantly younger than the overall prison age. Seventy-six per cent of the SDG group members were under the age of twenty-five at the time of their most recent incarceration, as compared to only 63 per cent of the general Concord population. Nevertheless, despite their youth and hence the shorter time in which to accumulate records of arrest and conviction (particularly if time was served between convictions), the SDG members are drawn from a slightly more hard-core recidivist reservoir.

The organization seems to consist of men less likely to be reached by the traditional types of rehabilitative therapy. Here, however, if their recidivism is a disadvantage, their youth is an advantage. The young, rehabilitation workers maintain, can be reformed (because they can be re-formed) more easily than the old—except for the very elderly, who retire from crime much as people do from other occupations.

SDG is modeled after AA and other self-help groups in that it is open to anyone who has the necessary desire to help himself and others (except that it is not always easy to enter). As such, there is always a strong possibility (which certainly pervades AA's own prison efforts) that these groups will attract those seeking to exercise undue influence over others. That this has not occurred in SDG is in part demonstrated by the racial composition of the group, one that is rather unique in light of what many inmates and staff members quite readily admit is the prison's racist atmosphere. One study revealed that more than 25 per cent of SDG's members were Negro, as compared with only 19 per cent of the general prison population. In all SDG programs, the Negro-white balance is well maintained, and the relationship between members of different ethnic groups seems, at least on the surface, to be exemplary. Of SDG's out-of-prison activities, only the South Boston youth group is composed entirely of whites, and that is due to the segregation of the community. The racial success of SDG seems to be an indication that the major and manifest purpose of the group, self-betterment of those involved, has been undermined neither by prejudice nor the manipulation of others—in many cases, an early manifestation of racial prejudice.

SDG is presently functioning with ex-convicts as staff, and with both ex-convicts and current prisoners as members. The paid (ex-inmate) staff consists of three men—

the executive director and two full-time assistants. The executive director is a strong personality, and his responsibilities include most of the group's functions: fundraising, maintaining and furthering public relations, conducting and participating in group meetings (both inside prisons and out), preparing newsletters for outside members and reports for the board of directors, and counseling members. This latter task, though most time-consuming, also most significant for the individual, covers employment, drivers' permits, education, and the numerous other problems arising from the specific and debilitating status of being a parolee. The assistants help the director with many of these tasks, and, in addition, both maintain contact with members through street and home visits, and work with the youth group in South Boston on a daily basis.

Since SDG has no dues structure, the funds used to meet expenses and to implement new programs come from private foundations and individual donors. As a matter of principle, SDG declares its unwillingness to accept money from the state or federal governments; it fears that strings will be attached which will make the organization a vassal rather than an independent movement. Nevertheless, they have accepted anti-poverty monies, if not directly from the OEO, from a group funded by it; in fact, they have actively sought such funds. To date, funds have been received sufficient only to meet current expenses, not to expand the program into the areas that SDG wishes to enter, or to hire the staff that the group claims to need. As in many other organizations, its ambitions are beyond its budget, and it is constantly looking for patrons, angels, and wealthy foundations.

The work of SDG can be divided into four more or less separate programs: the groups that meet inside prisons, those that meet outside in the community, the woman's auxiliary (which contains SDG members, their wives and girl friends), and the South Boston youth group. Each program seeks to operate on the same principles and with the same aims and methods, differing only in its respective location and the composition of its members. But the major success of SDG must be judged by what happens to its people outside prison, to the central group of ex-inmates.

Meetings of the SDG central group of outsiders are structured according to methods outlined in an SDG brochure. It contains the group's preamble (a sort of statement of principles), the seven points, a brief constitution, bylaws, and a prayer with which meetings are closed. Discussion leaders, or chairmen, rotate at meetings. After the preamble has been read, the person whose turn it is to lead the group chooses one of the seven points as a focus for discussion. Sometimes the discussion revolves closely around the chosen point, at other times it wanders. At these meetings, the men appear always to be honest with themselves and each other. Men who have so long worn the mask of the hardened criminal frequently display tenderness and sentimentality. In reviewing the circumstances that led them to a life of crime, they speak of their inability to respect, then their subsequent rebellion against, authority. At times they seem to repeat statements heard or read; if the analysis is not original, nevertheless it is the application of learned material to the understanding of self.

The SDG image of its mission is to try to find a way for ex-convicts to get what they want out of life—but to get it in a legal and respectable manner. When a member is released from prison, he is very impatient to catch up on everything he feels he has missed during incarceration: sex, good food, liquor, and money. Whatever he may have told social workers and sociologists about his longing for the warmth of his family and the reassurance of his church while in prison, his actions upon release are rarely a literal translation of these verbal responses. SDG recognizes these more basic desires, both their legitimacy and their imperious nature; it knows that, if not satisfied or controlled, new frustrations may lead to new and early difficulties. The group meets the ex-convict upon release, inquires where he will spend his first nights, and arranges that he receive some money from its loan fund. Even if the man has a job and starts to work immediately, he may not receive his first pay check for two weeks.

At the meetings of ex-convicts, financial problems, drinking, emotional needs, sex, family difficulties, general frustrations and fears, and harassment—all the factors which the members contend were responsible for leading them into crime, then into recidivism—are aired in the attempt to prevent the repetition of the pattern. The services that SDG can offer to ex-convicts are discussed, so that they may know what to expect and, more importantly, what the limits of these expectations should be. Once trust is established, based neither on fantasies nor falseness, the strong bond thus developed both strengthens the organization and aids the member.

At meetings attended by wives and girl friends, domestic and sexual problems are discussed with as much frankness as in guided group therapy. The members claim to be searching for the path of propriety, for guidelines in locating the norms, but at the same time they display a need for reinforcement of behavioral patterns about which they harbor serious doubts. The group draws out, in what is often heated cross-discussion, material which a one-to-one relationship seems to inhibit. In the end, the members can find protection and support for faltering self-images through this "ventilation" group therapy.

SDG meetings are anything but dull. A moment of silence is a rarity, and there is never any lack of subject matter at the ventilation sessions. Although this is true of many groups of people, it is especially so when the problem that brings the group together is that of being a convict or ex-convict. Here one finds people with deep hostilities and resentments, people usually more aggressive than retiring who have spent considerable time unable to articulate and vocalize. Given the opportunity, everything they have to say spills over.

At the meetings held in prison, the director, John Anthony, is something of a hero; his advice is always sought, and he is unlikely to be challenged. His thorough familiarity with the convict's problems and state of mind, his ability to talk the convict's language, and his readiness to offer himself as living evidence that the square world can be conquered—all this provides an atmosphere conducive to cementing the bonds between SDG and the prisoner.

The enthusiasm of SDG in-prison meetings also derives from the fact that they provide the only opportunity for the men to talk with each other as a group unhindered by the presence of professionals and guards. This deep-going resentment and suspicion of authority has been one major factor in discouraging prisoners from utilizing professional therapy programs (of which there are very few operating in prisons anyway), and in turning them to groups like SDG.

SDG's mistrust of corrections professionals and their rehabilitative methods is fully returned. In fact, as SDG sees it:

> They are afraid of us. They don't want to be proven wrong by a bunch of cons, who they feel are definitely inferior to them. So they do all they can to keep us in. They look at us as a bunch of

troublemakers because we dare to challenge the status quo and the methods of treatment which have been proven time after time to be totally ineffectual.[30]

How does one evaluate SDG? It cannot be denied that the group suffers a major decline when its men leave prison. This might be interpreted as evidence that the convicts use the program as a mechanism to escape boredom and manipulate officials to hasten their release; even if true, however, this would not prove that SDG lacks rehabilitative value. There are a number of reasons why loyal in-prison members quickly lose sight of the group once paroled. Many members are released to areas of Massachusetts where no SDG meetings are held. Only those men residing in Boston or Springfield are, in fact, able to attend regularly scheduled meetings. Furthermore, many members claim that the help they received from SDG while in prison was sufficient to effect their rehabilitation; in short, they no longer need the group. From the officials' point of view, a fair percentage of individual parole officers will not permit their parolees to attend SDG meetings; with official policy vague, these officers are allowed to follow their own judgment. Finally, many ex-convicts who have continued to attend SDG meetings complain that they lose much of their force and meaning on the outside. In prison, SDG affords an opportunity for interaction, the exchange of confidences, and a little privacy in a world where nothing is private. On the outside, there are activities and people to turn the ex-convict's attention (and his possible search for help) away from SDG. Among these outside people, stigma can sometimes be reduced by avoidance of the past, even by concealment; in SDG, one sees in the other ex-inmates a mirror image of oneself.

Does this mean that SDG should restrict itself to an

organization of inmates, one which the member leaves
when the prison gates open, and which differs from other
such groups only insofar as its civilian leadership consists of ex-prisoners? SDG is not pleased with such a prospect. No organization likes to relinquish any sector of its
potential membership. Self-perpetuation dictates that
SDG's drive to retain the parolee must be continued. In
this respect, the organization is planning what it calls
a "dynamic program" so that contact with the released
men will not be lost. The leaders envision outings, social
events, and what has been termed an "all-the-way" house.
The latter, which would be set up with the help of a college
or university, would provide housing for members as well
as counseling from the SDG staff. But it would differ from
most existing halfway houses in that it would be staffed
and operated completely by ex-convicts. Nonetheless, such
an "all-the-way" house would face many problems. Even
while denouncing the professionals, the ex-convicts staff-
ing it would tend in their own way to become more and
more professionalized; even while helping them, they
would tend to become more alienated from the newly
released men. As yet, however, the all-the-way house remains to be established.

The final test of SDG and movements like it will
probably not be made by measuring their success in
helping members cope with problems like stigma, except
in the most indirect sense. Important as stigma is, it is
not easily enough quantified; it cannot be punched on a
computer card. Besides, the public does not really care
about this. What counts for SDG and other groups, in the
minds of both public officials and the public itself, is the
rate of recidivism. Will their members slip as often as
those who do not go through their programs? That is the
crucial question.

The Department of Correction has done a study of the rate of recidivism of SDG's members, and compared it to the rate for the general Concord population.[31] First, the expected rate of recidivism for both groups was computed; the figures were 57.9 per cent for SDG and 56.0 for all former Concord inmates. The difference in this expected rate is hardly significant. However, using forty members of SDG who had been out of prison for two and a half years, it was found that their actual rate of recidivism was 60 per cent. Unable to attain accurate records of attendance at meetings, or to establish a workable method of determining who could be considered SDG members, the Department of Correction researchers simply chose the first forty persons who had had contact, no matter how little, with the organization.

The defenders of SDG denounced these findings. They pointed out that SDG itself does not consider a man a member until he has attended at least a dozen meetings. Compared with statistical studies on the successes of psychoanalysis, in which those who do not attend at least twenty-five sessions are usually excluded from consideration, SDG's requirements are quite conservative.

In the dispute over these findings, the Department of Correction withdrew its figures, then subsequently issued them in a circular labeled "not for publication." Even this circular, distributed only to members of the Department, should have been left undistributed in the view of SDG leaders. Although prefaced by a recitation of the shortcomings of the data, it contains the following statement which SDG insists is far more likely to remain in the minds of readers than are the qualifying remarks:

> The expected recidivism rate for the SDG participants was 57.9 per cent, while the actual recidivism rate was 60.0 per cent. Since the actual return

rate was slightly higher than the expected rate, it appears that the SDG program did not have an impact in reducing recidivism for the first forty participants who were released to the community.[32]

When the Department of Correction utilized all SDG members who had been out of prison for one year—a total of seventy-two men—the return rate was only 27.8 per cent. What it was for all prisoners after one year is not revealed. In the end, this statement also became a focus of dispute, and was finally deleted from publication.

Using a total of ninety-three members, SDG itself claims a recidivism rate of 26 per cent. Furthermore, leaders state that only five of the twenty-four members returned to prison were accused of new offenses; the others were arrested and returned only for parole violations and—in SDG's view—minor ones at that. In SDG's figures, however, the 74 per cent of successes was based on a record of remaining free from reimprisonment for a period of six months or more; here may lie yet another source of discrepancy.[33]

In the end, it becomes impossible to settle this dispute between SDG and the professionals. Only an impartial research team, committed neither to self-help nor to its annihilation, can evaluate SDG's success. At this point, neither the group itself nor the corrections personnel constitute such an impartial body.

What of the future of SDG, and the many other movements among convicts and ex-convicts described here? For the most part, they still involve only work with inmates; the proposal to use rehabilitated ex-prisoners to assist in, or even lead, the rehabilitation of those still requiring aid is yet to be developed. But it probably will be, not only because an atmosphere of self-help conducive to such experimentation now exists, but because results in professional rehabilitation have been discouraging. Anything is worth trying now.

But the problem of resocialization of the former convict remains: the finding of good employment, the reduction of stigma, and the acceptance into the full life of the community. Perhaps what we will see in this respect is the use of a combination of the techniques of group therapy, civil rights protest, and education of the public; in fact, we already have the prototypes of this kind of movement in Johoso, the Fortune Society, and the Self Development Group.

8. Dwarfs:
little people with big problems

"Think Big."
—*Slogan of Little People of America*

The stigmatizing of the sick, the disabled, and the deformed is an old story. Primitive peoples feared and punished the physically afflicted; they considered them as evidence that the gods were angry, or as witches and purveyors of evil.

This mystical-religious interpretation particularly pervaded the attitude toward birth defects. Continuing through medieval times, the blind and deaf were avoided, especially by a pregnant woman whose child might be similarly afflicted by her sight of them. Whenever evil befell a community, the physically handicapped were the first to be blamed. Although little was known of contagion, communities in which lepers lived were not content to isolate them, but treated them with hatred and contempt.

Even in this era of rationalism and science, superstition has not disappeared from society's attitudes toward the

handicapped and the ill. People continue to be uncomfortable in the presence of those with physical defects. It has
not been long since an aura of shame surrounded the
victims of tuberculosis and cancer.

Within organizational society, several groups of people
with physical defects and ailments have been formed:
paraplegics, epileptics, people who have undergone ileos-
tomies and colostomies,[1] and sufferers from various
forms of dwarfism have all organized. Of these groups,
the undersized have been making an extraordinarily courageous effort to solve their difficult, almost insuperable,
problems through organization.

The mention of dwarfs may conjure up the image of
Snow White's delightful helpers, or a memory of charm-
ing drawings in a child's edition of *Gulliver's Travels*. It
is a far cry from such images to the real world in which
these people live. When you meet a dwarf, you will hear
the story of a lifetime of travail, of staring eyes, rejection
by friends and sometimes even family; of difficulties in
obtaining employment; of being addressed as though retarded; of being humiliated as a child and, in later life,
being shunned by adults. To aid themselves in solving
these problems and others, the dwarfs have formed a
self-help group known as the Little People of America.
It has the dual aim of helping members cope with personal
difficulties and of ameliorating the hostile social atmosphere in which they live.

It is not known how many people of insufficient growth
there are in the United States. One estimate puts the figure at 25,000; it is based on the number of people believed
to be so short that height represents a central life problem
for them.[2] Among many physicians specializing in fields
closely related to growth, it is somewhat arbitrarily stated
that a male who fails upon maturity to reach the height of
four feet ten inches and a female who fails to reach the

height of four feet eight inches are sufficiently below average to be considered undersized. But dwarfism has broad social consequences which go far beyond these purely physiological considerations.

The determination of insufficient growth in children is sometimes expressed as the difference between chronological age and expected age mean-height. Thus a girl chronologically fourteen years old whose height is 118.75 cm. (46.7 inches) is the height-age of seven years and six months. That is, at the age of fourteen, she is the same height as the average girl of seven and a half. A nine-year-old male whose height is 85.15 cm. (33.5 inches) is the height-age of two years and two months.[3]

Dwarf and *midget* are two terms generally applied to these undersized people, but they are popular rather than medical words. In everyday parlance, a dwarf exhibits bodily proportions unlike those of most persons: in the most common form, he has extremely short legs and arms (the former bowed), a normally developed torso, a large head, sometimes a flat nose, an unusual distribution of body weight at the lower end of the back, and short, stubby fingers that hang somewhat limply from the joints. This condition, a congenital one that is sometimes hereditary, is known as achondroplasia or achondroplastic dwarfism, and usually results in growth somewhere between forty-eight and fifty-six inches.

Midgets—again the term is used in its popular sense; it must be emphasized that midgets are not a single physiological entity—are normally proportioned but extremely short people. When they are less than four feet tall at maturity they tend to be slightly stocky. Midgets have been exploited in circuses, particularly by Barnum who made an international celebrity of Tom Thumb (he grew to only three feet, and married a midget a few inches shorter than himself).[4]

Stunted growth brings many difficulties and disadvantages. People are often evaluated according to their apparent age, and size is one criterion of that evaluation. Thus, one behaves toward a person as though he were of the age that his stature suggests; one also expects mental responses commensurate with that incorrectly estimated age level. This process results in a babying of the dwarf; furthermore, it can cause poor mental development by denying him the challenge of interaction on his mental age level. As a child, he is treated as if he were several years younger than he is; as an adult, he is frustrated and humiliated by such everyday experiences as being unable to reach a telephone in a booth.

Whereas adults generally behave toward a dwarf (the word is used here to denote all undersized persons) with polite evasion, children often treat him with cruelty. One mother writes:

> My son is age seven, weighs 29 lbs., and is 37¾ in. tall. Recently, another boy in the school yard picked Jeff up by his coat collar and swung him back and forth in pendulum motion. This boy held him up, ridiculing Jeff and bragging of his own strength. When he tired of his game, he dropped Jeff to the ground. A sympathetic bystander (3rd grader) picked Jeff up and carried him to the teacher supervising the playground. This teacher had Jeff stay by her until he felt better and was able to move under his own little strength.
>
> After this story unfolded before me, I realized that Jeff could very easily have choked to death, but for the Grace of God. I had the natural impulsive reaction. I wanted to do some choking of my own. Instead, I went to the phone and called the principal. Much to my surprise, this incident had

not been reported. The principal's reply? "Ha, ha, ha, children will be children." The next day during a conference with this principal I was asked why my boy had not reported this incident to his home-room teacher. I couldn't answer. I didn't know. Two weeks later Jeff let it slip. It seems that be-cause Jeff had previously received so many severe bumps in school, his teacher had told him that if these things kept occurring, he would have to leave school. . . . No, I haven't gone back for another con-ference yet. But when I'm fully under "control" I will. No, I don't want to shelter my "little" boy. I just want him to grow in age, even if he can't grow in size.[5]

There have been many organizations *for* the ill, far fewer *of* the ill. Groups have raised money, conducted research, done lobbying; one such organization has been formed to concern itself with problems such as those de-scribed by Jeff's mother. Called Human Growth, Inc., it describes itself as "primarily an organization of the par-ents and friends of children with severe growth disturb-ances." Members, most of them parents, raise funds to support medical research, and give each other moral sup-port in meeting their problems. To a certain extent, they bear the stigma of having produced a defective child: essentially, however, theirs is a stigma fallout, or what Goffman calls "courtesy stigma."[6] They have organized to learn how to live and act in a role for which they are unprepared, that of being parents of a visibly handicapped child. At present Human Growth is attempting to induce people to leave their pituitary glands to a tissue bank for use in hypopituitary cases, one form of dwarfism which now seems capable of scientific control.[7]

In turning from Human Growth, Inc., to Little People

of America, one moves from those concerned with a problem to those directly involved, from help to self-help.
Little People of America consists mainly of severely undersized persons; infrequently a normally sized family member will join as an expression of solidarity. Although LPA
takes in all dwarfs, the achondroplastics seem to domi-
nate; the more normally proportioned (or midgets, as the
public would call them) are ambivalent in their attitudes
toward the organization.

On a national scale, LPA has somewhat less than a thousand members, a small percentage of those eligible.[8] It
conducts national conventions and district meetings, the
latter bringing together some thirty or forty people who
often travel great distances for the monthly get-togethers.
Despite the publicity that LPA has received in magazines
and on television, it is little known outside its own ranks.
When interviewed, several doctors deeply interested in
growth (particularly pediatric endocrinologists) had a
vague idea that such a group existed, but did not know its
name or how to locate it. Even more revealing was the response from a prominent attorney, himself a dwarf, who
had spoken at a meeting of Human Growth, but had never
heard of LPA.[9]

LPA has tackled the herculean job of helping to improve
the self-image of people in a world in which, literally and
figuratively, they are looked down upon. "Think Big" is
LPA's slogan, put forward precisely because it is the reverse of what many members do. Scholarship funds, assistance to members in financial difficulty, an adoption
service—these are among LPA's accomplishments. In itself, the adoption service illustrates the severity of the
dwarfism problem: on the one hand many of the dwarfs
are without children, or fear having them; on the other
hand, and more importantly, normal parents find themselves with a handicapped child (in achondroplasia cases,

the handicap is usually recognizable at birth), whom they frequently offer for adoption. This fact alone, that parents *give away* an achondroplastic child, indicates the strength of the stigma.

In the language of those short of stature, a dwarf is a little person. LPA offers advice to parents, normal or little, on bringing up these little persons. Much of this advice seems far more sound than that encountered in professional literature on rehabilitation. For example, the president of LPA suggests:

> In the case of a nickname, there is a very simple way to handle this problem, even though many little people rebel in being singled out this way. Rather than to counterattack with some other equally obnoxious name, the best way to avoid being called Shorty or Midget is to ignore it, pure and simple. If a person persists and blocks your way, you can simply say, "Oh, were you calling me, I didn't hear my name mentioned." Then if the little person continues to refuse to be interrupted by use of any but his real name, the tormenter will cease and desist.[10]

In a study of LPA, Martin Weinberg found that most of the members look to it for social benefits.[11] This goal is not unexpected. Dwarfs live in a world in which their possibilities for social contact are limited. They are deeply restricted in finding partners for sex, love, and marriage. Thus any means by which such men and women can meet one another is fully exploited. While many handicaps and diseases, particularly stigmatizing ones, limit people in their selection of marriage partners, the dwarfed man is further limited by the general societal insistence that the male must be at least as tall as, and preferably taller than, the female.[12] This insistence places the achondroplastic male in a double bind; he can seldom find a normally sized female to court, both because of his condition and his desire to avoid the Mutt-and-Jeff caricature.

Most of the members of LPA whom Weinberg interviewed were single; unmarried people make up 65 per cent of the organization, as compared to about 22 per cent for the general population of the same age group.[13] When I asked LPA members what they had gotten out of the organization, I received enthusiastic replies from the married, but somewhat wan answers from the single. By far the most enthusiastic came from those who, with broad smiles, said "I met my wife"—or husband, or sweetheart —at an LPA convention or a meeting.

While LPA meetings offer a remarkable opportunity for socializing, many members sit alone, unable or unwilling to speak except when approached. When I engaged a brilliant high school girl in conversation, I learned that she was planning to go on to college to study sociology; bubbling over with youthful excitement, she seemed the very prototype of adjustment. She came from a family of normal stature; when I met her father, he regarded her with the eyes of the traditionally (even stereotypically) loving parent. At the same meeting, however, an older woman spoke to me of her hatred of the streets, of how she never leaves her house from one week to the next, save for the LPA meetings, because she knows that people are staring at and talking about her. Though her strong paranoia is filled with obvious fantasy, it has no doubt been fed by reality. For this woman, then, LPA constitutes her only social life.

At one meeting I attended, many members sought me out privately, as if their problems of loneliness and despair could somehow be solved by counseling or a cathartic process. Perhaps they did not understand the difference between the sociologist and the social worker, or the sociologist and psychologist. At any rate, they looked to me for advice on and answers to extraordinarily difficult questions. One young man to whom I spoke, John, appeared to me to be about twenty-five; when I mentioned my estimate, he replied that he was ten years older. Unlike people of normal stature, for him my error was not a compliment. Extremely well proportioned (thus popularly a midget), John would have been considered strikingly handsome had he not stopped growing when he was four feet six inches. Up to that height, he had developed normally for his age; once growth ceased, he was taken to many specialists, but without results. When I asked if he had tried human growth hormone, the pituitary gland extract, he replied: "I can't get it—it's in short supply. They need it for kids. And it probably won't help me because I'm not a pituitary case. Besides, it's certainly too late." Like many others at the meeting, he was well informed on his particular medical condition.

John lives a lonely life. All his friends are married, and he says, with some resignation: "It's hard for a single guy to keep up with married friends. Even normal single guys." Nor has he been able to make it socially with a bachelor crowd. "I just don't fit in." So he goes home at night after work, and reads, watches television, or broods over his bleak future. He has lunch with the men in his office, but they never invite him to their homes. Above all else, he wants romance, sex, and friendship, but LPA cannot offer it to him.

"Why not?" I asked.

"Because most of them are achondroplastics, and I guess I'm prejudiced. I shouldn't be, but I am. I don't want to go out with a girl like that, and I don't even want male friends like that. I'm uncomfortable with them."

"But you still come to the Little People meetings?"

"Maybe there'll be a little girl—a short girl—but some-one like me."

Like many organizations, LPA functions on both a na-tional and a local (or district) level. One of its major prob-lems is that the district groups seem to be at a loss for functions to perform, other than simply providing a place for men and women to meet each other. They are not social clubs where members share an interest, hobby, or avocation; what they do share are physical character-istics which are insufficient to make the meetings impor-tant unless the discussion centers strictly around the problems of being little. Thus LPA's members are caught in a contradiction: they want to meet one another, but, once they do, there is no purpose, goal, or structure to their meetings—nothing to bind them to the organization. If they avoid the problems encountered in being little, they lose any *raison d'être;* on the other hand, if they center the meetings around such problems, members say that they came to get away from them.

An LPA meeting therefore becomes something like a philatelists' gathering at which there is no discussion of stamps. Once the meeting is called to order, announce-ments are made: Susan moved out of the district, Jane is getting married, and we have a new member here today, Carl, but let's not forget an old face that we haven't seen for a long time—and everyone smiles as Lewis is given the welcome deserving of the prodigal son. No, everyone does not smile; that is an exaggeration. Some sit, somber and unhappy, even through the frolicsome parts of the ses-sion. There is a report on dues, on the state of the treasury, on a communication from the national office. Old business, new business, points of order—all give an air of legitimacy to the meeting, but much of it is busy work. The main point before the refreshments are served is a discussion of where the next meeting is scheduled to take place. After coffee and cake, the socializing begins—the manhunt and the womanhunt, the pairing-off into small groups, the exchange of ideas and the search for advice. If nothing else, this socializing seems to be the group's main, though unstated, purpose.

Like many organizations, LPA's functions on the national level are more clear-cut.[14] To support the national group, local chapters and members are necessary; but these chapters are not necessary for the fulfillment of the national goals. Thus, a local LPA group becomes only a monthly meeting place, while the national association is a cadre organization where a few do all the work while the rest tag along. Moreover, the fear of making the marginal life of LPA meetings the only life of the little people seems to inhibit more socializing among the members.

Some come to a meeting, even two, then are not seen again. This characteristic is found in many organizations of both the deviant and the normal. But why does it happen in LPA? When asked, one of the activists had a ready explanation:

> "They come looking for a husband or wife or sweetheart or someone. They heard it's a marriage mill. And the first or second meeting they don't meet someone they could go for, so it's no use. They get discouraged. That's all they were looking around for in the first place."

> "But once you've got them, even for one afternoon, a captive audience—maybe you could offer something else?"

> "No, absolutely not. Not if they come with that in mind. You don't know little people. I know them."

This is a difficult argument to rebut.

Still other little people cannot be prevailed upon to come to meetings at all. They believe that the organization represents a turning inward, despite the fact that LPA's national leadership strongly urges members to mingle in the world of the normally sized. Leaders warn them not to retreat into a separate community of their own, but, instead, to join (in addition to LPA) the local Democratic or Republican club. (They do not mention conservative or liberal, John Birch or communist groups. The deviant cannot afford a double stigma.)

There is also a third type of little person who refuses to attend meetings because he fears to mingle in a world inhabited by people like himself.

"Why?" I asked.

"Because they just don't want to be with people who look like they do."

"Why?" I insisted with what must have been annoying perseverance.

"I don't know," the district leader replied. Then he added hesitantly, as if himself fearing to articulate the answer: "Maybe it's because they don't want to see what they look like."

What type of adjustment can dwarfed persons make? The president of LPA urges that they relinquish any dream of a magic pill. They must, he says, accept the permanence of their condition.[15] On the other hand, many little people simply deny the need for adjustment. They reject the notion that they have a problem, specifically a problem of "spoiled identity." While they admit that being little is a handicap, they refuse to concede that it is debilitating. There are compensations to being little, they maintain—even advantages.

The friends of the little people, fearful of not being compassionate enough to the suffering, go even further than the sufferers themselves. The father of one girl told me, "It's only our prejudice that makes us see the achondroplastics as sick. After all, there are advantages in being small. This is the age of rockets and spaceships, and who knows, maybe space on a ship to the moon will be so valuable that we will have to man it with little people." Possibly. But it is more likely that this reply is the rationalization of a man who has watched the inadequate struggles of his handicapped daughter to handle overwhelmingly difficult problems.

Nor are the professionals, in their compassion, free of similar thinking. "Many dwarfs are able to have children who may or may not themselves be dwarfs," writes John Money of Johns Hopkins. He then continues:

> People may argue about the advisability of reproducing when there is a risk of producing a dwarf. The positive side of the argument is that a male dwarf should deliberately mate with a female of the same type in order to continue the strain and produce, eventually, a new subvariety of the human race.[16]

Out of sympathy for those in distress, how can one so easily forget the depths of their anguish—or the dangers of propagating it?

LPA publishes a news letter which does not present an image either of what the organization is or what it might become. Rather, it is concerned only with organizational matters for their own sake: the next convention, the district meetings, the growth in membership. And yet, at the same time, the leadership encourages scholarship (and scholarships), aids medical research, and, above all, has accumulated a remarkable amount of experience in handling the social aspects of problems of dwarfism.

Thus, the major problem of the dwarf may be one of accepting self without accepting the negative evaluation of others. The president of LPA points out that little people are certainly different "and have only to look in the mirror to assure themselves of this." He continues:

> The best way to handle this problem [of self-acceptance], in my estimation, is for another person to apparently read this person's mind and express out loud all of the hidden feelings, desires and questions that he will have had over the years. Of course, this is a shocking experience and should not be attempted by an amateur.[17]

The president may be right. LPA members could well benefit from self-help, mutual-exchange therapy—not the kind that attacks or ventilates, but the kind that offers help *by* those who have reached a better solution of a problem *to* those who are still grappling with that same problem. This is, after all, AA once again, with the better adjusted acting as sponsors and examples, ones who ask the neophytes: "If I can do it, why can't you?"

9. Mental patients:
are they their brothers' therapists?

Angel or demon,
Everywhere I have seen that shadowy friend,
Wherever I wanted to sleep
Wherever I wanted to die
Wherever I touched the earth,
On the path I followed,
Sat a stranger clad in black
Who resembled me like a brother.
   —Alfred de Musset

This country has become mental-health conscious. That large numbers of Americans are mentally or emotionally ill—most of them dangerous to no one but themselves, but a few dangerous to society at large—has come to be taken for granted. Once highly stigmatized, the mentally disturbed are now accepted with sympathy. Freud and psychiatry have obliterated old notions of people possessed by witches and devils; even the once pejorative terms for a mental institution (such as *loony bin* and *nuthouse*) have ceased to be used seriously.

Nevertheless, the ex–mental patient, seeking once again to function in the world, is still forced to conceal his institutional past; he is still pursued by the shadows of his own biography.

With the growing use of group therapy, the idea of former mental patients meeting to ventilate their difficulties, protect themselves against the world, and yet find methods of returning to it, began to take hold. This movement has been called "the new therapy" or "the new group therapy";[1] despite its frequent lack of professional guidance, even its anti-therapeutic bias, it has gained the support of some psychotherapists.

To date, there have been a few national organizations and several hundred independent self-help mental-health groups or clubs, the latter usually having a following or membership of about twenty to thirty people each. The largest and most enduring of the national groups is Recovery, Inc., which today claims hundreds of branches and a membership of more than five thousand. Neurotics Anonymous International Liaison has a scattering of groups and a couple of hundred faithful followers. Schizophrenics Anonymous maintains branches in half-a-dozen cities but probably numbers no more than a hundred people who attend meetings with sufficient regularity to be considered members. SA has also undergone fission, with its Cleveland group establishing itself as Better Health, Inc. And there are other organizations on the periphery of this movement.

Recovery, Inc., the best known of the new therapy groups, was organized under the leadership of the late psychiatrist Abraham A. Low. He remained the professional in charge of Recovery until 1952, at which time he encouraged it to become a self-help organization.[2] Low died two years later; since that time Recovery has been following the path he laid down. In 1968, it claimed to have 641 branches located in thirty-six states and three Canadian provinces.[3]

Recovery now calls itself an "association of nervous and former mental patients." So long as it remained strictly an ex-patient (or, more specifically, an ex-inmate) group, it clearly attracted only those who had been sufficiently disturbed to need care, even institutionalization. Now that it has broadened its scope to include "nervous" people (a compromise between the mildly stigmatizing term *neurotic* and the more lay-oriented term *nervous breakdown*), it attracts those who have never been under care and mingles its avowed aim of "self-help after care" with the almost inevitable aim of "self-help group therapy." Still based almost completely on Low's work, the organization has tended to become cultist, and has many of the elements of a social movement rather than a social or self-help club.

Unlike many of the other new therapy groups, Recovery specifically does not seek to supplant therapy; on the contrary, it states that, as an organization, it "does not offer diagnosis, treatment, advice or counseling, and it does not supplant the physician. Each member is asked to follow the authority of his own physician as part of his training."[4]

The organization publishes a journal entitled *The Recovery Reporter;* distributes an information sheet to new and would-be members, and a pamphlet which describes its "systematic method of self-help after-care"; sells the books and records of its founder; and holds regular meetings. While Recovery has taken over from AA the first-name anonymity, unlike that organization and almost all others of a self-help nature, it has a clear-cut list of members who pay annual dues. It is thus one of the few self-help groups that can count its members; as of January 1, 1968 it listed 5,712.[5] It is probable, however, that the group's influence extends beyond this figure, with several thousand more occasionally attending meetings without signing up. For most, membership involves attending a weekly meeting for about two hours, and receiving Recovery's bulletin.

Membership in Recovery does not seem to become a way of life or dictate constant interaction; as such the degree of rapport between individual member and organization may be minimal. While no analysis of Recovery's membership is obtainable, this writer gathered the impression from talking to members and visiting meetings that it has attracted mostly urban, middle-class white persons. Catholics and Jews may be overrepresented out of proportion to their total numbers in the national population, the Jews perhaps because of their involvement both in social movements and in psychotherapy, the Catholics because of Recovery's emphasis on faith as a means of recovering one's mental equilibrium.

In addition to its journals and pamphlets, Recovery also publishes a directory which lists the full names of its leaders in thirty-seven areas (thirty-five geographic ones in the United States, and one in Canada, plus the independent headquarters in Chicago) and the location of meeting places in these areas. For meetings, almost all of which are held in churches and temples, the areas are further broken down into groups. These groups are concentrated in the heavily populated states, especially those in which the national organization got started: Illinois, Ohio, Michigan, New York, and California; on the other hand, they are sparse in the deep South, with only one in Georgia, and none in Alabama, Mississippi, and South Carolina.[6]

As an organization, Recovery has gone through various stages; hence to go to the early writings of Low to understand its present theoretical basis may be misleading. Nevertheless, his 1950 book, *Mental Health Through Will-Training: A System of Self-Help in Psychotherapy as Practiced by Recovery, Incorporated*, remains the organization's bible. By 1966, the book was in its fourteenth edition.[7]

Low developed his therapeutic technique largely as a reaction against psychoanalysis and as a manifestation of his belief that man can control his mental and emotional life, and hence his conduct. "Adult life is not *driven* by instincts but guided by Will," he states,[8] using this last word in a sense almost opposite to its meaning for Schopenhauer. For Low, will is free will, the determination to act, self-control, belief in oneself and in one's consciousness. It is Coué brought up to date, made reasonable and rational.

In a sense, Low did not start Recovery; rather Recovery came to him. It was originally founded by thirty former mental patients who had regained their health; that they had been severely ill is indicated by the fact that they had had shock treatments "and/or other therapies" as patients at the Psychiatric Institute of the University of Illinois Medical School, with which Low had been affiliated.[9] For three years the organization was limited to ward patients; in 1940, it expanded to include psychoneurotic out-patients of the institution; after that, it started to recruit members from Low's private practice. Emphasizing self-help, it offered its services as a means of saving the physician's time and the patient's money; it sought to prevent recurrences of mental ailments "and to forestall chronicity in psychoneurotic conditions." In essence, what it was developing at the time was a type of group therapy.

In its original conception, Recovery's work centered largely around the problems that the ex-patient encounters returning to society; it did not seek specifically to continue the therapy without the therapist. "Returning home," Low states, "the patient still suffers from restlessness, tenseness, and preoccupation. His inability to relax is aggravated by the sense of being stigmatized." And again: "Feeling stigmatized, the patient becomes self-conscious and introspective." He may become alarmed if he has difficulty sleeping; that alarm in turn produces more sleeplessness, fatigue, imaginary symptoms, and fear of a relapse. Recovery started out to treat these problems.

In Low's view—later Recovery's—patients are better equipped than physicians to sell mental health to each other because the patient is always suspicious of the physician who (in the patient's mind) is unwilling to state that his condition is incurable. What the patient needs essentially is to believe, and to have that belief reinforced, that while his condition is chronic, its sensations can be endured, its impulses controlled, and its obsessions checked. In this respect Low and Recovery advocate the AA technique of sponsor and role model:

> The fellow sufferer who explains how he "licked" his frightful palpitations after years of invalidism cannot possibly be suspected of trying to sell something. That "colleague" is convincing. He convinces the novice that "chronic" conditions are not hopeless.[10]

In Recovery's early stages, Low developed a technique of group therapy that dispensed with the presence of the professional therapist. Nonetheless, the therapist did receive regular reports on thrice-weekly meetings from the panel leaders. One evening a week, the therapist conducted "a group psychotherapy class," the exact nature of which is not clear: was it therapy itself, or a class in how to conduct therapy? Finally, on Saturday afternoon, he held a public meeting "attended by the patients, their relatives and friends."

Between meetings, any patient who suffered a "setback" (the equivalent of the AA slip), in the form of being tortured by "that awful fatigue" or another symptom, was advised to contact a veteran Recovery member immediately after the symptom had reappeared. This was a combination of conventional psychotherapy—except that the therapist or a substitute was on call at all times—and the AA sponsor system:

> The assurance offered by the veteran is in accord with the language used by the physician, and the interpretations given to the novice coincide with those used in the physician's classes and in his writings. New members are assigned to veterans whom they may call in distress. The veteran functions in the capacity of the physician's "aide."[11]

For the ex-inmate, Recovery offered more than continued therapy and, in the absence of the therapist, reinforcement of the latter's teachings. It offered opportunities to socialize with others having similar problems who, it was hoped, would be tolerant and understanding. At this point in Recovery's history, the members were said to have had "an almost unquenchable thirst for social contacts." They visited in each other's homes, went to shows, concerts, and museums together, had bowling groups and hiking groups—even sewing circles.

> Consciously or unconsciously, the trend is to break through the dismal isolation and loneliness which have always been the blight of neurotic or postneurotic existence. The patients state it explicitly that formerly they were lonely individuals, now they are thoroughly integrated with the rich, pulsating life of a closely knit group.[12]

This was the nature of Recovery under the guidance and direction of Low. Although the organization began to grow and change after his death in 1954, it retained his works as a philosophic and therapeutic basis, but as is often the case after the death of the man who was founder and undisputed leader, his printed word became a revelation, his works a set of scriptures.

To contact Recovery today, one makes a telephone call; in the larger cities, calls are generally handled by an answering service to whom one gives his name and address. Several days later a mimeographed sheet arrives, giving the times and places of meetings. I followed this procedure. No one invited me to a meeting, or inquired if I was in difficulty. Unlike the Good Samaritan, the Helping Hand, and other European groups, and unlike organizations in the United States primarily designed to aid people who call for help when they are on the verge of suicide, Recovery is not for emergency situations. It sends a sheet and tells you where to go for a meeting. I went.

Arrived at the meeting place, I watched the regulars come in, occasionally nodding at one another and taking their seats. My efforts to mingle, to inquire about the organization, were rebuffed. "If you're not a member," I was told, "then just take a seat in the back. You'll be allowed to listen, but not to talk or ask questions." As soon as the meeting was called to order, the chairman announced that no one could take notes.

The chairman (or group leader) and her assistant sat at the front of the room. A businesslike manner pervaded the meeting, a manner formal rather than friendly, one that often bordered on the authoritarian, even the angry. The atmosphere was that of a schoolroom, whose adult pupils were subdued like children. The meeting opened.

"We will start by reading from page 130," the chairman said. "Joan, will you read from page 130, starting at the last paragraph?" Page 130 of what? There was no need to mention the name of the book.

Joan took her copy of Low and began to read. "I want you to understand what is meant by the word 'total experience,' " she read. A few sentences later, she came to the passage: "Experiencing security they will all be largely devoted of . . ."

"Devoid of, Joan," the chairman interrupted.

Joan went on. "Devoid of, excuse me, devoid of strain, tenseness, commotion, and excitement." By this time, of course, Joan was anything but devoid of strain and tenseness.

Once Joan—with obvious relief—finished her paragraph, the chairman called on Harry. "We are on page 131, starting with: 'A total has parts.' "

"I'm sorry, my glasses are broken," a middle-aged man replied sheepishly.

A look of dismay crossed the face of the chairman. She looked around. Some of the group were eager to be called on; others looked apprehensive, sinking down into their seats, hoping not to be noticed.

"The young lady over there, what is your name?"

"Laura Jones, Mrs. Laura Jones."

"Now, Laura, when I asked for your name, I wanted only your first name. You must never give a last name in Recovery. Are you a member?"

"Yes."

"Then you should know that. Laura, will you please read, starting on page 131, 'A total has parts.' "

"I'm sorry, I lost my book," Laura meekly confessed.

I closed my eyes. Surely, I thought, we were going to have the true nature of the fantasy revealed. In my mind, I could anticipate the words, "Lost your book, you naughty crook, then you shall have no thera-pie!" No, they were of course not forthcoming, these words; instead, Laura got an impatient look from the harried chairman, who turned back to Harry.

"Since you broke your glasses, there's no use just staring at the book. Will you lend it to Laura?"

And so it went, until five people had read from the book. Then the therapy began.

Members were called upon to volunteer some experience of the past week which illustrated overanxiety, fatalism, or defeatism: these were the symptoms the group was alerted to. The volunteer was to relate how he would have reacted before Recovery, then how he'd handled the matter on the basis of Recovery's teachings. The format was all laid out; one could not deviate.

One young lady told how she constantly fears her mother's death. That week, she had been unable to leave the house to go to work because she fantasied her mother would die if she departed.

"Is your mother sick?" a member asked.

"No. But I still think she might die."

"How old is she?" another member asked. Told that she was fifty-four, and in good health, the member replied, "Well, everyone is going to die sometime. Your mother probably has many good years ahead of her, so just stop thinking such nonsense."

The chairman interrupted: "We have to ask her how she would have reacted before Recovery, and how she acted now in Recovery."

The fearful girl apologized plaintively. "But I didn't react *any* different."

The chairman was flustered. The reply was not part of the script. "Well, let us show you what you're doing."

The members started to analyze the girl's behavior. They explained what she was doing wrong; they berated her for her incorrectness. They quoted Dr. Low; then they argued over what Dr. Low had said, and what he'd meant by what he'd said, and what he would have said had he lived to say what he didn't live to say.

During the therapy session, the members used—and seemed to derive a great sense of belonging from—the special language of the organization. When a member noted certain symptoms pinpointed in Low's philosophy as self-defeating, he did not merely note them, he "spotted" them. And when he handled a matter in keeping with Low's teachings, he gained confidence in himself which, in the Recovery jargon, meant that he "endorsed himself." Throughout the meeting, members spotted and they endorsed, competing as to who spotted something first, and searching for opportunities to use the ritualistic words.

At the time that he wrote, Low mentioned some groups operating outside Chicago. One, in Denver, was under the guidance of a local psychiatrist. Others were in the hands of ex-patients. That the latter procedure has become official policy is indicated by this statement from the organization:

> Dr. Low established that professionals may attend meetings to observe, but they may not participate unless, of course, they are nervous or former mental patients themselves. This only strengthens and preserves the self-help aspects of the meetings.[13]

The Recovery groups that I visited were led by ex-patients, all of whom seemed deeply distressed. Some were meek and passive, others angry and hostile. Less than in any other group of people with severe problems did I find that they were satisfactory role models (although, as will be brought out shortly, another group of mentally ill, Schizophrenics Anonymous, was similarly led by deeply disturbed people).

What had happened to the outings, picnics, sewing circles, walks—the activities in which people would find companionship and mutual acceptance that they could not locate in a hostile and stigmatizing world? Inquiring about social activities, I learned that in New York there was almost no social interaction among members. According to a recent report on the organization:

> Social activity is kept to a minimum. While members are encouraged to associate during meetings on an informal, friendly basis, they are often known to each other only by first names and last initials, a practice which invites comparison with Alcoholics Anonymous.[14]

Quite obviously, then, Recovery has changed over the years. What started as a mutual self-help group, supervised by one doctor, and consisting of his own patients—all of whom had been treated with similar therapy—has blossomed into a many-therapist, many-therapy movement (and sometimes a therapy movement without a therapist). The member is now urged "to follow the authority of his own physician or other professional." That such professionals often advise their patients in directions other than Low's makes for frequent difficulties—ones, however, that are not handled within the format of the group.

One psychiatrist has summed up Recovery's program:

> The principles of Recovery as established by Dr. Low included the idea that it represented self-help toward rehabilitation and that some continuing psychiatric supervision of individuals who had been mentally ill is useful, even if not intensive. In practice, the Recovery groups have been established in centers where psychiatric help is generally readily available so that the problem of the untreated individual in Recovery should very rarely come up.[15]

Neurotics Anonymous (or Neurotics Anonymous International Liaison, to differentiate its initials from those of Narcotics Anonymous) is closely patterned after AA. It was founded by a man who describes himself as "a recovered neurotic and an arrested alcoholic."[16] He became convinced that the AA technique would work for those with emotional disturbances; when he tried it on a non-alcoholic neurotic woman, and it worked (both the diagnosis and the cure were judged by the untrained alcoholic), he felt that he had the basis of his organization. A small group, NAIL probably numbers not more than a couple of hundred adherents, and puts out a mimeographed monthly bulletin called, rather pretentiously, *Journal of Mental Health*.

One issue of the journal published three brief autobiographical statements, one each from an AA, GA, and NAIL member, which purportedly demonstrate that alcoholism, compulsive gambling, and neurosis are one and the same: "the identical illness which varies only in detail." Incidentally, most AA members would deny this statement: it runs counter to their contention that there is nothing wrong with alcoholics except alcohol—and certainly not neuroses.

The editor of the journal notes that alcoholics, gamblers, and neurotics "are exactly alike in the illness *and* in the recovery." The three organizations, he points out, even use the same program, and it works for everyone: "All of us are, indeed, brothers, and the variations in detail are no more than if one of us likes chocolate ice cream and the other likes vanilla."[17]

There are some questionable assumptions in this statement. On the one hand, it suggests that these three groups of people are similar because they all have emotional ailments which differ only in behavioral symptoms (another way of saying that all alcoholics and compulsive gamblers are neurotics). On the other hand, the editor goes on to state that those with emotional ailments are in no way distinguishable from other (normal) people: "We are first of all human beings and preferences hardly separate us into unique categories," he concludes.

Local NAIL groups are small, informal, and, from this observer's experience, quite friendly. AA is copied mechanically; at the meetings, in fact, having no literature of their own, members simply use AA books and, as they read, change *alcoholic* to *neurotic*. Any difficulties, such as passages referring to the resort to alcohol, are quickly glossed over. For the confused newcomer, who may think that he has walked into the wrong meeting, there is a brief but patient explanation of this process.

Once formalities have been dispensed with, the members discuss their experiences, observations, difficulties, and problems. In trying to build up each other's self-confidence, they seem to be closer to Albert Ellis and his rational-emotive psychotherapy than to any other school; nonetheless, they are really too fluid to be affiliated with any school.[18] They urge each other not to be perfectionist, not to be afraid of undertaking a project that may lead to defeat, and not to be easily upset by difficulties, either real or imaginary. When asked what they had achieved through NAIL that could not have been obtained without the group, almost all spoke enthusiastically:

"I reduced my anxieties."

"Now I sleep—and if I don't sleep, I don't worry—I just get up and read."

"I had been at a complete standstill. I had been in therapy on and off for fifteen years, and once I came here, I learned to stop blaming my husband for things, and to assume responsibility myself. The program tells us you don't blame others for your condition. It is within you."

"Many thoughts are thrown out during the course of a

meeting. We may not buy them the first and second and third time, but suddenly it begins to take shape within yourself—and this is where I get my help, from this group."

Listening to the members' stories, I was impressed that those who regularly attend the meetings are not severely disturbed. That they have problems, there is no doubt; but they are not searching so much for therapy as for a set of rules to guide their lives. They have found in each other reinforcement of these rules. "When you see twenty or thirty faces and they're all trying to live by the same principles and they tell you they're making it, you feel there must be something to it."

One of the negative aspects of this group is its self-labeling. Neurosis is a term that entered the language on the crest of the Freudian wave; afterward it came to be used in two somewhat contradictory manners: first as a self-judgment that minimizes emotional illness by reducing it to humor—"that's my neurosis" was an early form of the later "that's my hangup"; and secondly as a sneering, pejorative term, a hangover from the era when the emotionally disturbed were scorned. Neither use of the word betrays the recognition (one inherent in the outlook of this group) that neurosis is a real illness to be respected for its maiming, destructive effects. Any group of people calling themselves neurotics may make it difficult for others to take the problems of those people seriously.

Although schizophrenia is a severe ailment, it is a poorly defined one which remains the subject of extensive psychiatric study. Originally, as used by Bleuler, who seems to have created the term, it meant split personality.[19] In severe cases, it denoted the Jekyll-Hyde condition, or referred to people with assumed fantasy identities—Jesus Christ or Napoleon, for instance. Recently, it has come to be used for a wide range of mental illnesses, particularly those in which there is a feeling of disembodiment.

Schizophrenics Anonymous is in many ways the most curious of the self-help groups. Certainly the modeling of this organization along the lines of AA leaves much to be desired—as well as feared. Whatever truth there may be to the maxim that only an alcoholic can help another, there is considerable doubt about the validity of its application to the schizophrenic. That SA members can be very damaging to one another does, in fact, become quite apparent at the meetings.

Schizophrenics Anonymous had its first meeting in Canada in 1964. A man using the pseudonym of Gregory Stefan, who had been in and out of mental hospitals, went to an AA meeting and happened to meet there two people who were not alcoholics:

> I told them I was not an alcoholic either; that I was a schizophrenic. They replied that they were also schizophrenics, but that they had found something in AA that they had not found in any other group: this spirit of fellowship. It had given them a place to come twice a week for social contacts and friends.[20]

On October 15, 1964, eight schizophrenics met with Abram Hoffer, director of psychiatric research at the University Hospital in Saskatoon, Saskatchewan. Gregory Stefan had brought these people together after the encounter at the AA meeting. According to Hoffer, Stefan was thinking: "If it does this for alcoholics, and these two schizophrenics, why don't we have a similar organization for schizophrenics?"[21] At the first meeting, Hoffer was present; after that, he "refrained from attending meetings, having informed the group that they would be on their own."[22]

It was a banding together of lonely people. As stated by Stefan:

> I am especially keen on this idea of Schizophrenics Anonymous. Schizophrenia is a very lonely disease; an intense feeling of loneliness was the most common complaint I heard from fellow schizophrenics.[23]

Schizophrenics Anonymous denies the definition of schizophrenia as a split personality. "It is a biochemical disease which upsets body chemistry . . . and is characterized by (1) changes in perception such as seeing, hearing, tasting, etc., (2) difficulty in judging whether these changes are real or not."[24] Its cause is clear: biochemical changes which lead to the production of toxin materials prevent the brain from working normally. But there is a cure: "The niacin therapy is a successful treatment."[25]

Then there are the twelve steps of SA, starting with the admission that the person was powerless over schizophrenia, and followed by eight traditions. They end with the assertion of anonymity as their spiritual foundation.[26]

Like alcoholism, SA maintains, schizophrenia can be arrested, but despite the use of the word *cure*, one is constantly admonished never to go off vitamin therapy. And certainly do not rely on psychoanalysis, dismissed by one of the leaders of a New York group with the rather flippant remark: "SA is not concerned with our members' past, but with their future."

The basis of the SA approach to aiding schizophrenics is chemotherapy (and especially the use of vitamins), combined with some measure of self-help. For any member to question the efficacy of vitamin therapy is a form of heresy. All the honest and valid answers known on schizophrenia have been obtained by a handful of doctors of whom SA members are the true followers.[27]

Every new member is given a test (known as the HOD test, after Hoffer, Osmond, and Desmond, the men who initiated it), to determine if he is schizophrenic. On cards, the test lists such statements as: "Sometimes I find myself talking inwardly to myself"; "Sometimes I have visions of God or of Christ"; "Sometimes the world seems unreal"; "I often hear my own thoughts outside my head"; and "I hear my own thoughts as clearly as if they were a voice." The individual places the cards in a true or false pile, and each affirmative answer entitles him to a given number of points. A high score means that he is a schizophrenic, a low one that he is normal.

At one meeting, a woman asked, "What if you feel that you have some problems similar to those discussed here tonight, but you got a low score, say only nine points, on the HOD test?"

Immediately the group leader took the floor. In a ringing voice of denunciation, like a fire-and-brimstone preacher, he told the woman that she had probably lied to herself and to the examiner when she took the HOD test. Therefore she was even more schizophrenic than the others because she could not recognize her symptoms. She'd better get into the program and start taking vitamins mighty quick.

When I pointed out to one of the best-adjusted people present that the leader seemed to be too ill himself to give therapeutic advice, he smiled as if I had complimented the group. "Of course," he said, "that's just what qualifies him. He's a real schizophrenic!"

What seems to have been lost in SA's effort to emulate AA is a differentiation between role models in the two forms of disability. An alcoholic need only stay away from

drink to be identified as arrested—perhaps a superficial
standard, but one that does provide legitimacy for the role
he assumes in seeking to aid the newcomer who might
still feel uneasy about his ability to overcome the bottle.
However, the degree to which a person formerly depressed, paranoid, or in other ways suffering from mental
illness (schizophrenic or other) is now functioning in a
less self-defeating manner is not so easily measured, particularly by untrained laymen who may be more distressed than he.

Thus in SA, as in many other groups, there is the almost
inevitable problem that the persons giving advice are not
only untrained and ill-prepared for that function, but that
they may advise out of their own needs rather than those
of the patient. That this problem is to some extent true of
the trained professional cannot be gainsaid, but it is a
shortcoming not inherent in his being professional; on the
other hand, it does inhere in the very condition of mental
illness.

It is indisputable that the leader of a self-help group of
mentally ill persons acts as a therapist; this is not the less
true whether the people have been diagnosed by others or
by themselves, or whether they are under the care of professionally trained persons or are receiving no such aid.
But when these leaders are extremely ill, as is often the
case, one is reminded of the words of Gregory Stefan:

> I believe that a therapist must always be stronger
> and healthier than his patient; for in this critical
> confrontation, either he succeeds in lifting the
> patient up to his level or the patient may well drag
> him down. The stronger of the two personalities—
> whether it is healthy or sick—is likely to win out.[28]

SA's Cleveland chapter has recently disassociated itself
from the parent organization to become Better Health,

Inc.[29] While there seem to be some programmatic differences between the groups (Better Health has condensed
the twelve steps of SA, and has revised and adapted the
eight traditions, now called ten guidelines), the suspicion continues that disassociation represents the same
sort of fission found in the homophile movement: a struggle for hegemony, leadership, and power leading to the
search for programmatic differences, rather than those
programmatic differences in themselves leading to a new,
and necessary, regrouping of forces.

Perhaps the most important and serious development
in the self-help movement among the mentally ill can
be found in local social and friendship clubs. Usually not
led by a trained therapist, but sometimes utilizing a social
worker or some other counselor, these clubs are often
limited only to former mental patients and presently
(often severely) disturbed persons. They exist in many
cities, but their efforts to form a national coordinating
council have thus far met with only meager success.

A few years back a directory of these clubs was compiled.[30] While the directory is now out of date—one sign
of the clubs' ephemeral character—in themselves their
names make interesting reading: Comeback, Friendship
Club, Stairways, New Horizons, Social Renascence, Mental Health Club, and AFTLI (the Association of Feeling
Truth and Living It).

One of the best-known and most enduring of these clubs
is Fountain House in New York, described at some length
by Victor Goertzel, John H. Beard, and Saul Pilnick.[31]
They report that in 1948, "a small group of patients in
Rockland State Hospital banded together under the name
WANA—We Are Not Alone." After their release, they met
on the steps of the New York Public Library, and soon
thereafter, through the aid of interested citizens, obtained

a clubhouse of their own. The four-story brick house had a patio and a fountain (hence the name). Although Fountain House, having been founded by ex-patients to assist both themselves and those still inmates, has the reputation of a self-help group, it does provide professionally directed rehabilitation. Nonetheless, there is a good deal of patient participation and what might be called patient power. The members meet not only at Fountain House but in small patient groups in their neighborhoods.

The ex-patient club movement seems to be quite popular in England; that the groups are not self-help to the exclusion of help from others is, however, quite apparent.

> They are run by a variety of bodies, some of them by local authorities, hospitals and local associations of lay people who are interested in mental health. Quite a number of very good ones are also organized by the Institute of Social Psychiatry.[32]

The well-known existentialist-psychotherapist, R. D. Laing, together with a number of colleagues, has formed one of these organizations.[33] Called the Philadelphia Association, it "has set up small experimental residential centers, run on household lines, where people live a community life together." Some of the residents have been diagnosed as schizophrenic or otherwise mentally ill; others are doctors, social workers, and allied professionals. Whether this experiment in living together as equals, in which the mentally ill are afforded dignity and control over their own lives, can long endure will be a matter of great interest to all those involved in the mental health problem.

In Johannesburg, South Africa, there is a club of people who either feel that they are suicidal or who have attempted suicide at one time; they have banded together as a fraternity of hope. Their name, Suicides Anonymous (at least one other group of this name has been reported, although its existence has not been verified), seems unnecessarily self-stigmatizing. Suicides Anonymous is a serious effort to overcome self-destructive drives, not a fantasy of people pretending to be denizens of a shadowy world that hovers between life and death; thus a name more inspirational and therapeutic can surely be found.

Any mental health club that functions without professional guidance faces obvious dangers; but for those who simply need the hand of friendship, one that can assist them to return to the world and overcome the stigma of being an ex-inmate, perhaps the advantages of such a club can outweigh the liabilities. While some clubs offer only authoritarianism, rigidity, and poor advice, others afford the social acceptance which can put the individual on the road to self-acceptance. Some clubs will help him return to the world of the mentally healthy; others will protect him sufficiently so that he will not seek to make that long and difficult journey.

Henry Wechsler has pointed out that one takes a major step merely by joining a self-help club: the act implies the voluntary acceptance of the ex-patient role.[34] Some discharged psychiatric patients, he states, are anxious to sever their connection with anything that reminds them of the hospital; they shun the company of others like themselves, or of those who know their past. Rather than join an ex-patient group, they wish to "pass," in much the same way that homosexuals do. However, for certain patients, Wechsler writes, "the act of passing may not be possible or desirable. These persons continue their association with other mental patients or with psychiatric facilities."[35]

One early consequence of being a member of such a group, Wechsler further points out, is that the person begins to consider himself similar to other ex-patients and "different from other persons in the community."[36] Does a person discharged from a mental institution see himself primarily as an ex-patient? Is this view the result of self-identification and self-labeling? Or is this labeling imposed on him by others (but one which he nevertheless accepts)? In either case, some ex-patients seem to be extremely conscious of that specific role; they seek shelter among others like themselves, and fear release into a world which, presumably, is made up only of normal people. Some such former patients develop great dependency on their club, and find it increasingly difficult to graduate from it. This is more likely to happen in a live-in than a once-a-week meeting situation, but although such dependence is decried and denounced as a crutch, for some it may be more fulfilling than the loneliness and lack of confidence, the fear of their incompetence, and the awareness of stigma deriving from their past, with which so many of these people live once they have walked out of the gates of an institution.

10. Truth or compassion?

Since de Tocqueville's early statement on the pro- liferation of organizations in America, numerous other writers have remarked on the large numbers of such groups and the wide spectrum of people they en- compass. But until a generation ago, it is doubtful that many persons would have dreamed that open, publicly acknowledged, formal organizations of deviant and stig- matized groups would be so apparent on the American scene. Whether organized as expressive associations for the gratification of the members' special pleasures, or as mechanisms for exerting pressure on both government and public for the purpose of furthering specific interests, these organizations are today interwoven into the fabric of contemporary society.

In general and with few exceptions, they have had a good press, from both the mass media and social scientists (although the latter have not been as friendly to Synanon as they have been to other parts of this movement). So severe have been the problems that many of these people have faced, so courageous have been their leaders in their willingness to struggle against overwhelmingly strong odds, so unjust has been their treatment at the hands of the public and government, that social scientists have applauded, often with little firsthand knowledge, every one of their organizational efforts. Deviants, particularly those who are victims without being victimizers, have found in sociologists a group anxious to express their friendship and understanding. And when the victims have decided that they will fight for their goals, either to change themselves or to alleviate their condition by changing others, their motives have seemed so lofty that it has been difficult to criticize any of their actions.

It is not unexpected, then, that internecine battles for power and strong-arm methods involving threats and even blackmail should have been concealed from public view. Every organization projects an image that it wishes the world to accept; groups of deviants do not differ from other associations in this respect, although, of course, their projected images may be less congruent with the public's view of the world. What is unusual is that so many of these organizations (again with the exception of Synanon) have had a sort of immunity from serious scientific study. They have coopted the social scientist to become, in the guise of researcher, the witting or unwitting publicist. From that scientist, and sometimes by him, the history of the group is carefully concealed, ideological distortion is glossed over, and successes exaggerated, while the danger of such actions, either to members or to those many others sharing a special status with members, is seldom even considered. The groups have had the benefit of uncritical whitewash.

While many deviant organizations put forward exaggerated claims of their own following, in this respect they do not differ from other political, social, and special-interest groups. Moreover, organized deviants seldom speak for the mass of the unorganized, only for a fractional percentage of their members; the organizations' rates of success, as judged by the numbers of people who have, through them, either overcome a stigmatizing problem or adapted to it, are to be considered self-serving declarations never subject to verification. All this would not be surprising, however, were it not for the complicity of the social scientist in these patently false presentations.

Despite expectations of exaggeration, it is nevertheless difficult not to be shocked to read in *L'Express*, an influential and generally reliable French publication edited by Jean-Jacques Servan-Schreiber, that "Americans can claim eight million homosexuals, boys and girls, who have been officially counted in the United States. They are grouped in vast organizations like the Daughters of Bilitis or the Mattachine Society."[1] Disregarding the peculiar terminology, "boys and girls" for men and women, and the inexplicable reference to their having been "officially counted," one is still brought up short by that figure of eight million grouped in "vast organizations." Eight million! Why, there are not even eight thousand in the homophile organizations, probably only a half or a quarter of that figure!

French excesses aside, one of the accomplishments of the organizations of deviants is that they have brought together for ease of study a relatively high concentration of people who would otherwise be difficult to locate, or, if located, unrepresentative of those sharing a given status. For researchers seeking to investigate gamblers, homosexuals, and others bearing an invisible stigma, the organizations offer a ready supply of subjects. In the absence of such groups, the behavioral scientist has usually turned—although he does not have to do so— either to gamblers or homosexuals in prison or to psychotherapists. However, the homophile movement has been particularly vociferous in insisting that prisoners and therapy patients are unrepresentative of homosexuals, and Mattachine and DOB (not to mention SIR and Vanguard), offer examples of better-adjusted sex deviants, in trouble neither with the law nor with themselves. Even when one turns to such a visible stigma as dwarfism, it is still difficult for the biological or social scientist to locate any large number of such people through ordinary medical channels; the researcher is therefore grateful for the resources of Little People of America.

The gratitude is mutual. Organizations offer their services gladly; they like to be studied, and constantly boast of the cooperation they have given the world of science. Cooperation is one of the self-justifying functions that gives legitimacy to these associations. But it is still likely that members of these groups are just as unrepresentative of all those sharing their status as are those recommended by psychotherapists or corrections officials. Although one can learn something about homosexuality by studying members of a homophile organization, he must always be aware that such members are more skilled at, and have a greater vested interest in, the game of putting on the investigator than are other homosexuals. In addition, a very real selectivity operates when one studies a group which contains only a fraction of 1 per cent of all those sharing the studied characteristic. In this respect, Joseph Scimecca,[2] whose work with gamblers I have briefly mentioned earlier, sought to overcome this difficulty when, during his research, he asked himself how compulsive gamblers in GA differed from those not in GA or those who had not sought to kick their habit.

Even dwarfs, in fact, may not constitute inside LPA the same populace they do outside. It is quite possible that LPA only attracts or holds on to certain types, or that the dwarf's experience in LPA modifies his outlook to the extent that it is not the same as that of another dwarf who has not been exposed to the organization.

For research purposes, the concentration of large numbers of deviants in organizations brings forth the further danger that some of these persons have been studied and observed so frequently that their organization provides a sort of zoo-type framework for them. Studies of deviant behavior and deviant status, unless handled with consummate skill and the highest ethical standards, can be an invasion of the very private life of sensitive persons; their delicate balances can easily be upset by encounters with ill-trained students or personnel. And such invasions are no more justified because the persons are begging for such exposure.

In this age of mass communication, particularly of television, the organizations of deviants have had a field day. Both the deviants and their leaders have been gratified at their high degree of exposure. Sometimes they count their successes by the number of programs on which they've appeared because the programs represent propaganda for their views. Following such appearances, the organizations receive numerous telephone and mail inquiries, perhaps even invitations to appear at women's clubs or schools.

In the view of the leaders, such opportunities for publicity are welcome. But public exposure is not so one-sidedly an asset. It is entirely possible that, commingled with a little pity, the public reaction is mainly one of reinforced contempt and ridicule when, for example, FPE or COG appears on the air to "educate" people about transvestism or transsexualism. There have been no studies to determine the effect on the listening audience of programs in which the "organization line" on homosexuality is put forward by a Mattachine or DOB leader; nor has anyone determined whether an old-fashioned position of enlightened criticism ("These people are disturbed and sick, but they deserve sympathy, not scorn") would affect the public in a way beneficial to the homosexual in our society. Moreover, what of the effect of such programs on youths who are still searching for their sexual identity? The generally negative attitude toward censorship, and the concomitant favorable view of freedom of opinion and inquiry, should not prevent us from facing this issue.

In short, public exposure can lead to either understanding or ridicule; perhaps the same program can result in both. Too frequently, however, the organizations have sought publicity for its own sake, not for any goal toward which they're working. But this, too, is understandable in terms of the nature of deviant organizations: whatever good or harm publicity brings to the deviants themselves (members *and* nonmembers), it almost invariably strengthens their organizations.

The social scientist, like others—and perhaps more so than most others—suffers from underdog ideology. While there is considerable doubt whether the American public at large has any real sympathy for the underdog, or whether this alleged sympathy must also be seen as a self-serving pat on the back, it is beyond doubt that the deviant has gained almost the total sympathy of sociologists. "Whose side are we on?" asks Howard S. Becker in a presidential address by that title before the Society for the Study of Social Problems.[3] Lest anyone not know the appropriate answer, he makes it explicit: we, the social scientists, are—or at least should be—on the side, for instance, of prisoners against guards in the sense that we study "the prison through the eyes of the inmates and not through the eyes of the guards or other involved parties." The same is true of most other victims of social containment against those who would control them: we should present their view of reality, the underdogs' view, as the real, legitimate one.

However, the fact that we are on their side, that we portray the world as they see it, should not prevent us from understanding that not every act of the deviants in dealing with both their problems and the hostile public is necessarily in the best interests either of themselves or that public. We must not be seduced either by our sympathy for the sufferer or by the hostility to the perpetrators of injustice which we share with him, into fighting with weapons we have not forged, ones which could well lead only to defeat. By definition, the champion of the underdog is on the side of the oppressed in the sense of supporting that great goal, the abolition of stigma; yet he must not be on that side in the sense of offering support for any theory and strategy which he might consider false, misleading, or self-destructive. To use an expression coined by a writer speaking of white workers in the civil rights movement, the social scientist should not enter into "voluntary servitude."[4] Not only must he retain his critical objectivity while remaining an ally of those he befriends, but he must always see the two factors—objectivity and commitment—as having no possible long-range conflict. In dealing with organized deviants, the social scientist could use as his model a statement from Spinoza: "I have made a ceaseless effort not to ridicule, not to bewail, nor to scorn human actions, but to understand them." From this, he can proceed one step further: once he has understood —in all understanding's possibly critical ramifications— he can help.

In searching for a clue to understanding these organized

people, one might start off with the nature of America as an extremely pluralistic society, one formed of large numbers of ethnic and other heterogeneous groups, and one moreover whose quickly changing and highly advanced technology has produced a rapidly altering social scene in which conflicts of interest abound. These conflicts arise between the young and their parents, the highly educated and the less so, the squares and the dropouts, the haves and those striving to have, as well as those racial groups whose struggles with each other have recently come so sharply into focus. These conflicts point out the diversity of the ways of life, values, and interests of that larger body, the American people. Once that diversity is recognized, struggles take place for influence, power, and recognition, for social acceptance and social change. From such struggles—even from the felt need for them—organizations are born.

While there is pressure to conform in America, the country takes pride in both its tolerance of nonconformists and the contributions which they make to society. Provided that he operates within certain socially stipulated limits, the nonconformist is almost glorified; however, when he goes outside these limits, he is pilloried. And these limits may lie precisely at the point where nonconformity coalesces with deviance: in fact, this statement becomes tautological if one defines deviants as socially disapproved nonconformists.

Any society which tolerates and, at times, even glorifies nonconformity cannot fail to arouse in its deviant members the hope that they too may one day enter its mainstream, if not by becoming conformists themselves, then by forcing a redefinition of their deviant characteristic as acceptable nonconformity. While the special status that marks such people as different from others would remain (that is, they would continue to be defined as a homosexual, ex-convict, or dwarf), the social disapproval attendant on that status would be lifted. Once the status had ceased to be a stigma, the person would no longer be a deviant, except in the statistical sense of that word.

One of the problems facing leaders of public opinion—in fact, facing the leaders of movements of deviant persons themselves—is how to alleviate stigma without reducing preference for the "normal" or majority condition. That this task has largely been accomplished in the case of blindness and deafness (although many deny that stigmatization has disappeared entirely from either case, it is certainly less prevalent and less strongly felt than in centuries past) would indicate that it can also be accomplished for dwarfism, mental retardation, and severe emotional illness—even for sexual deviance. That people struggling against such stigma have fallen into the habit, one which I find both fallacious and difficult to resist, of glorifying their condition, considering it as good as the normal, is readily understandable.

No less understandable is the fact that deviants have now begun to organize. But such organization should never be taken to mean that they have "nothing to lose but their chains." Just the opposite: their rising social expectations have provoked both the need to attain greater dignity and the belief in the possibility that such attainment is within their reach.[5] Now, for almost the first time on any large scale, these people, formerly leaderless, mute in a society that was deaf to their cries of tragedy, have demanded to be heard.

Americans, more than but not excluding other nationalities, are living in an age which Amitai Etzioni has labeled the epoch of "the active society."[6] Man, he writes, "has the ability to master his internal being, *and the main way to self-mastery leads to his joining with others like himself in social acts.*"[7] Three major components, Etzioni continues, are needed for active orientation: "a self-conscious and knowing actor, one or more goals he is committed to realize, and access to levers (or power) that allow resetting of the social code."[8] Of the third component, perhaps it should be added that the belief that people have such access will be sufficient to motivate them to form an organization, even if it leads them into blind alleys.

The active society is apparent to anyone opening a morning newspaper or listening to the latest news broadcast. America is a society on the move. People have discovered that the American dream of self-improvement, if it is to be realized, must be achieved by collective, not individual, action. In a society in which people are not defeated quietly, it's Benjamin Franklin's aphorism: "If we don't hang together, we will hang separately." True, the Molly Maguires hung together, then hanged separately, but, in so doing, they forced changes in a society that denounced—and hanged—them.

Organization, once reserved for movements possessing a pretense of respectability, at least among their own adherents, has now become a force among those fighting to enter precisely that respectable world. What started with alcoholics could not help but spread—in a society of superactivism, of an almost infinite variety of acting-out groups, of outcasts not yet suppressed in any totalitarian fashion—to homosexuals, ex-convicts, and dwarfs.

By organizing, however, these people have necessarily fallen into the pitfalls that inhere in organization. Ideological distortion, selective interpretation of the world, the assumption of a new mask (the mask of organization) with the abandonment of the old—all are seen more frequently than not. Furthermore, many of these difficulties have been overlooked in the past, primarily by the deviants, but also by their friends in the normal world.

One of the traps of organization is that it can cause a further chasm between the deviant minority and the dominant majority. This is not an ideological chasm so much as a physical or interactionist one; that is, organization may provide a small social structure for an independent world of deviants, all bound together by one characteristic, moving within a single circle and hence less within the world at large. It is the problem of separatism versus integration, of whether a man finds comfort and protection within a group of people like himself where stigma is lessened and acceptance taken almost for granted, or whether he is better off to ignore the special trait as being of no more significance in social life than, say, lefthandedness, and thus mingle with people of all types and predilections.

In a discussion of marginal men, Everett C. Hughes has pointed to the possibility that they may choose, or be forced into, social isolation, rather than struggle for integration with others:

> Sometimes it happens that marginal people establish and live their lives in a marginal group, hardly knowing that they are doing so. There are whole segments of marginal society, with their marginal cultures among various ethnic and religious groups in this country, some of whom even develop a distinguishing speech. Large numbers of unmarried career women in American cities live in essential isolation from other women and with only formal contacts with men. In addition, there are other marginal groups who are not quite aware of their marginality, by virtue of living together a somewhat insulated life, but who are, furthermore, made up of people of the most diverse backgrounds; people who have in common, to

start with, nothing but their marginality. They are
to be found in cities and especially among young
people. They are the American Bohemians.[9]

Hughes's description here, of "people who have in common, to start with, nothing but their marginality," could
apply to deviant and stigmatized people even more precisely than to the bohemians he mentions. Thus the question which I raise is twofold: first, whether social isolation with others like himself is desirable for the individual
deviant, and, secondly, whether that isolation will be fos-
tered by the act of organization. It has been feared by
some that organization can lead only to further alienation
from society; on the other hand, from a long-range view,
this alienation can be considered a temporary retreat that
will eventually serve as a bridge to a fuller, more genuine
return to society.

One is finally led to ask whether the movements of deviants are successful. There are many criteria by which
one may judge success: endurance, number of members,
and amount of publicity. But all are relatively unimpor-
tant beside the one basic question: to what extent have
these movements alleviated human suffering? That AA
has helped its members—although, I suspect, less frequently than it claims (and what organization does not
claim more success than it has actually had?)—seems apparent. That many former inmates of mental institutions
have received friendship and the encouragement to face
life from association with their fellows (particularly from
the role models of those who have left these hospitals to
become apparently well-functioning persons) would likewise seem to be almost indisputable.

I have suggested in this work that the very real help that
some (even many) have received from deviant associa-

tions should not encourage us to gloss over the errors, shortcomings, possibly even the harm that these groups might cause. Social science, despite the highest of motives, loses all objectivity when its analysis is designed to see good (or bad) in a movement only because it consists of people who are oppressed, suffering underdogs. Such analysis is shortsighted as well as nonscientific; in fact, it is nonanalytic. In the long run, the errors and difficulties, the outright lies and distortions made by the aggrieved, or on their behalf, must be exposed and corrected if the suffering itself is to be alleviated.

Although AA and similar groups have been designed specifically to aid the individual, they have actually played a major role in changing social attitudes toward both their members and outsiders in similar situations. The very reverse may be true for groups like Mattachine: designed, at least on a manifest level, to change society's attitudes, they have instead been more influential on homosexuals themselves, both Mattachine members and outsiders. That is, many homosexuals—organized or not— have received an enhanced feeling of self-worth from knowing that there are homophile spokesmen, groups, and magazines, as well as homophile pickets in front of the White House. This fact should not, however, blind the social scientist to the possibility that some impressionable people may be unwittingly or unfairly reinforced in their deviance by such movements, and, as a result, led to many years of loneliness, frustration, and unhappiness. Nor should one fail to understand the ideological and organizational motivations—all not always reputable—that produce a particular view.

Success, in summation, should be viewed not only in terms of the individual member or the individual organization, but in terms of deviant societies as a collective movement; their effect should be considered not only on the self-image and life style of the deviant—on how he is viewed and labeled by others—but on currents and directions in the entire society. In that sense, the overall organized movement of deviant people, as I see it, is certainly useful; if it does not always do good for the deviants themselves, it does do good for the society in which their associations thrive. Although theirs is the voice of the distressed, it is also that of the rebels, of people who, often for reasons beyond their control and their understanding, have challenged the taken-for-granted world of others, and are therefore causing those others to reflect on that world, provoking self-doubt where there was once complacency, and marshaling the forces of change. Theirs is the socially useful role—one today accentuated by organization—of marginal people who because of their marginality become instruments of skepticism for what can be a world of smugness.

The days of passive acceptance of one's fate are over, whether for welfare clients or for ex-convicts. In the secular society, no one is predestined to purgatory, neither symbolically in this world nor religiously in the other. If a man today cannot change the condition that constitutes a handicap, then he changes the situation in which it becomes a handicap. People have decided that they can decide their own fate now. In so doing, they will naturally commit excesses; they will do the outrageous (or what is viewed as outrageous by many not in their group), and they will defend what to others seems absurd. What matter, though, when their acts are viewed in a wide sweep as part of an outcry against injustice, rather than in a narrower range of whether a single scientific contention is correct?

This is a period in American and probably world history when everyone is fighting for rights—his and everyone's.

Only a few years ago, the use of the word *rights* for ex-convicts would have been an absurd contradiction; these people were only tolerated by the public, had to hide lest their stigma be exposed, and inherently had no rights except those that were thrown to them, like crumbs to an animal. Today it is generally conceded that ex-convicts should have rights, that ex–mental patients (even those presently confined) should have dignity, and that homosexuals should be considered part of humanity; those who now deny these contentions are increasingly called to answer by outraged citizens. Today there is almost, but not quite, a complete turn of the table: those who would deny rights and dignity to the deviant must slink backward, admit to being prejudiced, and conceal their illiberal views as they might a discreditable stigma. Certainly it has become improper to stigmatize, and to the extent that this development is the result of the existence of organizations of deviants (rather than the result of conditions making possible such existence), to that extent this movement has made a remarkable contribution to intergroup tolerance and liberalism in America.

In the end, what seems most to be under attack by the societies of deviants, albeit frequently without their realization, is stigma itself. That many of these organizations, certainly their members, have internalized the stigmatization process and express it toward others—even toward themselves—should surprise no one. They are products of a society that has rejected them; thus they are no less its products either when they accept some of that society's judgments or when they turn around and reject those who have rejected them. Furthermore, people reinforce their own righteousness and normality, even their own humanity, when they differentiate themselves from others who are despised and cast out. Thus, those who have been cast out by society may have a strong need to rejoin humanity (in their own mind) by separating themselves from other stigmatized persons.

The movement of organization among deviants is part of a land on the march. It is Mississippi Summer and SDS, anti-war demonstrations and sit-ins. Students are protesting, and welfare recipients are demanding; policemen stage job actions, and no one knows who next will occupy a building, or where. Everyone is organizing and fighting for rights; in a society which guarantees them the right to conduct such a fight, it is only natural for ex-convicts and homosexuals to join the ranks.

People who once were told, "Go fight City Hall," heard in the tone and context of that expression a clear indication that such a fight was futile; now these same people interpret the statement as an imperative command. They fight City Hall without fear—and with success. City Hall remains "them"—the others—the rule-makers who have cast out the deviants from society, but now the deviants are fighting back. Although there are many pitfalls in their struggle, it is good for American society that, through organizations, such people do fight back.

Notes

Chapter 1. Organizations of deviants
in a nation of joiners

1. This group is briefly discussed in Hans Toch, *The Social Psychology of Social Movements* (Indianapolis: Bobbs-Merrill, 1965), pp. 16–17.

2. *Encyclopedia of Associations* (Detroit: Gale Research Co., 1968).

3. Early American secret societies are discussed by Charles W. Ferguson, *Fifty Million Brothers: A Panorama of American Lodges and Clubs* (New York: Farrar & Rinehart, 1937). The theme is also analyzed by Arthur M. Schlesinger, Sr., *Paths to the Present* (New York: Macmillan, 1949), Chap. 2, "Biography of a Nation of Joiners." This essay appeared originally, in essentially the same form but more fully annotated, in *American Historical Review*, L (1944–45), 1–25.

4. Erving Goffman, *Stigma: Notes on the Management of Spoiled Identity* (Englewood Cliffs, N.J.: Prentice-Hall, 1963), pp. 1–2.

5. *Ibid.*, p. 3.

6. *Ibid.*, pp. 3–4.

7. Marshall B. Clinard, *Sociology of Deviant Behavior* (New York: Holt, Rinehart and Winston, 1963), p. 22.

8. Albert K. Cohen, "The Study of Social Disorganization and Deviant Behavior," in Robert K. Merton, Leonard Broom, and Leonard S. Cot-

trell, Jr., eds., *Sociology Today: Problems and Prospects* (New York: Basic Books, 1959), p. 462.

9. The differentiation has not been sufficiently investigated by those writing on this subject. See, for example, the articles collected in Howard S. Becker, ed., *The Other Side: Perspectives on Deviance* (New York: Free Press, 1964).

10. Alexis de Tocqueville, *Democracy in America* (New York: Vintage ed., n.d.), II, 114.

11. *Ibid.*, p. 118.

12. "The Differential Political Activity of Participants in a Voluntary Association," *American Sociological Review*, XXIII (1958), 524–532. Maccoby notes that his definition is a modification of one found in *Our Cities: Their Role in the National Economy*, Report of the Urbanism Committee to the National Resources Committee (Washington, D.C.: Government Printing Office, 1937), p. 24.

13. Schlesinger, *Paths to the Present*, p. 38.

14. *Race Questions, Provincialism, and Other American Problems* (New York: Macmillan, 1908), p. 239.

15. Jack Alexander, "Alcoholics Anonymous," *Saturday Evening Post*, CCXIII (March 1, 1941), 9 *et seq.* This was the lead article in the magazine; it has been reprinted by AA as a pamphlet entitled, "The Jack Alexander Article About AA."

Chapter 2. Alcoholics

1. Some of this historical information is taken from Sister Joan Bland, *Hibernian Crusade: The Story of the Catholic Total Abstinence Union of America* (Washington, D.C.: Catholic University of America Press, 1951).

2. An excellent history of the Father Mathew movement is given by Milton Andrew Maxwell, "Social Factors in the Alcoholics Anonymous Program" (doctoral dissertation, University of Texas, 1949). See also John Francis Maguire, *Father Mathew: A Biography* (New York: D. & J. Sadlier, 1864).

3. The historical roots of this group are traced by Maxwell in "Alcoholics Anonymous Program." Good related material is also found in John Allen Krout, *The Origins of Prohibition* (New York: Knopf, 1925), pp. 77–80.

4. "Alcoholism: Attitudes and Attacks, 1775–1925," *Annals*, CCCXV (January 1958), 17.

5. Maxwell, "Alcoholics Anonymous Program," offers some information on this group. There is also a book by the group's founder, Robert J. Patterson, *The Happy Art of Catching Men: A Story of Good Samaritanship* (New York: G. H. Doran, 1914).

6. *Alcoholics Anonymous Comes of Age: A Brief History of AA* (New York: Alcoholics Anonymous Publishing, 1957), p. 39.

7. I have leaned heavily for my history of the Oxford Group on Hadley Cantril, *The Psychology of Social Movements* (London: Chapman & Hall, 1941; new ed., New York: Wiley, 1963). While it cannot be denied that Cantril's description is unfriendly, it is nevertheless sound, well-documented history, as well as brilliant analysis.

8. *New York World-Telegram*, August 26, 1936, in Cantril, *Psychology of Social Movements*, 1963 ed., p. 152.

9. *Ibid.*

10. Printed in many places by AA, including *Alcoholics Anonymous Comes of Age*, p. 50.

11. "The Role of Alcoholics Anonymous as a Therapeutic Agent" (master's thesis, University of Wisconsin, 1949), Appendix.

12. For a research study on the group, see Margaret B. Bailey, "Al-Anon Family Groups as an Aid to Wives of Alcoholics," *Social Work*, X (January 1965), 68–74.

13. *New York Times*, June 18, 1968.

14. *The Cured Alcoholic: New Concepts in Alcoholism Treatment and Research* (New York: John Day, 1964).

15. D. L. Davies, "Normal Drinking in Recovered Alcohol Addicts," *Quarterly Journal of Studies on Alcohol*, XXIII (March 1962), 94–104.

16. Cain, *Cured Alcoholic*, pp. 70–71.

17. *44 Questions* (New York: Alcoholics Anonymous World Services, 1952), p. 5.

18. Cain, *Cured Alcoholic*, p. 63.

19. *Ibid.*, p. 63.

20. *Ibid.*, p. 66.

21. "Alcoholics Anonymous and Professional Relations (An Exploratory Study)," speech presented at the annual meeting of the North American Association of Alcoholism Programs, Portland, Oregon, September 30, 1964.

22. *Ibid.*, p. 6.

23. "Alcoholics Anonymous: Dangers of Success," *Nation*, CXCVIII (March 2, 1964), 212–214.

24. *Ibid.*, p. 214.

25. *Ibid.*

26. Harrison M. Trice, "Evaluation of Alcoholics Anonymous," *Third Southeastern School of Alcohol Studies* (Athens, Ga.: Center for Continuing Education, University of Georgia, 1963), p. 144.

Chapter 3. Gamblers, addicts, illegitimates, and others

1. Gabriel Tarde, *The Laws of Imitation*, trans. by E. C. Parsons (New York: H. Holt, 1903).

2. The list was compiled by Maurice P. Jackson in 1962; it is entitled "Their Brother's Keeper," and is discussed in Chapter Nine, below.

3. "The Facilitation of Gambling," *Annals*, CCLXIX (May 1950), 21–29.

4. Several articles on the relationship of gambling to crime are reprinted in Robert D. Herman, ed., *Gambling* (New York: Harper & Row, 1967). The entire question was brought before the public in the course of the televised hearings of the U.S. Senate investigation into gambling and organized crime (McClellan Committee), August 1961. See also *Task Force Report: Organized Crime* (Washington, D.C.: Government Printing Office, 1967).

5. Some of this literature has been summarized by Robert M. Lindner, "The Psychodynamics of Gambling," *Annals*, CCLXIX (May 1950), 93–107.

6. Albert H. Morehead, "The Professional Gambler," *Annals, ibid.*, p. 84.

7. "Gamblers Anonymous," pamphlet published by Gamblers Anonymous, n.d.

8. "The Sociology of the Compulsive Gambler" (master's thesis, New York University, 1965).

9. "Inspirational Group Therapy: A Study of Gamblers Anonymous," *American Journal of Psychotherapy*, XVIII (January 1964), 115–125.

10. Synanon, the well-known group designed to rehabilitate addicts, is discussed in Chapter Six, below.

11. Most of the remaining material on NA comes from Sherman W. Patrick, "Our Way of Life: A Short History of Narcotics Anonymous, Inc." in Ernest Harms, ed., *Drug Addiction and Youth* (Oxford: Pergamom Press, 1965), pp. 148–157. In addition, NA testimonials are quoted from the *Newark Evening News*, March 29, 1963.

12. Patrick, "Our Way of Life."

13. *Ibid.*

14. *Newark Evening News*, March 29, 1963.

15. *Ibid.*

16. Patrick, "Our Way of Life," p. 150.

17. *Ibid.*

18. The figure of seven million is cited by Dorothy A. Purser, "Methods of Stimulating Community Action on Illegitimacy," National Council on Illegitimacy, 1965, mimeographed. The same figure is used by Clark E. Vincent, *Unmarried Mothers* (New York: Free Press, 1961), p. 261.

19. The best effort to account for the social hostility toward illegitimacy is found in Kingsley Davis, "Illegitimacy and the Social Structure," *American Journal of Sociology*, XLV (September 1939), 215–233.

20. This theory, known as labeling, is expressed in two works by Edwin M. Lemert, *Social Pathology* (New York: McGraw-Hill, 1951) and *Human Deviance, Social Problems, and Social Control* (Englewood Cliffs, N.J.: Prentice-Hall, 1967). See also Howard S. Becker, *Outsiders: Studies in the Sociology of Deviance* (New York: Free Press, 1963) and Howard

S. Becker, ed., *The Other Side: Perspectives on Deviance* (New York: Free Press, 1964).

21. *Alcoholics Anonymous Comes of Age: A Brief History of AA* (New York: Alcoholics Anonymous Publishing, 1957), p. 241.

22. *Ibid.*

23. *The Social Psychology of Social Movements* (Indianapolis: Bobbs-Merrill, 1965), p. 72.

24. *Ibid.*, pp. 72–73.

25. *Ibid.*, p. 74.

26. "Overeaters Anonymous," brochure published by Overeaters Anonymous, n.d.

27. Of the organizations in this list, Adults, Recidivists, Teen-agers, and Youth are discussed in more detail in Chapter Seven, below, and Checks briefly mentioned in that chapter. Neurotics and Schizophrenics are discussed in Chapter Nine; in this same chapter, a few words are devoted to Suicides. Priapics Anonymous appears in a novel by Twiggs Jameson, *Billy and Betty* (New York: Grove Press, 1968).

Chapter 4. Homosexuals

1. Much of the material in this chapter appeared in my doctoral dissertation, "Structure and Ideology in an Association of Deviants," New York University, 1966.

2. See A Note on Sources, following, for discussion of the work of Hirschfeld.

3. See A Note on Sources, following, for discussion of the work of Carpenter.

4. Gordon Allport, *The Nature of Prejudice* (Garden City, N.Y.: Doubleday, 1958), pp. 147–148.

5. Alfred C. Kinsey, Wardell B. Pomeroy, and Clyde E. Martin, *Sexual Behavior in the Human Male* (Philadelphia: W. B. Saunders, 1948).

6. I obtained information on this group through extensive personal interviews with many of the former leaders and members.

7. This organization was described to me by several former members.

8. Marvin Cutler, ed., *Homosexuals Today: A Handbook of Organizations and Publications* (Los Angeles: One, Inc., 1956).

9. *Ibid.*

10. *Ibid.*

11. Louys was a minor French writer of the aesthetic-decadent school, popular at the turn of the century, and best known for his novel *Aphrodite*, of which there have been many translations and many editions. *The Songs of Bilitis* was originally published in French as a translation from the Greek, but this was a spoof or a hoax; an English translation first appeared in 1904 and has been reprinted many times since.

12. The differentiation between expressive and instrumental groups is

made in the sociological literature on voluntary associations. See particularly C. Wayne Gordon and Nicholas Babchuk, "A Typology of Voluntary Associations," *American Sociological Review*, XXIV (1959), 22–29.

13. Information on these agencies has been given to me by Alfred A. Gross and Fredric Wertham; I have also had access to the annual reports and other documents of the George W. Henry Foundation.

14. I have interviewed many former leaders involved in this struggle, and have had access to documents concerning it.

15. Goffman, *Stigma*, p. 25.

16. Howard S. Becker, "Deviance and Deviates," *Nation*, CCI (September 20, 1965), 115–119.

17. Edwin M. Schur, *Crimes Without Victims: Deviant Behavior and Public Policy: Abortion, Homosexuality, Drug Addiction* (Englewood Cliffs, N.J.: Prentice-Hall), pp. 96–97.

18. The concept of sympathy for the underdog as causing a distortion of one's view of the deviant has been brought forward by David Bordua, "Recent Trends: Deviant Behavior and Social Control," *Annals*, CCCLXIX (January 1967), 149–163; see also Edward Sagarin, "Ideology as a Factor in the Consideration of Deviance," *Journal of Sex Research*, IV (1968), 84–94.

19. This is probably the most civil-rights-oriented group in the homophile movement; location may be the major reason for this.

20. From various mimeographed and multigraphed documents, a prospectus, and from information supplied by officers of the organization.

21. See the decision of the Supreme Court of the United States, in the case of *One, Inc. v. Olesen*, 355 U.S. 371 (1958).

22. Most of the information in this paragraph comes from the bulletin of the National Coordinating Council. I have also seen some of the literature, mimeographed documents, and other material distributed by individual groups, including the Student Homophile League of Columbia University.

23. This quotation is from the front page of an undated *Vanguard* publication, probably issued in August 1966. Several other issues of *Vanguard* appeared, none of which have dates, and in some issues the name of the organization sponsoring the publication is "Circle of Loving Companions."

24. *Ibid.*, p. 7 (of unnumbered pages).

25. *A Brief of Injustices*, Council on Religion and the Homosexual, Inc., San Francisco.

26. *One*, January 1965.

27. Multigraphed bulletin issued by MSNY, entitled "Mattachine," n.d.

28. *Mattachine Newsletter*, March 1964, p. 11.

29. *Eastern Mattachine Magazine*, July 1965, p. 23.

30. Albert Ellis, *Homosexuality: Its Causes and Cure* (New York: Lyle Stuart, 1965).

31. Evelyn Hooker, "The Adjustment of the Overt Male Homosexual," *Journal of Projective Techniques*, XXI (1957), 18–31.

32. MSNY bulletin (see note 27).

33. *Mattachine Gazette* (publication of the Mattachine Society of Washington, D.C.), II (Spring 1964), 5.

34. *Ibid.*, p. 4.

35. *One*, August 1965.

36. *Mattachine Newsletter*, August 1964, p. 11.

37. Rita La Porte, "The Causes and Cures of Heterosexuality," *The Ladder*, XI (September 1967), 2–5. Previously, the same journal (in March 1966) had dealt with this same theme in an article by Judith Rascoe, "Creeping Heterosexuality: America's No. 1 Social Problem," reprinted from the December issue of a publication called *Grump*.

38. From a private document in the files of MSNY.

39. MSNY bulletin (see note 27).

40. *Mattachine Newsletter*, June 1964, p. 2.

41. *Ibid.*

42. *Mattachine Newsletter*, May 1964, p. 5.

43. Irving Bieber, "Speaking Frankly on a Once Taboo Subject," *New York Times Magazine*, August 23, 1964, pp. 74 *et seq.*

44. *Mattachine Newsletter*, October 1964, p. 15.

45. Paul H. Gebhard, John H. Gagnon, Wardell B. Pomeroy, and Cornelia V. Christenson, *Sex Offenders: An Analysis of Types* (New York: Harper & Row, 1965), pp. 275–276.

46. Jerzy St. Giza and Wieslaw Morasiewicz, "The Role of Seduction in the Genesis of Environmental Homosexuality: A Medico-Legal Study," in *Current Projects in the Prevention, Control, and Treatment of Crime and Delinquency*, VI (Winter 1964–65), 202.

47. See Edward Sagarin, book review, in *Crimonologica*, IV (November 1966), 48–51, in which two works on this theme are jointly reviewed: John Gerassi, *The Boys of Boise: Furor, Vice, and Folly in an American City* (New York: Macmillan, 1966), and Robert H. V. Ollendorff, *The Juvenile Homosexual Experience and Its Effect on Adult Sexuality* (New York: Julian Press, 1966).

48. Sir John Wolfenden, *et al.*, *Report of the Departmental Committee on Homosexual Offences and Prostitution* (London: Her Majesty's Stationery Office, 1956). The sections of the Wolfenden report dealing with homosexuality are reprinted in Edward Sagarin and Donal E. J. MacNamara, eds., *Problems of Sex Behavior* (New York: Crowell, 1968); see particularly page 129 of this edition.

49. Schur, *Crimes Without Victims, passim*.

Chapter 5. Transvestites and transsexuals

1. Havelock Ellis seems to have originated the term eonism, and wrote

one of the first studies of the phenomenon: *Studies in the Psychology of Sex*, VII (New York: F. A. Davies, 1928).

2. Jan Waldiner, *Transsexualism: A Study of Forty-three Cases* (Göteborg, Sweden: Scandinavian University Books, 1967), gives the following as a definition of transsexualism (p. 30): "A condition in which the subjects are convinced that they belong to the opposite sex and want a surgical change in their external sex characteristics, which are a source of disgust and torment."

3. *Ibid.*, p. 2.

4. Charles Winick, "The Beige Epoch: Depolarization of Sex Roles in America," *Annals*, CCCLXXVI (March 1968), 18–24; also Winick, *The New People: Desexualization in American Life* (New York: Pegasus, 1968); and Winick, "Dear Sir or Madam, as the Case May Be," *Antioch Review*, XXIII (Spring 1963), 35–49.

5. Daniel G. Brown, "Transvestism and Sex-Role Inversion," in Albert Ellis and Albert Abarbanel, eds., *The Encyclopedia of Sexual Behavior* (New York: Hawthorn Books, 1961).

6. Brown's definition (*ibid.*, p. 1012) of transvestism is given as follows: "Transvestism is limited to and refers only to the desire for and act of wearing the clothing of the other sex."

7. *Turnabout*, 1964.

8. Some of the information about FPE was supplied in a personal communication from Virginia Prince; some of it from the files of *Transvestia*; and, finally, some information is based on the work of H. Taylor Buckner, "Deviant-Group Organizations,'" (master's thesis, University of California, Berkeley, 1964).

9. *Ibid.*, pp. 137–186.

10. *Ibid.*, p. 180.

11. *Transvestia*, February 1965.

12. *Ibid.*

13. According to Waldiner (*Transsexualism*, p. 1), the term *transsexualism* was introduced by two writers at approximately the same time: Harry Benjamin, "Transsexualism and Transvestism as Psychosomatic and Somatopsychic Syndromes," *American Journal of Psychotherapy*, VIII (1954), 219, and E. A. Gutheil, "The Psychologic Background of Transsexualism and Transvestism," *American Journal of Psychotherapy*, VIII (1954), 231. However, Benjamin seems to have used the term in an earlier paper, "Transvestism and Transsexualism," *International Journal of Sexology*, VII (August 1953).

14. Harry Benjamin, "The Transsexual Phenomenon," *Transactions of the New York Academy of Sciences*, XXIX, Ser. II (February 1967), 428–429.

15. From *The Village Voice* (December 1, 1966), cited by Richard Green, "Physician Emotionalism in the Treatment of the Transsexual," *Trans-*

actions of the *New York Academy of Sciences*, XXIX, Ser. II (February 1967), 443.

16. For a discussion of the conversion operation, see Leo Wollman, "Surgery for the Transsexual," *Journal of Sex Research*, III (May 1967), 145–147; and Wollman, "Transsexualism: Gynecological Aspects," *Transactions of the New York Academy of Sciences*, XXIX, Ser. II (February 1967), 463.

17. There is widespread opposition to transsexual surgery in the medical profession on moral and religious grounds. For a report of an attempt to assay "physician emotionalism" on the subject, see Green, "Physician Emotionalism," p. 441. In California, and no doubt in many other states, some physicians fear that performance of the surgery may lead to prosecution under sections of the penal code dealing with the crime of "mayhem" (California Penal Code, Section 203).

18. Harry Benjamin, *The Transsexual Phenomenon* (New York: Julian Press, 1966).

19. At the present time, performance of sexual conversion operations in the United States is limited to a few hospitals. For a few years, such surgery has been performed on a small scale at Johns Hopkins (see *Time*, December 2, 1966), and it is now being considered at Stanford University Hospital (*San Jose Mercury*, January 3 1969).

20. Leon Festinger, *A Theory of Cognitive Dissonance* (Evanston: Row, Peterson, 1957).

21. Lemert, *Social Pathology*.

22. For a discussion of personality characteristics of transsexuals, as revealed by psychometric instruments, see Waldiner, *Transsexualism*, pp. 47–58; and Ruth Rae Doorbar, "Psychological Testing of Transsexuals," *Transactions of the New York Academy of Sciences*, XXIX, Ser. II (February 1967), 455–462.

23. The female counterpart of the somewhat more common, and certainly more publicized, male transsexual surgery is discussed by Wollman, "Surgery for the Transsexual."

24. Waldiner (*Transsexualism*, p. 9) cites as a distinguishing characteristic of transsexualism the fact that transsexuals "want one kind of treatment only—'a change of sex'; they never want to be 'cured' of their 'aberration.' " Note his use of quotes. The same author points out, p. 21, that not all authorities in the medical profession favor such operations: "One serious objection to surgical treatment is that, if the subjects change their minds about their sexual role afterwards, nothing can be done to put them right again anatomically. This is not purely an academic question—cases of this kind have been reported. Again, some patients have great difficulty in adjusting themselves to the change in their anatomy. This is why reports of operations in these cases often cause a storm of protest from colleagues." And even more significant is a previous pas-

sage, pp. 20–21: "Operations of this kind are one of the most controversial issues in the subject of transsexualism. Many believe that one should not give in to the demands of the patients for operation, because this alleviates the condition only for a time, and because it is never possible to change a person's sex completely." References have been omitted from these quotations.

25. The statement is taken from a paper by a graduate student, James P. Driscoll, "The Transsexuals" (unpublished). Several other references to this paper will be made, as Driscoll's observations may have significance insofar as his views, and those of others with similar attitudes, when expressed to the transsexuals themselves, could act as reinforcements for their own way of structuring reality; second, he offers interesting verbatim replies from transsexuals to some of his questions, although I do not accept his implicit or explicit interpretations of these replies.

26. The term is Benjamin's, and may be of more than passing significance.

27. Harold Garfinkel, *Studies in Ethnomethodology* (Englewood Cliffs, N.J.: Prentice-Hall, 1967), Chapter Five, "Passing and the Managed Achievement of Sex Status in an 'Intersexed' Person, Part 1," pp. 116–185. To understand the full significance of this case, one must read the key to the mystery contained in "Appendix to Chapter Five," pp. 285–288. Apologies are offered, however, for spoiling the story by revealing the end.

28. One member openly avows an intention to commit suicide if "she" is ever again arrested and placed in jail. Histories of suicide and self-mutilation are not uncommon among transsexuals. See I. B. Pauley, "Male Psychosexual Inversion: Transsexualism," *Archives of General Psychiatry*, XIII (1965), 172. Pauley found that in a study of one hundred cases of transsexualism, thirty-five had threatened suicide, seventeen had actually attempted suicide, and eighteen had attempted amputation of offending portions of their body.

29. Erving Goffman, *Asylums* (Chicago: Aldine, 1959), pp. 12–43.

30. See Eugene J. Webb, Donald T. Campbell, Richard D. Schwartz, and Lee Sechrest, *Unobtrusive Measures: Nonreactive Research in the Social Sciences* (Chicago: Rand McNally, 1966).

31. Driscoll, "Transsexuals."

32. See Benjamin, *Transsexual Phenomenon*, and see also my own very critical remarks on this book, "Ideology as a Factor in the Consideration of Deviance," *Journal of Sex Research*, IV (May 1968), 84–94, with a rejoinder by Benjamin, "Comments to E. Sagarin's Article," *ibid.*, p. 95.

33. Some members of COG have reached such a plane of identification with the opposite sex that they actually look forward to a day when "advanced surgical methods" will afford them the ultimate feminine

fulfillment represented by biological maternity. Of the known tendency for some males to fantasy that their bodies have actually taken on certain of the specific qualities of women (e.g., menstruation, capacity for child-bearing, etc.), see C. E. Allen, *A Textbook of Psychosexual Disorders* (New York: Oxford University Press, 1962), p. 243; for an older work, see Magnus Hirschfeld, *Sexual Anomalies and Perversions* (London: Encyclopedia Press, 1938), p. 169. A recent discussion along such lines is presented by John Money and Geoffrey Hosta, "Negro Folklore of Male Pregnancy," *Journal of Sex Research*, IV (February 1968), 34–50.

34. This is true in most American cities, particularly Los Angeles, where the police department wages an unrelenting war on the city's sexual deviates; for an enlightening report on the Los Angeles police vis-à-vis sexual deviants, see E. Havemann and P. Welch, "Homosexuality in America," *Life*, LVI (June 26, 1964), 72–74.

35. Becker, "Deviance and Deviants," pp. 115–119.

36. Minutes of the Police Community Relations meeting, held February 13, 1968.

37. Under Section 415 of the California Penal Code ("disturbing the peace"), an officer has no alternative to arresting a transsexual if a private citizen "reads her" and makes a complaint. An earlier penal statute making it unlawful to wear the clothing of the opposite sex has been declared unconstitutional, as has that portion of Cal. P.C. 650½ permitting the arrest of one who "outrages the public decency," e.g., by dressing as a member of the opposite sex in public.

38. Police Community Relations minutes, February 13, 1968.

39. It must be understood that this policy derives largely from the general reluctance of the district attorney to prosecute, and judges to convict, individuals for "transsexual offenses," as well as the police department's desire to use the community of sexual deviants as a mechanism for crime control.

40. One local radio station has expressed interest in doing a program on COG, while several graduate students of social work at the University of California, Berkeley, plan to film a meeting for didactic purposes. The group has allowed contact between members and news media on a rather selective basis, since the past exposure of some obviously disturbed individuals has resulted in adverse publicity.

41. Police Community Relations minutes, February 13, 1968.

42. What is stated in this paragraph is the theme of a body of sociological literature, too significant to be passed over lightly, and too well known to warrant citation. Among others, many others, one can cite Thurman Arnold, *The Folklore of Capitalism* (New Haven: Yale University Press, 1937), p. 357: "The creed of any institution is public presentation of a drama in which the institution is the hero. The play is spoiled unless the machinery behind the scenes is carefully concealed." More recently, there is Anselm L. Strauss, *Mirrors and Masks: The*

Search for Identity (Glencoe, Ill.: Free Press, 1959), and Erving Goffman, *The Presentation of Self in Everyday Life* (New York: Doubleday, 1959). This theme is explicitly applied to a voluntary association by Aaron V. Cicourel, "The Front and Back of Organizational Leadership: A Case Study," *Pacific Sociological Review*, I (Fall 1958), 54–58.

43. The paranoia of the transsexuals is discussed by Waldiner (*Transsexualism*, p. 8): "The victims [of transsexualism] often grow more and more suspicious of their fellow-men who they feel make no effort to understand or help them. The end result is often a conviction that one is being persecuted."

44. This chapter also has its denouement in the form of an afternote. As the book goes to press, I learn that COG is no more, and that CATS continues to exist, a small group struggling to survive and to carry on the work of COG.

45. Driscoll, "Transsexuals."

46. *Ibid.*

47. Emile Durkheim, *The Division of Labor in Society*, trans. George Simpson (New York: Free Press, 1964 ed.), pp. 84ff.

48. Kai T. Erikson, *Wayward Puritans: A Study in the Sociology of Deviance* (New York: Wiley, 1966), p. 4.

Chapter 6. Synanon

1. President's Commission on Law Enforcement and Administration of Justice: *Task Force Report: Narcotics and Drug Abuse* (Washington, D.C.: Government Printing Office, 1967). Here it is contended that reports of an addict population as high as 200,000 in the United States "are without a solid statistical foundation."

2. Narcotics Anonymous is briefly discussed in Chapter Three, above.

3. Jonathan O. Cole, "Report on the Treatment of Drug Addiction," in *Task Force Report*, pp. 135–137.

4. *Ibid.*

5. Guy Endore, *Synanon* (Garden City, N.Y.: Doubleday, 1968), p. 81.

6. *Ibid.*, p. 133.

7. *Ibid.*, p. 191.

8. See particularly Albert Ellis, *Reason and Emotion in Psychotherapy* (New York: Lyle Stuart, 1962).

9. Endore, *Synanon*, p. 135.

10. Lewis Yablonsky, *The Tunnel Back: Synanon* (New York: Macmillan, 1965), p. 142.

11. *Ibid.*, pp. 142–145.

12. Endore, *Synanon*, p. 37 (ellipses in original).

13. Daniel Casriel, *So Fair a House: The Story of Synanon* (Englewood Cliffs, N.J.: Prentice-Hall, 1963).

14. Endore, *Synanon*, p. 17.

15. *Ibid.*, p. 52.
16. *Ibid.*, p. 53.
17. *Ibid.*, p. 89.
18. Robert Martinson, "Research on Deviance and Deviant Research," *Issues in Criminology*, I (1965), 238–245.
19. This is a quote by Martinson from Yablonsky.
20. Edgar Z. Friedenberg, "The Synanon Solution," *Nation*, CC (March 8, 1965), 256–261.
21. Peter Collier, "The House of Synanon," *Ramparts*, VI (October 1967), 47–54.
22. *Ibid.*, p. 52.
23. Friedenberg, "Synanon Solution," p. 260, emphasis in original.

Chapter 7. Convicts and ex-convicts

1. *The Effectiveness of a Prison and Parole System* (Indianapolis: Bobbs-Merrill, 1964), Chapter 2, "How Many Prisoners Return?," pp. 13–35.
2. Glaser cites some conflicting statements, as in John Bartlow Martin, *Break Down the Walls* (New York: Ballantine Books, 1954).
3. "Some Action Proposals for Utilization of Ex-Offenders," in "Experiment in Culture Expansion," Report of Proceedings of a Conference on the Use of Products of a Social Problem in Coping with the Problem, Norco, California, July 10–13, 1963, sponsored by the National Institute of Mental Health; mimeographed; see p. 142.
4. Glaser, *Effectiveness of a Prison and Parole System*, p. 405.
5. Perhaps the best description of black nationalist movements in prison, and the effect of such movements on rehabilitation, is found in *The Autobiography of Malcolm X* (New York: Grove Press, 1965); see also Eldridge Cleaver, *Soul on Ice* (New York: McGraw-Hill, 1968).
6. The organization is called the Leavenworth Epilepsy League, and it publishes a mimeographed quarterly, *The Epi-Gram*.
7. See, for example, Lloyd W. McCorkle, "Guided Group Interaction in a Correctional Setting," *International Journal of Group Psychotherapy*, IV (1954), 199–203.
8. "Social Psychological Foundations for Using Criminals in the Rehabilitation of Criminals," *Journal of Research in Crime and Delinquency*, II (July 1965), 49–59; also "Changing Criminals: The Application of the Theory of Differential Association," *American Journal of Sociology*, LXI (September 1955), 116–120.
9. Chester D. Poremba, "Group Probation: An Experiment," *Federal Probation*, XIX (September 1955), 22–25.
10. Albert Eglash, "Youth Anonymous," *Federal Probation*, XXII (June 1958), 47–49.
11. Roger Vaughan, "The REAL Great Society," *Life*, LXIII (Septem-

ber 15, 1967), 76–91. A former student, Steven Eric Edelman, gathered further information on this group for me.

12. Albert Eglash, "Adults Anonymous: A Mutual Help Program for Inmates and Ex-Inmates," *Journal of Criminal Law, Criminology and Police Science,* XLIX (1958), 237–239.

13. The description of this organization is taken from the annual reports of RA Fellowship Trust, and from personal interviews and studies that I conducted while in London in July 1968.

14. The information in this section was supplied by the various branches of the John Howard Society of Canada, in response to a written questionnaire which I distributed. See also *News Letter* of John Howard Society of Alberta, May 1966, pp. 1–3; further information about Dead Numbers is found in the same *News Letter,* May 1967, pp. 1–3.

15. Bill Sands, *My Shadow Ran Fast* (Englewood Cliffs, N.J.: Prentice-Hall, 1964) and *The Seventh Step* (New York: New American Library, 1967).

16. *Seventh Step,* p. 224.

17. *Ibid.*

18. Material for this section was obtained from Hartford, Connecticut, newspaper clippings, from some circulars issued by The Inn, and from personal interviews with Robert Glazier by Howard Ramer, then a graduate sociology student at the University of Connecticut.

19. *Time,* XC (September 22, 1967), 82–83.

20. Information on the organization came from personal interviews with its executive secretary, perusal of its bulletins and news letters (mimeographed material), and radio and television programs I heard and lectures I attended.

21. From the society's mimeographed letter, dated Mid-March 1968.

22. The material on SDG, which makes up the remainder of this chapter, was obtained by William C. Kuehn, and analyzed and written by Mr. Kuehn and myself. He obtained his data by personal interviews, attendance at many meetings, studies of tapes of meetings that could not be attended, perusal of files and documents of the organization, and other methods.

23. Timothy Leary has told the story of his experiences with the prison inmates in his autobiography, *High Priest* (Cleveland: World Publishing, 1968), pp. 173–211.

24. *Ibid.,* p. 182, emphasis in original.

25. *Ibid.,* p. 201.

26. "The Self Development Group," a printed booklet issued by the organization, n.d.

27. *Ibid.*

28. A discussion of this theme is found in C. Wayne Gordon and

Nicholas Babchuk, "A Typology of Voluntary Associations," *American Sociological Review*, XXIV (1959), 22–29.

29. The findings used in this section are taken primarily from Ann Fuller, "An Analysis of the Self Development Group at Concord," distributed by the Massachusetts Department of Correction, January 10, 1968, Publication #849.

30. From an interview with James Kerrigan at MCI-Norfolk, May 2, 1968.

31. Massachusetts Department of Correction, "The Self-Development Group and Recidivism," May 8, 1968.

32. *Ibid.*

33. Self Development Group, Inc., "Progress Report," January 1, 1968, p. 12.

Chapter 8. Dwarfs

1. Among the best-known such groups is the Paralyzed Veterans of America, Inc.; there is a Colostomy Association in Los Angeles; "patient groups" of epileptics exist, but are rare.

2. Human Growth, Inc., in one of its bulletins writes: "Accurate statistics are unavailable, but there are probably half a million or more children who are stunted, somewhat fewer with excessive growth, infinitely more with pathological weight problems." It is doubtful, however, if the half million are (or are in danger of becoming) dwarfs. Many of them are late growers, and others will be somewhat shorter than they would prefer, but within the range of socially acceptable height.

3. Ernesto Pollitt and John Money, "Studies in the Psychology of Dwarfism. I. Intelligence Quotient and School Achievement," *Journal of Pediatrics*, LXIV (March 1964), 415–421.

4. Victor A. McKusick and David L. Rimoin, "General Tom Thumb and Other Midgets," *Scientific American*, CCXVII (July 1967), 103–110.

5. From a mimeographed letter, addressed to members and friends of HGI, May 1967.

6. Goffman, *Stigma*, pp. 30–31.

7. A two-page history of the organization, entitled "History of Human Growth, Inc.," has been distributed in mimeographed form; also a pamphlet entitled "Dwarfism . . ."

8. *Newsletter*, Little People of America, Inc., January–February 1967, reported a membership, as of December 1, 1966, of 730.

9. Private communication.

10. Private communication from the president of LPA.

11. Martin S. Weinberg, "The Problems of Midgets and Dwarfs and Organizational Remedies: A Study of the Little People of America," *Journal of Health and Social Behavior*, IX (March 1968), 65–71.

12. Height as a factor in mate selection is usually given scant attention by psychologists and sociologists; I believe that it is given a great deal of attention by mate selectors. A rare article on this subject is one by Hugo G. Beigel, "Body Height in Mate Selection," *Journal of Social Psychology*, XXXIX (1954), 257–268.

13. Weinberg, "Problems of Midgets," p. 69.

14. The differentiation between the functions of local branches and the national offices of voluntary associations has been made by several sociologists; see, for example, Gordon and Babchuk, "A Typology of Voluntary Associations."

15. Private communication.

16. John Money, "Dwarfism: Questions and Answers in Counseling," *Rehabilitative Literature*, XXVIII (May 1967), 134–138.

17. Private communication.

Chapter 9. Mental patients

1. O. Hobart Mowrer, *The New Group Therapy* (Princeton, N.J.: Van Nostrand, 1964).

2. Low has himself told the story of the organization of this group: "Recovery, Inc.: A Project for Rehabilitating Post-Psychotic and Long-Term Psychoneurotic Patients," in William H. Soden, ed., *Rehabilitation of the Handicapped: A Survey of Means and Methods* (New York: Ronald Press, 1949).

3. Recovery, Inc., "1968 National Directory," p. 2.

4. Recovery, Inc., "Offering a Systematic Method of Self-Help After-Care" (Chicago, 1967), p. 10.

5. "1968 National Directory," p. 2.

6. Based on information in "1968 National Directory."

7. Abraham A. Low, *Mental Health Through Will-Training: A System of Self-Help in Psychotherapy as Practiced by Recovery, Inc.* (Boston: Christopher Publishing House, 1950; 14th ed., 1966).

8. *Ibid.*, p. 12.

9. Low, "Recovery, Inc."

10. Low, *Mental Health Through Will-Training*.

11. *Ibid.*

12. *Ibid.*

13. "Offering a Systematic Method . . . ," p. 10.

14. " 'Self-Help Psychotherapy' as Practiced by 'Recovery,' " *Roche Report, Frontiers of Hospital Psychiatry*, March 1, 1965, p. 2.

15. *Ibid.*, p. 9.

16. Private communication.

17. *Journal of Mental Health*, III (September 1967), 5.

18. See particularly Albert Ellis and Robert A. Harper, *A Guide to Rational Living* (Englewood Cliffs, N.J.: Prentice-Hall, 1961).

19. For background on the concept of schizophrenia as well as the term, see Marvin K. Opler, "Schizophrenia and Culture," *Scientific American*, CXCVII (August 1957), 103–110. Opler traces the word to Paul Eugen Bleuler's 1911 work, *Dementia Praecox, or Group of the Schizophrenias*, trans. Joseph Zinkin (New York: International Universities Press, 1952).

20. John Ralph McDonald, "Schizophrenics Anonymous: An Experiment in Group Self-Help" (master's thesis, St. Patrick's College, University of Ottawa, 1967), p. 36. The passage quoted is from a taped interview of McDonald with Abram Hoffer, in which Hoffer is quoting Stefan.

21. *Ibid.*

22. *Ibid.*, p. 39.

23. Gregory Stefan, *In Search of Sanity: The Journal of a Schizophrenic* (New Hyde Park, N.Y.: University Books, 1965), p. 232.

24. "Introducing Schizophrenics Anonymous International," booklet, n.d.

25. *Ibid.*

26. *Ibid.*

27. The two men whose theories are most closely followed are Abram Hoffer and Humphry Osmond. Hoffer, director of psychiatric research at the University Hospital in Saskatoon, Saskatchewan, and Osmond, director of the Bureau of Research in Neurology and Psychiatry of New Jersey Neuro-Psychiatric Institute, have collaborated on a book, *How to Live with Schizophrenia* (New Hyde Park, N.Y.: University Books, 1966). Hoffer is also author of *Niacin Therapy in Psychiatry* (Springfield, Ill.: Charles C. Thomas, 1962).

28. Stefan, *In Search of Sanity*, p. 234.

29. *Better Health*, I (1968), published by Better Health, Inc.

30. Maurice P. Jackson, "Their Brother's Keepers: A Directory of Therapeutic Self-Help Groups, Intentional Communities, and Lay Training Centers," Urbana, Ill., 1962.

31. Victor Goertzel, John H. Beard, and Saul Pilnick, "Fountain House Foundation: Case Study of an Expatient's Club," *Journal of Social Issues*, XVI (1960), 54–61. Several other references to Fountain House are found in the bibliography at the end of this article.

32. The movement is described in a mimeographed bulletin, "Therapeutic Social Clubs," Institute of Social Psychiatry, London, n.d. The quote is from a private communication.

33. Private communication.

34. Henry Wechsler, "The Expatient Organization: A Survey," *Journal of Social Issues*, XVI (1960), 47–53.

35. *Ibid.*

36. *Ibid.*

Chapter 10. Truth or compassion?

1. *L'Express*, August 12–18, 1968, p. 50. Lest the reader, incredulous, question my translation, I quote the original: "En compulsant les statistiques, les Américains peuvent en effet constater qu'il existe 8 millions d'homosexuels, garçons et filles, officiellement recensés aux Etats-Unis. Ils sont regroupés en vastes organisations comme les Filles de Bilitis ou la Mattachine Society."

2. Joseph Scimecca, "The Sociology of the Compulsive Gambler" (master's thesis, New York University, 1965).

3. Howard S. Becker, "Whose Side Are We On?" *Social Problems*, XIV (Winter 1967), 239–247.

4. Charles J. Levy, *Voluntary Servitude: Whites in the Negro Movement* (New York: Appleton-Century-Crofts, 1968).

5. The theme that people rebel and revolt when their conditions are not at a nadir but are somewhat ameliorated is the subject of an article by James C. Davies, "Towards a Theory of Revolution," *American Sociological Review*, XXVII (1962), 5–19. Davies traces this theory to Marx and de Tocqueville.

6. Amitai Etzioni, *The Active Society: A Theory of Societal and Political Processes* (New York: Free Press, 1968).

7. *Ibid.*, p. 2, emphasis in original.

8. *Ibid.*, p. 4.

9. Everett C. Hughes, "Social Change and Status Protest: An Essay on the Marginal Man," *Phylon*, X (1949), 58–65.

After this book was first published, a left-wing homophile movement emerged. I analyzed this development in an article, "Behind the Gay Liberation Front," *The Realist*, No. 87, May-June 1970. The first book devoted entirely to the homophile movement, written by a participant and a partisan and containing a wealth of useful information and documents, was Donn Teal, *The Gay Militants* (New York: Stein and Day, 1971).

A note on sources

The most important single source for this book has been the deviant organizations themselves: their documents, magazines, bulletins, news letters, publicity statements, mimeographed sheets, private files, and, in a few instances, their books. In most cases I have supplemented these sources with personal interviews and by attending meetings. Although the latter cannot literally be called bibliographical material it has been among my best sources. Sometimes I did not personally attend the meetings but relied on reports prepared for me by persons whom I have identified; nonetheless, the interpretations of these reports have always been my own.

The phenomenon of organizations of deviant and stigmatized people has been almost nowhere discussed in sociological and psychological literature, although single organizations have occasionally been studied and analyzed. The forerunners of deviant organizations, religious sects and politically unpopular movements, have been the subject of many works, the most useful of which for my purposes has been Hadley Cantril, *The Psychology of Social Movements* (London, 1941, and New York, 1963). American fraternal organizations and so-called secret societies have been described by Charles W. Ferguson, *Fifty Million Brothers: A Panorama of American Lodges and Clubs* (New York, 1937), and Noel P. Gist, "Secret Societies: A Cultural Study of Fraternalism in the United States," *University of Missouri Studies* (1940). Although the two works are both good sources, Ferguson's is a popular and Gist's a scholarly presentation.

Closer to the theme of my own work is much of the material in Hans Toch, *The Social Psychology of Social Movements* (Indianapolis, 1965), inspired to some extent by the work of Cantril. While Cantril deals with many movements too clearly political to coincide with those I have studied, he does offer information that has proved invaluable to me, particularly his brief summary of the Oxford Group (Moral Rearmament), out of which AA grew. Toch's work, in addition to the light it sheds on activism in general, contains an excellent description of TOPS (Take Off Pounds Sensibly), an organization of the obese.

There is, of course, a tremendous literature on alcoholics, homosexuals, and the mentally ill, and a somewhat smaller literature on ex-convicts, gamblers, and those others whom I have studied. But much of this literature is only peripherally related to *organizations* of these deviants; thus, in most instances, it will not be mentioned here.

During the course of my work, I had occasion to read and reread many books and essays dealing in a general manner with voluntary associations, deviance, and stigma. Of the latter, I feel secure in mentioning only a single work: Erving Goffman, *Stigma: Notes on the Management of Spoiled Identity* (Englewood Cliffs, N.J., 1963). The related problem of courtesy stigma is treated in an excellent doctoral dissertation by Arnold Birenbaum, "Non-Institutionalized Roles and Role Formation: A Study of Mothers of Mentally Retarded Children" (Columbia University, 1968). The literature on deviance is by contrast vast; I should like particularly to mention Marshall B. Clinard, *Sociology of Deviant Behavior* (New York, 1963); Albert K. Cohen, "The Study of Social Disorganization and Deviant Behavior," in Robert K. Merton, Leonard Broom, and Leonard S. Cottrell, Jr., eds., *Sociology Today: Problems and Prospects* (New York, 1959); Edwin M. Lemert, *Social Pathology* (New York, 1951) and *Human Deviance, Social Problems, and Social Control* (Englewood Cliffs, N.J., 1967); Howard S. Becker, *Outsiders: Studies in the Sociology of Deviance* (New York, 1963); and the collection of essays edited by Becker, *The Other Side: Perspectives on Deviance* (New York, 1964).

There are numerous essays and several excellent unpublished doctoral dissertations on voluntary associations, but few books dealing with the phenomenon of joining. A data-laden work by Murray Hausknecht, *The Joiners: A Sociological Description of Voluntary Association Membership in the United States* (New York, 1962) has been valuable for me. A collection of articles has been edited by William A. Glaser and David L. Sills, *The Government of Associations* (New York, 1967). On the closely related theme of pressure groups and interest groups, organized and unorganized, the most helpful work is David B. Truman, *The Governmental Process: Political Interests and Public Opinion* (New York, 1960). There are many studies of specific organizations, an outstanding example being Sills's *The Volunteers: Means and Ends in a National Organization* (Glencoe, Ill., 1957). Studies of Alcoholics Anonymous are mentioned below.

Of the many fine theses dealing with voluntary associations in general, rather than with a specific one, the most helpful (titles omitted) have been: Morris Axelrod (University of Michigan, 1953); Bernard Barber (Harvard, 1948); Sherwood Dean Fox (Harvard, 1952); and Herbert Goldhamer (University of Chicago, 1942).

Among the most useful shorter pieces and essays on joiners have been: Arthur M. Schlesinger, Sr., "Biography of a Nation of Joiners," first published in *American Historical Review* (1944–45), and later reprinted in the author's *Paths to the Present* (New York, 1949); Gordon W. Allport, "The Psychology of Participation," *Psychological Review* (1945), reprinted in the author's *Personality and Social Encounter* (Boston, 1964); C. Wayne Gordon and Nicholas Babchuk, "A Typology of Voluntary Associations," *American Sociological Review* (1959); Mirra Komarovsky, "The Voluntary Associations of Urban Dwellers," *American Sociological Review* (1946); and Charles R. Wright and Herbert H. Hyman, "Voluntary Association Memberships of American Adults: Evidence from National Sample Surveys," *American Sociological Review* (1958). The foregoing is only a small sampling from a large and very helpful literature.

On one further theme that runs through this work, the literature is particularly sparse: anonymity and secrecy. Of those works extant, there is nothing I know of that equals the essay of Georg Simmel, "The Secret and the Secret Society," originally translated by Albion W. Small and published (under a slightly different title) in *American Journal of Sociology* (1906). In a new translation it appears in Kurt H. Wolff, *The Sociology of Georg Simmel* (New York, 1964). The theme of secrecy appears in Edward A. Shils, *The Torment of Secrecy: The Background and Consequences of the American Security Policies* (Glencoe, Ill., 1956), and in Vilhelm Aubert, *The Hidden Society* (Totowa, N.J., 1965). Most of this literature, as well as other on secret societies, deals with terrorist, criminal, and outlawed political groups; thus its relationship to my own work is tenuous.

Of the specific organizations discussed in this book, the literature I have used is as follows:

ALCOHOLISM: Alcoholics Anonymous has published several books, a regular journal (*The Grapevine*), and numerous booklets which it makes available to interested researchers. Its books include *Alcoholics Anonymous: The Story of How More than One Hundred Men Have Recovered from Alcoholism* (New York, 1939) (in a later edition [1955] the subtitle referred to "many thousands of men and women"); *The Twelve Steps and Twelve Traditions* (New York, 1953); *Alcoholics Anonymous Comes of Age: A Brief History of AA* (New York, 1957); and *AA Today* (New York, 1960), this last written by Bill W.

There are at least one hundred technical articles about AA, and innumerable popular ones; a bibliography of the former is available at small cost from the Rutgers Center for the Study of Alcoholism, New Brunswick, New Jersey. Abstracts of these articles are also available for a small fee. While I have tried to read all the articles, those that I have actually used are cited in the footnotes to Chapter Two.

Several books deal with AA, if not fully, at least in part; I cite two which, although they maintain opposite attitudes toward the association, have been particularly helpful: Irving P. Gellman, *The Sober Alcoholic: An Organizational Analysis of Alcoholics Anonymous* (New Haven, 1964), and Arthur H. Cain, *The Cured Alcoholic: New Concepts in Alcoholism Treatment and Research* (New York, 1964). The January 1958 issue of *Annals* contains important material on both AA and earlier movements of a similar nature. There are also many dissertations on AA, most of them favorable; many describe meetings of the organization or the results of interviews with members, others give information on the Washingtonians and other nineteenth-century movements. A few such dissertations are cited in the footnotes to Chapter Two.

Among the works on the general problem of alcoholism that I have found useful are: John Allen Krout, *The Origins of Prohibition* (New York, 1925); many works of E. M. Jellinek; the doctoral dissertation of Milton Andrew Maxwell (University of Texas, 1949); Sister Joan Bland, *Hibernian Crusade: The Story of the Catholic Total Abstinence Union of America* (Washington, D.C., 1951), and the report of the President's Commission on Law Enforcement and Administration of Justice, *Task Force Report: Drunkenness* (Washington, D.C., 1967). Material on alcoholism in general and AA in particular can also be found in two collections: Raymond G. McCarthy, ed., *Drinking and Intoxication: Selected Readings in Social Attitudes and Controls* (New Haven and New Brunswick, N.J., 1965), and David J. Pittman, ed., *Alcoholism* (New York, 1967).

GAMBLING: Gamblers Anonymous has published several pamphlets on its own. A number of newspapers have carried stories about the organization, including a rather lengthy discussion in the sports section of the *New York Times*, June 30, 1968. Gambling was also the subject of an issue of *Annals* (May 1950), while Gamblers Anonymous is studied in a master's thesis written by Joseph Scimecca at New York University, 1965. The organization is also described in an excellent article by Alvin Scodel, "Inspirational Group Therapy: A Study of Gamblers Anonymous," *American Journal of Psychotherapy* (1964). While many works on organized crime deal with gambling, they do not mention the struggle to overcome the temptation to gamble nor the organization formed for that purpose. A collection of articles on gambling, including Scodel's, appears in Robert D. Herman, ed., *Gambling* (New York, 1967).

ADDICTION: A few newspaper accounts and one article comprise the literature on Narcotics Anonymous; the article is by Sherman W. Patrick, "Our Way of Life: A Short History of Narcotics Anonymous, Inc.," in Ernest Harms, ed., *Drug Addiction and Youth* (Oxford, 1965). Many works provide a good background on addiction itself: among others, Isidor Chein, *et al.*, *The Road to H* (New York, 1964); John A. O'Donnell and John C. Ball, eds., *Narcotic Addiction* (New York, 1966), and the report of the President's Commission on Law Enforcement and Administration of Justice, *Task*

Force Report: Narcotics and Drug Abuse (Washington, D.C., 1967). The literature on Synanon is discussed separately.

ILLEGITIMACY: The adult illegitimate is hardly mentioned in the literature on illegitimacy, except in legal works dealing with inheritance rights. W. Boyd Littrell and I have written an unpublished article on this theme, "The Illegitimate Adult: Self-Stigmatization and Organizational Failure." For those wishing to pursue the general subject of illegitimacy, the outstanding work in this field is Clark E. Vincent, *Unmarried Mothers* (New York, 1961). Although the bibliography needs some updating, it is extremely useful. Aside from Vincent's work, no mention of this field should be made without calling attention to Kingsley Davis, "Illegitimacy and the Social Structure," *American Journal of Sociology* (1939).

OBESITY: In addition to the usual pamphlets, booklets, and newspaper publicity by and about organizations of the obese, Weight Watchers regularly publishes a commercial magazine. Other than that, most of the literature on the obese is medical, a little is psychological, and hardly any deals with the social aspects of the condition. Toch's discussion of Take Off Pounds Sensibly, previously cited, remains the best of the social analyses.

HOMOSEXUALITY: American homophile organizations have issued a great deal of literature; it includes news letters, magazines, mimeographed sheets, booklets, speeches, newspaper releases, and clippings. There is no research substitute for the study of *One*, *Drum*, *Vanguard*, *Mattachine Review*, *Mattachine Newsletter*, *Interim*, *The Ladder*, and other homophile publications. Those no longer being published should be perused with great care, in order to grasp the history of the movement and its changing character. A rather journalistic work on these groups has been written by R. E. L. Masters, *The Homosexual Revolution: A Challenging Exposé of the Social and Political Directions of a Minority Group* (New York, 1962). My own doctoral dissertation, "Structure and Ideology in an Organization of Deviants" (New York University, 1966), offers much greater detail than I was able to use in the chapter in this book.

While most of the literature on homosexuality is not helpful to a study of the homosexual organizational movement, I have nonetheless used several works from the Institute for Sex Research founded by Professor Alfred C. Kinsey: Alfred C. Kinsey, Wardell B. Pomeroy, and Clyde E. Martin, *Sexual Behavior in the Human Male* (Philadelphia, 1948); Alfred C. Kinsey, Wardell B. Pomeroy,

Clyde E. Martin, and Paul H. Gebhard, *Sexual Behavior in the Human Female* (Philadelphia, 1953); and Paul H. Gebhard, John H. Gagnon, Wardell B. Pomeroy, and Cornelia V. Christenson, *Sex Offenders: An Analysis of Types* (New York, 1965). Several articles on homosexuality have been collected by Hendrik M. Ruitenbeek, ed., *The Problem of Homosexuality in Modern Society* (New York, 1963). A psychoanalytic approach to homosexuality, with particular emphasis on therapy, is found in Irving Bieber, *et al.*, *Homosexuality: A Psychoanalytic Study* (New York, 1962); the topic is approached psychotherapeutically in Albert Ellis, *Homosexuality: Its Causes and Cure* (New York, 1965). An important landmark in this literature has been the famous Wolfenden report: Sir John Wolfenden, *et al.*, *Report of the Departmental Committee on Homosexual Offences and Prostitution* (London, 1956). Those sections of the Wolfenden report dealing with homosexuality, and the sections of the work of Gebhard, *et al.*, on homosexual child molestation, appear in a work which I co-edited: Edward Sagarin and Donal E. J. MacNamara, eds., *Problems of Sex Behavior* (New York, 1968). Finally, a great deal of factual information on homophile organizations has been assembled by Marvin Cutler, ed., *Homosexuals Today: A Handbook of Organizations and Publications* (Los Angeles, 1956).

No serious student of the history of the American homophile movement should ignore the life and work of the two most serious European predecessors, Magnus Hirschfeld and Edward Carpenter. The work of Hirschfeld is discussed in an article, Hedwig Leser, "The Hirschfeld Institute for Sexology," in Albert Ellis and Albert Abarbanel, *The Encyclopedia of Sexual Behavior* (New York, 1961). Hirschfeld was founder and leader of the Wissenschaftlich-Humanitäre Komitee and for many years edited the *Jahrbuch für Sexuelle Zwischenstufen*. Carpenter also headed an organization, although less influential, and wrote many books on homosexuality, including *The Intermediate Sex: A Study of Some Transitional Types of Men and Women* (London, 1908), *Intermediate Types Among Primitive Folk: A Study in Social Evolution* (London, 1914), and one section of his rather influential *Love's Coming of Age* (London, 1911) was devoted to this subject. In an autobiography, Carpenter acknowledged his own homosexuality.

TRANSVESTITES AND TRANSSEXUALS: The two journals published by and for transvestites, *Turnabout* (Abbé de Choisy Press, New York), and *Transvestia* (Chevalier Publications, Los Angeles) and their files will prove rewarding to the researcher. The transsexuals have also published some autobiographies, of which the best known is Christine Jorgensen, *A Personal Autobiography* (New York, 1967). COG has issued some leaflets and other mimeographed literature. I have also benefited from minutes of meetings between COG and both the police and other community representatives, as well as from studies of COG by graduate students. A master's thesis on transvestism that emphasizes the organizational aspects of the phenomenon (contrasting it to two nonsexual "way out" movements) was written by H. Taylor Buckner (University of California, Berkeley, 1964).

The first important book on transsexualism was Harry Benjamin's *The Transsexual Phenomenon* (New York, 1966). Although it contains a wealth of information, I have reservations about some of the author's viewpoints. These I have stated in an article, "Ideology as a Factor in the Consideration of Deviance," *Journal of Sex Research* (1968). A pamphlet by Jan Waldiner, *Transsexualism: A Study of Forty-three Cases* (Göteborg, Sweden, 1967) is even more useful than the clinical information that the title would indicate. Several brief statements and articles on this subject appear in the *Transactions of the New York Academy of Sciences* (February 1967). The chapter on a transsexual by Harold Garfinkel in his *Studies in Ethnomethodology* (Englewood Cliffs, N.J., 1967) is extremely important; it was written in collaboration with Robert J. Stoller, who is the author of a book having a great deal of information on this subject, *Sex and Gender: On the Development of Masculinity and Femininity* (New York, 1968). Transvestism and transsexualism cannot properly be studied apart from the problems of sex-role identification and differentiation, and on that theme I am indebted to Charles Winick, *The New People: Desexualization in American Life* (New York, 1968). Finally, the November 1968 issue of *Journal of Nervous and Mental Disease* is devoted entirely to transsexualism.

SYNANON: The Synanon literature is extensive, over and beyond the literature on addiction already mentioned. The most important single volume about the organization is Lewis Yablonsky, *The Tunnel Back: Synanon* (New York, 1965). Two other books that contain a good deal of useful material—although both authors are as uncritical as Yablonsky—are Guy Endore, *Synanon* (Garden City, N.Y., 1968), and Daniel Casriel, *So Fair a House: The Story of*

Synanon (Englewood Cliffs, N.J., 1963). There is also an extensive body of newspaper and magazine articles about Synanon. Three of these articles summarize among them what I consider the best analyses of the shortcomings and dangers of the movement; they are Edgar Z. Friedenberg, "The Synanon Solution," *Nation* (March 8, 1965); Peter Collier, "The House of Synanon," *Ramparts* (October 1967); and Robert Martinson, "Research on Deviance and Deviant Research," *Issues in Criminology* (1965).

EX-CONVICTS: Except for some autobiographical accounts, most works on ex-convicts deal with parole. The most thorough book along this line is Daniel Glaser, *The Effectiveness of a Prison and Parole System* (Indianapolis, 1964); but the reader should be warned that Glaser was investigating federal prisoners whose problems are quite unlike those of state prisoners in America, and further that Glaser's work has been severely criticized. As yet, there is no book on the organizations of ex-convicts or on the use of such persons as role models or therapeutic agents. This subject was, however, handled in a paper by William C. Kuehn, "Organizations of Inmates and Ex-Inmates," delivered at the American Society of Criminology meeting, Toronto, 1968. Several articles, some government pamphlets, and conference reports on convict organizations have appeared; the best of this material, such as the articles by Eglash and Cressey, is cited in the footnotes to Chapter Seven. For further information, see "Experiment in Culture Expansion," the report of a conference sponsored by the National Institute for Mental Health and held in Norco, California, in 1963; and a small government booklet with the excellent title, *Pros and Cons: New Role for Nonprofessionals in Corrections*, by Judith G. Benjamin, *et al.*, issued by the Office of Juvenile Delinquency and Youth Development, HEW (Washington, D.C., 1966). My material on the Self-Development Group came from the organization's files, public and private literature, and reports about SDG prepared by the Massachusetts Department of Correction. Important material on this group is to be found in Timothy Leary, *High Priest* (New York, 1968), and in several articles written by Leary and his colleagues for scientific journals, all mentioned in the bibliography in *High Priest*. Many other groups mentioned in this chapter have issued statements or bulletins to which I was given access; most of them have also had some local newspaper publicity that I have seen. Bill Sands has written two autobiographical works: *My*

Shadow Ran Fast (Englewood Cliffs, N.J., 1964) and *The Seventh Step* (New York, 1967), the second of which deals extensively with his ex-convict movement.

DWARFS: The Little People of America has a news letter and has issued its own publicity from time to time—as has Human Growth, Inc.; articles about both organizations have also appeared on occasion. In addition to this material, and to my own observations at meetings and discussions with members, I have had access to some of the correspondence of LPA leaders. Two social-scientific articles about dwarfism have appeared; the first deals extensively with LPA, the second with the general problem. The former is Martin S. Weinberg, "The Problems of Midgets and Dwarfs and Organizational Remedies: A Study of the Little People of America," *Journal of Health and Social Behavior* (March 1968); the latter is by Marcello Truzzi, "Lilliputians in Gulliver's Land: The Social Role of the Dwarf," which appears as a chapter in a collection edited by Truzzi, *Sociology and Everyday Life* (Englewood Cliffs, N.J., 1968). Some of the social-psychological aspects of dwarfism are considered in the following papers: John Money, "Dwarfism: Questions and Answers in Counseling," *Rehabilitation Literature* (May 1967), and Ernesto Pollitt and John Money, "Studies in the Psychology of Dwarfism. I. Intelligence Quotient and School Achievement," *Journal of Pediatrics* (March 1964). A more general review of the subject is by Victor A. McKusick and David L. Rimoin, "General Tom Thumb and Other Midgets," *Scientific American* (July 1967). Much of the remaining material on dwarfism is strictly medical.

EX–MENTAL PATIENTS: A few of the essays in O. Hobart Mowrer, *The New Group Therapy* (Princeton, 1964) deal with self-help therapeutic groups. Though now entirely out of date, Maurice P. Jackson, "Their Brother's Keeper" (Urbana, Ill., 1962), is a booklet consisting primarily of a list of self-help therapy groups.

Recovery, Inc., the best known and most publicized of the groups, is based on the works of its founder, Abraham Low, and particularly on his *Mental Health Through Will-Training: A System of Self-Help in Psychotherapy as Practiced by Recovery, Inc.* (Boston, 1950). In addition to a regular magazine, Recovery issues many pamphlets, leaflets, bulletins, records, and tapes. The organization has also been the subject of many papers by college students, several of which were made available to me.

Neurotics Anonymous likewise has a magazine (mimeographed), called *Journal of Mental Health*, and it publishes the usual smaller bulletins about itself. For a fuller understanding of this group, one should turn to the book which many of its members and local groups have adopted as their own, Albert Ellis and Robert A. Harper, *A Guide to Rational Living* (Englewood Cliffs, N.J., 1961).

Schizophrenics Anonymous, like the other ex–mental patient groups, issues its own bulletins and pamphlets. It has been the subject of one master's thesis, Rev. John Ralph McDonald (St. Patrick's College, University of Ottawa, 1967). A prime lay mover in the foundation of the organization was Gregory Stefan, who has told that story in an autobiographical work, *In Search of Sanity: The Journal of a Schizophrenic* (New Hyde Park, N.Y., 1965). The scientists whose tenets guide the organization are Abram Hoffer and Humphry Osmond, who together have written *How to Live with Schizophrenia* (New Hyde Park, N.Y., 1966). Hoffer is the author of several other books on treating schizophrenics. SA's offshoot, the Better Health Group, has also published some literature of its own.

Like homosexuality, the literature on schizophrenia in particular and on mental illness in general is too vast to warrant citation of any but the most pertinent material. The reader should certainly become acquainted with the writings of R. D. Laing, British existentialist psychotherapist, especially his *Schizophrenia: Sickness or Strategy* (New York, 1968). Two papers of special interest are Hyman Spotnitz, "The Borderline Schizophrenic in Group Psychotherapy," *International Journal of Group Psychotherapy* (1957), and Marvin K. Opler, "Schizophrenia and Culture," *Scientific American* (August 1957). For those wishing further to investigate the chemotherapeutic work of Hoffer and Osmond, see their papers "Nicotinamide Adenine Dinucleotide (NAD) as a Treatment for Schizophrenia," *Journal of Psychopharmacology* (1966), and Hoffer, *et al.*, "Treatment of Schizophrenia with Nicotinic Acid and Nicotinamide," *Journal of Clinical and Experimental Psychopathology* (June 1957). Without citing specific works, I should like to add that the chemotherapeutic contentions of SA have been challenged by many scientific authorities.

There is a sparse literature on independent ex-patient clubs, and many of these clubs have issued little bulletins of their own.

Autobiographical accounts have been most valuable to me in appreciating the anguish, difficulties, and frequently the bitterness of people suffering from many of the conditions described in this book. A few such autobiographies have already been mentioned in this essay; others, particularly those of the physically handicapped, are mentioned by Goffman in his work on stigma. In addition, there are numerous outstanding works by ex-convicts, such as *The Autobiography of Malcolm X* (New York, 1965), and Eldridge Cleaver, *Soul on Ice* (New York, 1968). Biographies of homosexuals can shed a great deal of light on that condition. The struggle with mental illness has been described in somewhat fictionalized but nevertheless authentic form by Millen Brand, *Savage Sleep* (New York, 1968), while the struggle with alcoholism was made famous by Charles Jackson in his novel, *The Lost Weekend* (New York, 1944).

Finally, it is from the creative artist that one can get the most profound insights into deviance and stigma. Few works display a greater understanding of homosexuality than those of Marcel Proust and André Gide, of dwarfism than that of Pär Lagerkvist, and of alcoholism than that of Malcolm Lowry. These writers were sociologists and psychologists expressing themselves by implication rather than explication; their insights are no less meaningful to us because their vision of humanity is expressed through metaphor.

Of these sources I have used, many are reliable and many less so, but the latter can be as valuable as the former. All printed matter by any organization, not only the types described here but any at all, must be looked upon as self-serving. What is said may be correct, but if so, this is usually a coincidence; that is, truth coincides with self-interest. Many of those writing about the organizations—not only journalists and students from whom more cannot be expected, and publicists who are paid for a task to be done, but scholars as well—turn out material as naive as it is obsequious. Yet their information can be revealing, if only in an unintended manner.

There is no substitute for primary sources, it is often said, but even these must be examined critically, without glorifying the material simply because it is primary. Tapes, informal structured and unstructured talks, interviews, questionnaires, unobtrusively developed data, attendance at meetings, socializing over a cup of coffee—these may often reveal more than the perusal of a statement of principles.

Index

A note on the author

After a career in business, Edward Sagarin returned to school in his mid-forties and received a bachelor's degree from Brooklyn College and a Ph.D. from New York University. He is the author of *The Anatomy of Dirty Words* and *Nymphomania* (with Albert Ellis), and editor (with Donal E. J. MacNamara) of *Problems of Sex Behavior*. Mr. Sagarin is now Assistant Professor of Sociology at the City College in New York, a vice-president of the American Society of Criminology, and a member of the editorial board of *Salmagundi*. His writings have appeared in the *American Sociological Review*, the *Journal of Sex Research*, the *Annals*, *New University Thought*, and *Criminologica*. Mr. Sagarin is married and lives in New York City.